Literary
Lunch

Literary Lunch

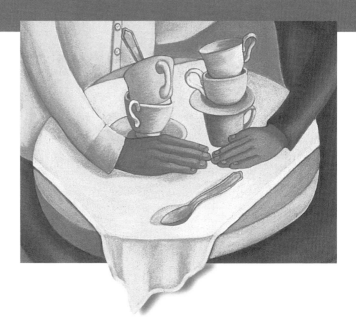

edited by
Jeannette Brown

with Flossie McNabb

KNOXVILLE
WRITERS'
GUILD

Knoxville, Tennessee

Printed in the USA

THE KNOXVILLE WRITERS' GUILD
P.O. Box 10326
Knoxville, Tennessee 37939-0326
http://www.knoxvillewritersguild.org

Contents

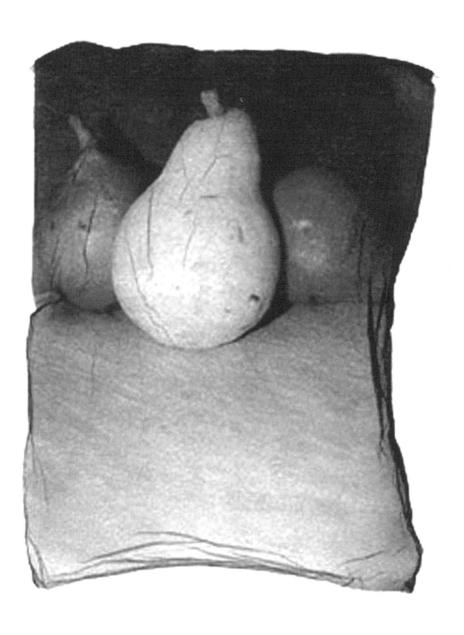

Lindsay Kromer / *Pears*

Introduction

"Food, glorious food."

Let's face it: food controls us. We retaliate by trying to control it, using it to make our lives memorable, or at least livable. From mother's milk to birthday and wedding cakes and, finally, to funeral casseroles, food is the major peg on which we hang our rites and rituals. We feast to celebrate promotions, diet when life becomes too rich.

Eating is nourishing, sensual, emotional, cultural, tempting, sacramental, disease causing/curing, sacrificial, comforting. It feeds or starves our addictions, cravings, and denials.

One reason good food is so alluring is that is reaches all our senses with its pleasurable scent, attractive presentation, specific consistency, and flavor, which sets off all the senses again. The smell of lasagna, popcorn, hot chocolate, fresh-baked bread and other childhood treats can set off pangs of hunger for the food itself or for the past. We don't want to taste the popcorn so much as to return to times when someone taller than us was worrying about war and the economy and the future so that we could concentrate on Roy and Dale and Trigger.

Yes, I'm a Baby Boomer. I've gone from thinking of saltines as a basic food group, through the macaroni-and-cheese as entrée, TV dinners as treats, tacos as exotic, to believing that French cuisine is the epitome of culinary sophistication. Our menus reflect our national culture and its progress; saluting the astronauts with Tang expressed the boldness and imagination of our country. Perhaps we currently have a touch of ennui. How else to explain our current preoccupation with the 1970's evening entertainment: a fondue pot? We are recycling our cookware fads. Chocolate or cheese?

Fondue pots or woks or crockpots can't turn some of us into cooks. We drift through Williams-Sonoma without fathoming the difference between a mincer and a dicer. We fondle apple corers, egg slicers, fruit-ball carvers and other mechanical delights, suspicious that one really good knife could perform the whole enchilada of kitchen tricks.

Years ago, I cooked for a man I was dating. I fed him the dainty single-girl dinners I made for myself: yogurt with peanuts or linguini with pesto. He was starving. He invited me to his apartment for dinner, a real dinner. We went shopping for the ingredients for his favorite food, spaghetti. We bought spaghetti, a jar of sauce, some ground meat, and two pots. I asked if he needed to buy flatware, too. No, he had plenty of plastic forks recycled from his forays through the fast food lane.

He became my chef. Having a personal chef is a privilege and no one should complain, but it is not without its quirks. For instance, my chef goes on what one might call benders. Perhaps obsession is a better term for making deviled eggs three times a week for a month, then waiting seven or eight years before needing to make that dish again. Homemade biscuits were popular for about two months; almost every day we had homemade biscuits, even for dinner with steak and potatoes. Then the biscuits disappeared.

My mother fuels these maniacal quests by sending recipes. "Mom, he's going through a cabbage phase." The incoming mail carries cabbage recipes torn from ancient cookbooks, Sunday newspapers, and scrawled on index cards; others are spoken over the phone, hurriedly because it is long-distance.

He has gone full circle from outdoor grill to kitchen Jenn-Air to George Foreman grill. He's back outside now, expanding his repertoire from a slab of red meat to a slab with grilled veggies.

Obviously, the man is obsessive/compulsive. You can see why I married him.

He didn't say a word when Poetry Maven Flossie McNabb and I converted the dining room and its huge table into the editorial office for *Literary Lunch*. He cooked extra-large dinners, creating leftovers for lunch, so we wouldn't have to stop reading and editing and organizing and all the other elements of making this communal, collective, comestible book.

It was hard not to nosh all day as we pored over well-written tributes to Krispy Kreme donuts, grandma's biscuits, fish and cheese grits, fresh tomatoes, sweet corn, and pie. Several of the offerings talk of hunger: Nikki Giovanni's prose/poem speaks to the hunger for learning; others hunger for lost loves or some unnamable longing. The events of 9/11/01 influenced several of the pieces. We read about grandmas who influenced young lives and in-laws who taught cooking skills as cultural lessons. We learned about food as an element of dating. And we took our time reading the most entertaining category—food as a metaphor for sex. An international flavor (pun intended) is provided by entrées describing food and/or relatives from Italy, Germany, Greece, Kazakhstan and Finland. Food-related paintings and photographs by seven artists appeal to our sense of sight through the display, presentation, or the isolation of food. We tried to find a scratch-n-sniff rubber noodle so readers could play with their food, too, but it didn't work out.

Nevertheless, we hope *Literary Lunch* sates your appetites.

Jeannette Brown
K-town, 2002

Acknowledgments

Literary Lunch is a publication and product of the Knoxville Writers' Guild, which supports beginning and established writers, as well as aspiring readers.

Many people were involved in creating this anthology. If we've missed anyone, we'll cut our tongues out. We'd first like to thank the contributors, some of whom created work especially for this volume. Also, thanks to Jo Ann Pantanizopoulos for suggesting that the Guild's fifth anthology be about food (she had just come off a Ruth Reichl bender); to Doris Ivie and Jim Johnston for sharing their experience on the previous Guild anthology; to Catherine Crawley for her heroic public relations efforts; to Tom Post for sharing PR and marketing secrets; to Julie Auer for guidance and wit; to Jackie Kittrell for her clever fundraising; to Diane Hanson of Hanson Gallery for representing Elizabeth Johns and putting us in touch with her; to Cindy Spangler for leading us to artists; to Marga Hayes Ingram for her knowledge of art and its technology; to J.T. Hill and Gary Biviano of Alcoa Primary Metals for cold cash; to Judy Loest for encouraging some really fine writers to write about food, and for her connections to Dr. Giovanni (and for all the other things she did; we would name her second assistant editor, but we don't want her to be blamed for anything); to Marybeth Boyanton for creating the name of this volume and for her "*New Yorker*" drawings sprinkled throughout; to Laura Still for her near daily deliveries; to the East Tennessee Foundation for support through their Art Fund of the East Tennessee Foundation program; to Allen Wier for helping us avoid a *faux pas*; to Suzanne Seton for assisting with details and paperwork; to Kay Newton, Doris Ivie, Linda Parsons Marion, and Judy Loest for their proofing expertise; to Mr. K's Used Books and CDs (Oak Ridge and Johnson City) for funds and support; and to the many others who found ways assist.

About the Cover Art

The day after I agreed to edit this anthology, I was driving down Kingston Pike and had to hit my brakes in front of Hanson Gallery. In the window was the perfect painting for our unnamed book about food. Inside, Diane Hanson told me the artist was practically local, just up the road in Bristol. Her name is Elizabeth Johns.

Diane said the name of the painting was "Talk Over Coffee."

The painting told a story, but I couldn't quite get it. Was it a Romance? Certainly, but the elongated proportions hinted at Fantasy. The closer I looked the more it became a Mystery. All those coffee cups; are they lingering so as not to part or are they unready to move on? Those closed lips: has it all been said or are they swallowing the truth? That tiny window could keep the world out or let light into a cell. The walls are bare; no artwork, posters, or family photos to tell whether they are at home or in a café. Their feet don't touch the floor, which is covered by a rug woven from Eden, knitting a tight coil of love. Or is it unraveling?

How can Ms. Johns offer so many perfect contradictions? How can she present so much information without giving anything away?

She explains somewhat in her Artist's Statement.

It is through her dream life, both sleeping and waking, that Elizabeth Johns taps into the images that she brings to life on canvas. Johns' work is primarily figurative with a strong narrative quality. When the images that appear to her, sometimes in dreams at night, but more often in a quiet or meditative moment in the day, are compelling enough, she attempts to capture them by setting them down on paper or canvas.

"The fascination for me," Johns explains, "is to pull images through from the unknown, to wonder about them, to sometimes understand their meanings later on, or sometimes not at all." Johns contends that images communicate in a different way than words, sometimes bypassing the naming and knowing part of the brain. Johns continues, "As much as I love stories and literature, stories are not always told in words. And the source of stories is not always in what is known. Images and ideas can come through from the unknown, from the mystery, if we leave the window open and allow it."

And so, it seems that Ms. Johns agrees with one of my favorite writers, Gertrude Stein, who said, "There ain't no answer. There ain't gonna be any answer. There never has been an answer. That's the answer."

Maybe, if I can quiet my inquisitive mind long enough to just enjoy the painting, the story will come to me intuitively.

— J.B.

Memory's Table

by Judy Loest

I am woman; therefore, I have cooked. Early on, however, I decided that "found meals" were my forte: a banana here, a piece of cheese there, or, more fortunately, another cook's largesse. I do cook on occasion, but it is usually the one-step variety: I steam broccoli, scramble an egg, bake a potato. So, when our writers' group announced its plans to publish a literary food anthology, I thought I would have nothing to say, that only people who love to eat and love to cook, people whose happiest experiences center around food would be able to contribute in a meaningful way. A food anthology implied, in essence, an epicurean paean, a buffet of prose in celebration of the most intimate of human acts: eating. Making a place at the table for someone who would happily sacrifice eating to reading or surfing the Web would be like giving space in a book on architectural design to someone who only drives nails and drives them purely for shelter.

But when I examined my relationship with food, I realized that I have a literary interest in food, an interest as passionate and authentic as the gastronomic. As a book lover, food interests me greatly—food as metaphor, as the catalyst of narrative and memory, and as a symbol of spiritual transformation (the convergence of the sacred and the profane). Food in fiction often creates place and character; food is to narrative what dress is to persona: it delineates history, social hierarchies, and economic class; it defines and reveals culture, serves as a driving force behind people's actions; and, out of all the significant aspects of community life, is perhaps the most effective, aside from blue jeans, at bridging ethnic boundaries. Throughout history, people have used food to mythologize the past, to enliven the present, and to celebrate faith. In all cultures, food plays a dominant role in ritualized celebrations—from the Hopi Corn Dance to the Jewish Bar and Bat Mitzvah, from the Afghanistan Festival of the Sacrifice (*Eid al-Adha*) to the Mexican Day of the Dead (*El Diá de los Muertos*)—and in the stories we tell in

constructing our personal life narrative. Food is to memory what the hinge is to the door, or, in keeping with the food-as-metaphor theme, the spice, the condiment, the leaven. It often acts as the catalyst for the memory to surface from the long heap of history, much the way Proust's madeleine sent him off on a 14-year-long reminiscence. And 14 years doesn't seem an exorbitant amount of time to devote to recovering what he called "lost time," memory beyond conscious recollection, memory triggered by uncontrollable, chance events and sensory impressions. As someone once said, the past is big because it's growing. Our early personal history begins to blur in the distance just about as fast as our skin loses its baby softness. Proust began the first part of his long novel cycle, *À la recherche du temps perdu* (*Remembrance of Things Past*), in 1913 when he was 42, an advanced enough age to require memory triggers in order to reconstruct the person he had been as a youth and to relive forgotten events. Food was the trigger he found most effective.

Like Proust, my life narrative owes much to food. I was born in a holler in a small farming community called Snowflake in the Appalachian mountains of Southwestern Virginia, a life so vastly different from the present that my images of myself as a child there are authenticated as much by the stories told about me as they are from actual remembered events. It was a life truly the stuff of fairy tales—the deep, primeval woods and tangled thickets where there were snakes but also wild blackberries, chinquapins, and papaws; the little one-room school with a bell tower and coal stove; our tiny house, the front half jacked up on stilts and overlooking a mountain stream, with an outhouse beneath a mulberry tree; the bounty of a vegetable garden; the wild animals that threatened our free-roaming chickens—with enough darkness and magic to inspire any writing brothers with a penchant for the grim. And much of both the darkness and the magic was intrinsically tied to food: the Halloween cakewalk at school when I was six and my mother won a chocolate cake for best costume, a frighteningly realistic bear suit cut from an aunt's old fur coat; the visit from California of my mother's prodigal brother whom she hadn't seen in twenty years and who made extraordinary chunky, spicy Southwestern chili, which, even today, can conjure up an image of him in jeans and plaid shirt with his tales of the West, of panning for gold and working on horse ranches during the Great Depression; the first time I witnessed a hog being slaughtered, the horrific sight of the dead animal strung up by its hocks for the blood to drain before the hide was removed; or the chicken with its wrung neck flopping about in the yard. Those images may be part of the reason I am a vegetarian today, although, then, the horror was forgotten as soon as I tasted my mother's fried chicken or my aunt's delicious cracklings—salty, greasy, crunchy bits of pig skin and fried-out pork fat which remains when pork is rendered into lard.

Who was I back then, what pulls the child I was out of the layers of "lost time" and into the flesh of memory? For me, it's the stories told about me, stories that can almost begin with, "Once upon a time, a little girl . . . " and which, if I look closely enough, have somewhere in them a particular food. I was the baby found under a log in the month of May, or so that was the answer given to my three-year-old cousin who later cried to go into the woods blackberry picking with the mothers because he wanted to find another just like me. I was the barefoot preschooler who, every day, carried my little pail across the hill to an uncle's farm and returned with it full of fresh milk, who once came home crying with it half-empty because a black snake had chased me. That was me, too, the toddler, barely walking, who was found sitting in front of the open refrigerator "shampooing" my hair with milk, which my mother swears to this day caused my hair to be curly.

Our memories are the stories we tell about ourselves, an internal documentary, which selectively expands with every waking moment, and which inexplicably punctuates the present like dreams in sleep. It's odd how some of our strongest memories can be tied to the simplest, most inexpensive dishes, such as the Broken Glass Jell-O Torte my mother served at a Tupperware party in 1963, the only party she ever hosted. Jell-O is much derided today, but in the Fifties and Sixties was the dessert *du jour,* touted in daytime television commercials and respected at the most sophisticated tables in the form of molded salad. The torte was one of those experimental recipes in *The Joys of Jell-O* cookbook in which three or four different flavors of individually chilled and cubed Jell-O are folded into a pineapple and whipped cream base, poured into a graham cracker crust, and refrigerated to set. That jewel-like dessert, cut into squares and topped with whipped cream, seemed the most festive and frivolous thing my practical mother had ever made, as surprising and incongruous as the party itself with matching napkins and paper plates and our small living room lined with folding chairs rented from the funeral home. Now, whenever I see Jell-O, I invariably remember our living room filled with happy homemakers penciling in Tupperware orders and balancing paper plates of Broken Glass Jell-O Torte.

My mother shares my lack of enthusiasm for eating and cooking, with good reason. For the first four decades of her life, getting and preparing food was hard work. Those gleaming jars of canned fruits and vegetables lining our cellar shelves were not products of creative domesticity à la Martha Stewart; they were necessary to a healthy diet through the winter months and represented hours of labor beginning with seeds saved from the previous summer's garden. While writing this, I harassed her with phone calls to corroborate certain facts, prodding her for her own special or unusual memories of food, but she insisted she couldn't remember any. At one point, exasperated, she said, "When are you going to be through with this crap? I'm tired of these questions about cooking." Cooking, after all, was a chore; I might as well have been asking about her memories of doing laundry. Having seen food in all of its stages, she has no illusions about it; when I explained polenta to her, she said, "Humph, that's nothing but cornmeal mush, what old people ate with milk on cold nights when they wanted a snack." Imagine, my foray into Italian cuisine (which, happily, only requires boiling water) reduced to Depression Era mush. But I persisted with my questions, finally pushing the right button by asking if she and my father had ever fought over food.

"The only real fight we ever had was over food," she said and began the story of the unbrowned biscuits. When my parents married, they couldn't afford new or even used appliances and, so, took the old wood-burning cookstove handed down from an aunt and uncle. Years of use had burned a hole through the partition dividing the firebox from the oven. Ashes were continually falling into the oven, and baked goods would burn before browning. One morning at breakfast, my father, who, at this point, still believed that no one could cook like his mother, made a smart remark about my mother's pale biscuits. My mother had a temper then and immediately slapped him across the face with a wet dishrag.

"He came up out of that chair mad as fire," she laughed, forgetting that she had been manipulated into talking about cooking, pleasantly smug over the memory of her youthful defiance. "I grabbed a chair by the back legs, and he grabbed the front. But since we were about the same strength (my father was tall but skinny as a rail), the chair only went straight up, and there we stood like two bulls with locked horns. Finally, I guess, seeing that was going nowhere, I let go and grabbed a stick of stove wood. He saw I meant business, dropped the chair, took off through the house, and jumped off the front porch. By the time he'd made it around the house and back in, he'd cooled off. He never said anything about my cooking ever again."

I don't think my father backed down solely out of fear or because, by nature, he was nonconfrontational; I think his common sense prevailed. I think he realized that my mother could be a fierce ally, that her fearlessness was one of the things that had first attracted him, and that it might be in his best interest to walk away. He was right, she did prove to be the rock upon which the marriage endured; and it wasn't long, probably as long as it took to buy a proper stove, before his palate switched loyalties and his wife's cooking began to taste better than his mother's. Those biscuits triggered a turning point in their relationship, and I'll bet he never ate another one of my mother's biscuits without remembering that incident.

Every family has its biscuit or Jell-O story, its fragments of "lost time" which link it to the remote past and comfort it during times of grief like a hearty stew in winter. And nowhere is food more an agent of memory than in death, when the body must both memorialize the deceased but also re-ignite the collective unconscious and its genetic urge to survive. Proust said that memory "is a rope let down from heaven to draw me up out of the abyss of not-being." Perhaps, because death *is* always in the background, and memory is the only thing that survives us, that pulls us from the abyss of nothingness, our bodies instinctively fuel the memory with food, insuring the cycle of birth and death and rejuvenation.

I remember my father's death when I was seventeen, the refrigerator packed with funeral food, how eating our way through all that food was somehow tied to getting through our grief, how eating those lovingly pre-pared casseroles was not pleasurable nor memorable but something we did to remind ourselves that life would go on. Once again, the living room was crowded with funeral home chairs, and people were eating off paper plates. In the Sixties, poorer people in the South still observed the tradition of a wake for the deceased, sitting up with the dead all night, talking and eating. My father's body had already been detained at the funeral home for a week while the Red Cross found and delivered my brother out of the jungles of Vietnam. After he arrived, the closed coffin, covered with sprays of mums and carnations, sat for two nights atop its draped rolling stand in our tiny dining room separating the living room and kitchen. People, passing back and forth in front of it, talked in low voices, and the house was filled with the smell of cold funeral flowers and food warming in the oven. The ancient ritual played out even in that infinitesimal spot on the wheel of time.

I don't cook, but I appreciate those who do, those who love to cook and love to share their cooking, people like my friend Nan who, her head shaved due to the ravages of chemo, served a five-course meal to two dozen friends, regaling us with her bald jokes and jumping to fill our glasses or pass second helpings as if we were the ones with cancer; like my Romanian friend who insists on scorching his eggplant on the burner before making baba ghanoush because it enhances the flavor even though it makes a mess and stinks up the house; like my mother's friend, now deceased, who, every Christmas, made seven or eight fresh coconut cakes to give to family and friends. I also appreciate those who do not particularly enjoy, nor are good at, cooking but who do it out of love and in good cheer, people like my childhood neighbor Agnes who, when I came home from school with the cafeteria recipe for peanut butter cookies, made them because my mother, who was then working outside the home, didn't have time, and, while baking, the cookies ran together to form one giant rectangular cookie, as crisp as a cracker; like my Aunt Opal who, while living with us during an economic downturn, exploded a pressure cooker full of bean soup and had to sweep beans from the ceiling and then sponge mop it before my mother got home from work. Bless all the sustainers, amateur and expert alike, for they nourish us, not just with food but also with memories, the sweet impossible blossoms that bloom again and again for us in unexpected moments, that remind us who we are and where we have been. ☕

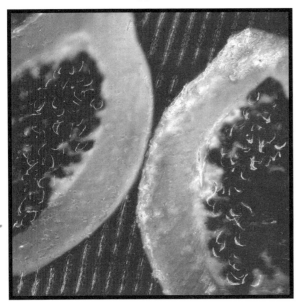

Lindsay Kromer / **Papaya**

the train to Knoxville
(for my father at Knoxville College)

an excerpt from *Quilting the Black-Eyed Pea* (HarperCollins)
by Nikki Giovanni

so what would you need? ten dollars more or less. maybe less. and uncle lee. you just needed someone to say you can go to college and there is a college for you and you have to get out of Cincinnati because if you don't you will probably go to Detroit or maybe Chicago but not back to Mobile or Birmingham not back down south where ugly ass white girls look longingly at you and call you nigger so maybe you will get lucky and find the ten dollars and maybe you won't but you better hurry because there just isn't much time for a sort of short guy to get a scholarship go to college when the sort of short guy is black

and everybody was happy that uncle lee was able to get that scholarship even though you wondered when you could do quadratic equations in your head why you had a basketball scholarship but you always knew that you had to take what they were giving since that was all you were going to get but you never fooled yourself about either the taking or the giving or the needing or the having you just sort of said to yourself I'll have to see what is being offered

and it's really hard to remember that mama bell whose name you called as you awaited the transition would be kind enough to put something in front of you that made sense for you to eat though by the time you talked about it she was one of the women in your life who unqualifiedly loved you though you were always smart enough to know that no one would unqualifiedly love you if they knew who you were

and you found the ten dollars because your friends were laughing and saying you don't want to go to college you can stay here and run the numbers and the women and make a lot of money but you had purchased that dream and you were determined to stay asleep and part of the ten dollars for the train fare to Knoxville came from the women who slept with you and who were kind to you because they knew you were a special person who could go left or right good or bad kind or mean but there was something in you that they liked and something in you that they recognized needed something they offered and even though they would have given you their hearts they decided to offer you a dollar a quarter a dime so that you could catch that train to Knoxville

and in segregated America in 1935 you go to a campus which welcomes you even though the upper classmen shave your head and laugh at the fact that you don't have any underwear on because underwear would have cut into that ten dollars or so that you needed to take a train ride south so you smile when you meet a girl with very long hair and a bit of a haughty air and you ask her out to share a cigarette which you smoke and vanilla wafers with marshmallow fillings which she eats and you tell her in no uncertain terms that you are the person for her and she will marry you and you two will have children and you will live together 'til death does part you and she laughs thinking you are kidding and probably the only other person who knows you never kid has not yet been born but when she is she will sing your praises because some folk think they can judge you and some folk think they know but no one understands what a step you took to board that train and now you sit in heaven watching over all of us

and we love you for all that you are have been will ever be because you always without a doubt without a qualification without a reservation loved us ☕

The Fall of Dorothy Speers
(or: Not All Reductions Occur in a Saucepan)
by Jack Mauro

I had forgotten the tale of Dorothy "Dodo" Speers and her fall from power. Only through a friend's casual remark was it brought back to me. The story itself, I beg to say, is not momentous; it simply has a modest place in my modest past. It is an heirloom of sorts, something maybe insignificant, yet one that pleased my mother and thrilled her mother before her; like a chipped Christmas ornament pulled out of the box every year, the tree is not the same without it.

Sara and I were in line at the food stand in our office building. A strange animal of a food counter it is, too. Fast food is married to a menu of leafy, non-fried items, and grease shares the stage with celery. One fidgets before ordering, faced with the dilemma of sacrificing a year of one's life or possibly adding a month or two.

A voice said, "Mayo?" and the patron directly before us said, "Oh, please!" As though this were an uncommon treat, like oranges in Victorian England.

Just then—happy occasion—Sara softly said, "You know, people are *afraid* of mayonnaise."

There was an unmistakably arcane depth to this assertion. I asked her to elaborate.

"It was on Oprah, or Sally. Or something. Anyway. They had this food expert on, and the audience was asking about safety issues with food preparation. Someone asked if mayonnaise was safe on potato salad if the potato salad was left outside, for a picnic."

I myself do not picnic, but suddenly shared in the need to know.

"Sure, it is," she replied. "The expert said it was totally safe. *Then,* someone asked about the safety of mayo on *egg* salad, if the *egg* salad was outside in a bowl for a few hours."

"Why would it be a different case?"

Sara turned to me a face exasperated with stupidity, either mine or that of Oprah's slower audience members. In any event, it is a surprisingly charming expression, whenever she wields it.

"Because people are morons. Hell, I don't know. But it gets better. Then someone *else* asked if you could keep BLTs wrapped in plastic without the mayo spoiling."

"So much fear. Over mayonnaise. Astounding." I ordered something with no dressing but much sugar. I'd die sooner but accomplish more in the time I had.

"Like I said. Morons." Sara chose fried chicken and a calmer, shorter life. And that was all there was to it.

Until we were back in the elevator, returning to the office. I read once that Alfred Hitchcock enjoyed nothing more than riding in a crowded elevator and blurting to an acquaintance, out of the blue, "I had no idea the old man would bleed so much." My intent was certainly not of a similarly mischievous nature, yet afterward it occurred to me that I may have generated something of the stunned silence Mr. Hitchcock so delighted in. For several others shared the car, no one was speaking, and the memory of the story came back to me.

"Mayonnaise actually destroyed the life of Dorothy Speers, where I come from."

I was of course not born when Dorothy Speers was smeared with disgrace at her own table. But it must have been something, then, to the women of my grandmother's hometown of Cookeville, Tennessee. As I get older, in fact, I more easily appreciate the drama.

Dorothy Speers was the great lady of Cookeville. That a humble little town should have a great lady is quite in keeping with the world as we know it. Ladders of society and standing are climbed with as much determination in a Southern village—if assembled with fewer and more splintered rungs—as in any thriving metropolis. I suspect that our nation's most skeletal outpost, boasting a population not exceeding double digits, has a great lady to guide it, most likely the woman who runs the combination post office and general store.

Mrs. Speers gave luncheon parties at her home. That, from everything I gathered at my grandmother's knee, was pretty much the source of her influence. She was no wealthier than any of the other matrons of Cookeville.

Her husband was a doctor, but there were other doctors in Cookeville. And her house was no more imposing, no more festooned with the day's fashionable names in furnishings, than many another on Main Street.

One lunch for her girlfriends. That was the beginning. Then a second. Then a regular weekday was set for the occasions. All very innocent, a perfectly natural progression into ritual. One wonders in retrospect if the Barbarians first knocked at a Roman door bearing Hun cake and primitive Schnitzel.

Propriety dictated, of course, that another lady or two of the circle would offer her own house, her own kitchen and cutlery, as a platform for the serious business of gossip and less compelling civic projects. But Dorothy's home was, really, so centrally ideal for everyone. "Besides, y'all know I just love to do it." This was Dodo's invariable stance. And she would put out, each time, successively more extravagant buffets. Each time, a member of the group would be that much more afraid to compete against Dorothy's fabulous fare.

By the sixth week, Mrs. Finching had made up her mind to insist that they all meet at her house. She was perhaps the first to perceive something other than altruistic bonhomie in the hospitality of Mrs. Speers. She was skewered on Dodo's shish kebobs. On the eighth week, Mrs. Grover gave the matter forethought and decided to offer the girls an English tea at her home. Dorothy's Italian feast smothered her intent in marinara and beat it down with garlic bread. There was no way to win. Dorothy just liked to entertain to an indefatigable degree.

By the third month, it was completely understood that generosity was not the true motivation in Dorothy's soul. It was power. This awareness crept up on the women of the group as such things do: slowly, imperceptibly, then crashingly overnight.

The overnight was a brief moment of sword-clashing, or butter-knife dueling. Mrs. Hanschmidt mentioned, over the remains of a superb Salade Niçoise on Dorothy's lace cloth, that, as they were all in accord over the issue of a church tag sale, they had better begin dropping off donations as early as possible.

"No. I really don't think that'd be the right thing to do, Mildred. Coffee?"

"I believe I will. But why not, Dodo? I thought we was all—"

"Here you are, honey. That's fresh cream, there. I just kept quiet, let you girls hash it out. But you'll remember, I said a while ago that the

Reverend Banks is being . . . looked into? The church accounts, and everything?"

Mrs. Hanschmidt took cream. There was surrender in the pouring of its richness into her cup, and she felt it. "I recall, surely. But the cause is still a fine one, and—"

"Damn silly to raise money when the need ain't even there. So I say, no. Now, *look*, everyone." A ceramic lid was raised, and the steam from fresh peaches filled the air. The ladies partook of the luscious fruit as Persephone ate the pomegranate in Hell. Every swallow was a signature to a declaration of dependence, every spoonful a curtsy in mute homage to the might of their hostess.

"Girls, girls! Pour some cream on 'em! There's plenty." The peaches— that is to say, Dorothy—won. There would be no tag sale.

In fairness to the ladies, they were not so shallow that their sense of right was eclipsed by gluttony. It was more a case of Dorothy's having employed a time-honored and virtually unbeatable strategy. She who dishes out the food is omnipotent. Children know it; animals know it. That day, in the picturesque dining room of a Cookeville two-story, a gathering of middle-aged women knew it too.

It was by her own hand that Dorothy Speers' reign ended. Quite literally, too.

Two years had come and gone, punctuated, not by weeks and months, but by tenderloins and little game birds, and casseroles and glazed loaves. Dorothy, like Cleopatra, was by no end hampered in her variety. If the salad served was nothing special, the beverage would be exciting and new. If the sliced steak was ordinary, the sauce would be daring and robust. Once, after the *foie gras* was cleared and just before the éclairs were set out—boldly Francophile was Dodo, that week—Mrs. Barry remarked to Mrs. Finching that she had it on good authority that Dr. Speers was given macaroni and cheese for his dinner, night after night. This was of course whispered.

Then Dorothy read an account of how the Duchess of Windsor rocked the English aristocracy by insisting upon club sandwiches for a garden party. Club sandwiches. Dorothy was intrigued. Yes. It would be different, daringly masculine, and tasty, too.

On that infamous day, all was laid out with Dodo's customary expertise. The sandwiches themselves were tidily cut for more genteel handling by feminine hands. Extra condiments were set out in gleaming silver goose-necks. A graceful little ladle was suspended in a cloud of mayonnaise.

The women sat, the women chatted, and the women ate. That day, Dodo's object was the installation of herself as chairwoman of the library drive. The subject was gently alluded to while she poured fresh apple juice for her guests. Apple juice, Dorothy said, was really the best complement to anything with bacon. Didn't they think? Prim mouths chewed while cowed heads nodded. The acquiescence was less in approval of the drink and more a premature resignation to the will of Mrs. Speers and her civic ambition.

Then—and my grandmother would giggle in the recalling of it—Dorothy moved to apply mayonnaise to her sandwich. The ladle, a fatally inappropriate implement for the condiment, betrayed its owner. Before it was returned to its station, it had left in its wake two dollops on her person. Two perfectly oval globs of mayonnaise decorated Dorothy Speers' blouse, like a pearl brooch. She was unaware of them.

Dodo was undone. No woman mentioned the accident to her dress, no one referred to the perfidious mayonnaise, and all exchanged traitorous looks. Thus the tiny clumps acted as punctures to Mrs. Speers and she deflated, minute by minute, before her friends' eyes. As Dorothy was dethroned by the twin blots, her guests were empowered by them. A silent *coup* in summer cotton and sensible shoes was staged around the Speers table. And all Dorothy knew was that, inexplicably, her pronouncements were suddenly being greeted by silence or with bland responses.

The library chair went to Mrs. Finching.

"Wild." Sara reached for my lunch refuse on her way to the trash. "Did she ever use mayonnaise again?"

"No one knows. They bribed the grocer, too. But—"

"But," Sara interceded, "you can make mayo at home."

"Exactly," said I. "Like poison, or a bomb." We went back to work. 🎩

Authenticity Quest

by Inga Treitler

Every Saturday morning, on an empty stomach, you set out in search of authenticity. You sashay along the cobblestone streets, snaking deftly through crowds, and around piles of vegetables and fruits at different stages of biodegradation.

The "North End." That name thrills. At first you don't know what it is the north end of . . . you never question what it is the north end of. It is a place name like any other—Arlington Heights, Marblehead, South Boston—all innocuous names bearing the meanings of embedded experience. Later, much later, you learn of the irony of that place called the North End, built, as it was by people who came from the south end of Europe and moved to the north end of Boston. You are so much a part of it—earth-toned and silent, dark-haired and untethered—it becomes a part of you. You carry the North End with you wherever you go. The North End is the standard of the authenticity you expect to find as you move through your life.

The people who live in the North End are southern and they live life just as their great-grandparents in Sicilia lived life. They carry a passion for fresh fruits of the fields and the oceans, blended simply for the extractions of sun, sea, and soil. These are the dark-skinned, dark-clothed, dark-haired sons and daughters of the ancient cultural Mediterranean core.

There is a vastness in all the connections to the very places the food comes from—connections through the people, the smells, the crudeness of those voices stretching back through generations of voices just like them, shrieking and bellowing out their produce in just the same way, with just the same seductiveness.

You step away from your small town car onto the cobblestones of that ancient city. You are tired and dulled by predictable insularity of suburban packaging. The vivid bouquet of scents knocks you refreshingly off your guard. You welcome the sharp acrid saltwater spray off Boston Harbor just upwind, fish just in on Nantucket trawlers, raw beef haunches hanging in front of butcher shops, suckling pigs on spits over low coals, rabbits strung up by long hind legs in shop windows (soft, gray fur coats and long ears intact), partridges and chickens (long, scrawny necks pulling toward the floor as if in a final yoga pose), sawdust soaking blood in dark corridors between vendor stalls, detritus from the fruits and vegetables dropped in haste or at day's end. You pirouette delicately around cheese wheels the width of a cow's stride.

First the cheese. You make a regular meal of sampling each kind, one more pungent than the next. These cheeses are gathered from cheese capitals of Europe: German cheeses, Italian cheeses, Dutch cheeses, Belgian cheeses, Swedish and Norwegian cheeses. So generously are the samples served up that you have learned to come with an empty stomach. Taste after taste, sniff after sniff, leaves you woozy with the ammoniac after-flavor. Lips smacking, face contorting, eyes rolling, you gradually choose those two or three cheeses you cannot live without. Putting in your orders with the rotund, aproned servers you stand back as they draw cleavers, blades flashing in the low light of Faneuil Hall, and find that perfect spot on the wheel of cheese that miraculously gives you the precise weight you hope for. Tucking precious chunks wrapped in white paper into string bags, you leave the dark interiors of Faneuil Hall to brave the crowds fighting for the attention of the fruit and vegetable vendors at the Haymarket. Outside, streets are richly blanketed with leaves of lettuce, skins of oranges, sparkling pomegranate seeds, oyster shells and countless unnamable artifacts of the busy market place crushed to a slippery pulp underfoot. Smells both nauseating and seductive sweep you off into the river of other shoppers, and you are met with the chaotic orchestration of vendors.

"Fi' fe' dolla'! Fi' fe dolla' beautiful fat green peppahs fi' fe dolla' goin' fast! Five fe' dolla'!"

"Fresh oysta's! Get a dozen! Common honey, getye' man some oysta's. He's lookin' a little wilted, sweethea't, Fresh oysta's! Smell those oysta's! Common sweethea't, put your nose right in theya. C'mon Jack, giveya sample, slide one down theya!"

"Case o' strawberries, fresh this morning. Case o' strawberries, three dolla's. Clean 'em up, you got some strawberry preserves. You don' like preserves, stick 'em in the freeza' fe' winta' eatin'. One case o' strawberries, three dolla's. Check 'em out sweetheart, they're as sweet as you ah! One case three dolla'!"

Flitting through the dense crowds, you dodge into collapsing doorways, duck under loads of fruit carried over the heads of vendors, slip behind benches out of the way of shoppers impatient to be the first to the front to snag a deal. Wondering at the strange offers uttered as warnings in growly, menacing voices—"Meat! Wanna buy some meat?!" The butcher looms suddenly above you, and you hear his suggestion week after week. Like everything else in this rich marketplace, the butcher's innuendo follows you from those impressionable years of your early adolescence into your adulthood. What did he mean? You wonder. Why did he scare you and excite you all at once? Everywhere, you learn, there is an innuendo, creating the thrill of forbidden lust. Not everything is what it seems.

Escaping monstrous crowds, you cram your way into impossibly minuscule shops. "Hot soup! Hot soup!" "Watcher back! Watcher Back!" Pairs of backpacked college students fleeing the uniformity of Harvard Square look on dazed, asking prices in Midwestern diction clashing with the fluid syllables of this pure vernacular—begging a connection to this mysterious hive. The North End is where immigrants have built their little Italy into the winding streets that follow the ancient paths of cows who meandered across colonial New England for so many centuries before the people took it as theirs.

The North End remains a pure and authentic enclave of ancient traditions. Your errand began in Faneuil Hall (Fan'l to you locals). Done with the wheels of cheese, you are ejected like a pinball out of Fan'l Hall's catacombs to drop into the alleys created by giddy makeshift stalls in the Haymarket. Finally, you end in the tiny residential streets of the Italian neighborhood where women heave their solidness from windows and chatter away in the southern Italian cadence—the day's gossip and news. You take your spot in the Café dello Sport with your espresso and cannoli sitting among old Italian men shouting at each other across dish-sized bistro tables. They are plotting, you fantasize, how to even the score with that other family who had crossed their turf.

The North End is not just a marketplace for food. It is a marketplace of relationships imagined and unimagined . . . of connections. The food comes out of generations of recipes, food combinations dreamed up only because it was a great season for raspberries this year and something had to be done with them all. In these streets of authenticity you dredge food

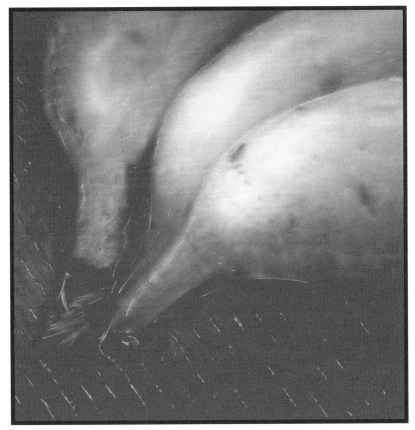

Lindsay Kromer / **Bananas**

from another place and time. Those are the connections and relationships you long for as you struggle to accommodate the alienating magic of mass marketing and ingenious packaging where clerks are far from the harvesting of the food and remote from the food preparation.

You carry the smells, sounds, feelings, textures, and relationships of the North End with you as you move from city to city, country to country. Sometimes you find it and sometimes you don't. When you don't find it, that oppressive homogeneity makes you look harder. You crave being a part of that marketplace of food, relationships and life. You find those marketplaces in the tiny islands of the Caribbean: vast marketplaces selling the freshest of fruits and vegetables. These marketplaces are the bustling centers of social life, food preparation, and romantic encounters for the islands' adolescents. You find them on the cobblestone *places* in Paris where farmers sell the vegetables they grow themselves on farms just outside the city, and fishermen sell oysters to ring in the New Year, harvested off the Brittany coast. You tell them about your family and about that beautiful *poulet* you have just purchased for dinner, and the farmers tell you that you must have the freshest peas to serve alongside the *poulet* and some new spring potatoes with your menu. Their food must be handled and served as if you are serving royalty and everyone will know which farmer's food you are preparing. They know you will come back next market day and tell them about the peas. And if you forget, they will ask. ☕

Ciudad de Los Tamales

by Jack Neely

The other day I went down to Market Square to see Mr. Perkins about some muscadine jelly. Not expecting much variety of fresh produce this early in the season, I didn't browse—but as I paid for the jelly I noticed, on the shelf near Mr. Perkins' scales, several fat little parcels wrapped in some kind of waxy paper and tied tightly in twine. "What are those?" I asked.

"Tamales," he said, and I felt stupid.

"Of course," I said. "I've just never seen them tied in that particular sort of a knot."

"They're not very hot," Mr. Perkins apologized. "You just boil them. Not for long, because they're fresh."

Mr. Perkins, who lives on his family's farm on the French Broad, says he ate homemade tamales when he was a kid, which was longer ago than most of our childhoods. "My mother wrapped them in corn shucks," he said. "That's the old-timey way."

His 83-year-old aunt made these tamales. If Mr. Perkins knows her recipe, he's not letting on, but he allows that she combines ground beef with some unspecified seasonings and cornmeal. I bought half a dozen for $3.50 ("you won't find them cheaper anywhere in town," Mr. Perkins said). I took them home, cut the twine with a knife, and boiled a couple of them for lunch. With some spicy barbecue sauce, they were good, very different from the greasy tamales you get in cans.

Many Knoxvillians of all ages say they were raised on tamales, store-bought and homemade both. It's a working-man's meal, one Mexican dish that somehow has never risen to *nouvelle* trendiness like the chalupa and the chimichanga.

The fact that there might be an "old-timey way" to make tamales in Knoxville may seem remarkable in itself. Until recently, we never had a Mexican population big enough to support a Mexican grocery. I don't even remember a Mexican restaurant in Knoxville before the unlamented Nixon-era Taco Rancho. The Mexican tamale—food historians believe it to be Aztec in origin—may seem the most un-Knoxvillian of foods.

Sometimes when I'm eating alone I dip into a weighty epicurean tome called *Southern Food*. Author John Egerton is a serious and respected historian of the Civil Rights movement and other regional issues, but in turn he's also a hedonistic reveler in Southern cuisine who can delineate the often-subtle differences in taste you might encounter in only an hour's drive through the South. *Southern Food* came out in 1987, and is still the definitive treatise on regional cuisine. It's a fascinating read, but it has very little to do with Knoxville, a city we have to admit has yet to establish itself in culinary circles.

In *Southern Food,* Egerton made only one positive mention of any Knoxville dish. It's not Greek pizza or metts & beans or Volburgers. It's a recommendation, in passing, of tamales. "At Charlie Green's Rib Shop in Knoxville, Tennessee," Egerton wrote, "you can get first-rate Chicano-class hot tamales wrapped in cornshucks or papers."

I'd never been to Charlie Green's, and the minute I read that I tried to look it up in the phone book. No luck. I drove around the usual barbecue routes. No trace of him anywhere. A few folks I spoke with recall a Mr. Green who sold tamales from a pushcart in Mechanicsville.

From old city directories I learned there was a place on University Avenue, next to the Beulah Church of God, called "Green's Hot Tamales." Green's closed around 1988—probably just a few months after Egerton's recommendation was published nationally.

Of course, Charlie Green and Sherrill Perkins were never the only guys who sold tamales hereabouts. In residential East Knoxville you sometimes see cardboard advertisements tacked on mailbox posts and porch columns: TAMALES $1. These places don't necessarily have business licenses or health department ratings, but I hear some of them serve some spicy tamales.

Knoxville's most conspicuous legal, license-on-the-wall tamale place today is on Magnolia Avenue, just past Scruggs's barbecue, but on the left; the flaming neon sign proclaims it to be *Mary's Hot Tamales*. It's a take-out shop with just one table and a large tapestry of da Vinci's *The Last Supper* on the wall. Mary's serves a few things like barbecue chicken, but it's clear that tamales—hot or mild, $1 each—are the specialty. The sign on the glass door assures you Mary also serves the Full House.

When I went by last week, Clara Robinson was in charge. A thin, energetic woman, she's from Greenville, Mississippi, by way of Chicago. She moved here in the '80s with her sister Mary Manuel. In 1989, the two opened Mary's Hot Tamales.

Clara Robinson and her sister grew up with tamales—Greenville is particularly known for them, another interesting fact you'll learn in *Southern Food.* John Egerton speculates the tamale percolated from Mexico along the Gulf Coast up the Mississippi River to Greenville, a Delta town.

Asked about their inspiration, Clara mentions the late Charlie Green. She knew him well. She says Charlie Green was also from Greenville, but moved here years before they did: "a *long* time ago," she says. "In the '50s, maybe." Green used to tell people his secret recipe was over a century old and came from a Mississippi slave family. Charlie Green took a liking to Clara and Mary, and bequeathed them his old Mechanicsville recipe. She and her sister are proud to keep the tradition going, and with a few alterations she doesn't care to discuss, they have. "It's more or less his recipe," she says.

Greenville has supplied Knoxville with at least three of our tamale masters of the last half-century. But Knoxville's tamale culture stretches back a good ways before Mr. Green.

There's a photo of the Greek-owned Biltmore Cafe on Union Ave., and the big sign advertising TAMALES. A license plate on a car indicates that it's 1935. Tamales were obviously an established favorite by then. Some speculate that tamales were one way Southerners coped with the Depression; cornmeal can stretch out one serving of beef into four servings of tamales. Others suspect local tamales go back farther than that. Knoxville's passion for tamales may be older than Volmania.

Clara says East Knoxville was home to a previous tamale legend her older customers call "Mr. Andrew." A few Knoxvillians older than Clara remember him. Harold Shersky, who once served kosher tamales in his deli, recalls Mr. Andrew around Central Avenue in the '30s. Mr. Andrew pulled his load of hot tamales in a metal wagon equipped with a portable stove and sold them for a nickel or a dime apiece.

Retired Gay Street insurance man and well-known rare-book scholar Ron Allen suspects the tamale man some remember as "Mr. Andrew" was one Andrew Taylor, who was a tamale vendor on Central Avenue from the '30s through the '60s. Allen says people drove to Knoxville just to buy Andrew's tamales. They were categorically different from all other tamales. Allen says the spiritual descendents of Andrew Taylor's legendary tamales were those at Sarge's Barbecue on Western Avenue, near New Gray Cemetery. Sarge's tamales were much thicker than anybody else's, and meatier, with a filling that's something like a dark, rich, smoky, finely ground beef sausage. Big "Sarge" Jackson retired from the barbecue business a couple of years ago, but he's said to be manufacturing tamales for friends in his home.

Allen and Shersky both remember another downtown tamale vendor who did most of his tamale-selling on Gay Street during the same era: a short, bowlegged fellow with a handcart. Allen says the guy's name was George, but he never knew his last name. He says George sold good tamales and, in season, ice cream.

Some folks think there's a season for tamales. Clara Robinson does. She closes her shop for a month or two during the hottest spells of summer.

When she and her sister moved to Knoxville years ago, there was one thing in particular that surprised her. Back in Mississippi, Clara says, they never dunked their tamales in chili. And before she came to Knoxville she had never heard of a Full House.

If Knoxville ever goes to war with the rest of the world, here's how to tell if someone's a spy: ask them what the phrase *Full House* means to them. Those words were familiar on several old-line Knoxville menus—at the Dutch Tavern in North Knoxville, Brownie's on Cumberland, and Gay Street's Rendezvous. Sarge offered a Full House, of course. It was a tamale or two dunked in chili, usually with crackers, cheese and maybe onions, a dish long known in Knoxville and maybe nowhere else as a Full House. It might have been our equivalent of Cincinnati's famous five-way chili. This poker hand is much scarcer than it used to be. Glenwood Sandwich Shop, northeast of downtown near Fourth and Gill, and Smoky Mountain Market, at the south end of the Henley Street Bridge, both offer old but fairly mild versions of the Full House.

Clara's a modest woman, but she says she serves the best Full House in town. I can't argue. Her tamales are plenty hot, submerged in spicy chili.

It's as fine a Full House as any I know. Some restaurateurs I've met say they're often frustrated by Knoxville's bland, unadventurous tastes in food, but when they say that, they're not talking about East Knoxville.

Some mourn that the Full House, arguably Knoxville's most distinctive epicurean tradition, may be dying out. But for the moment, it seems safe in the spicy hands of some Greenvillians who have perfected it.

(Portions of this essay appeared in the Metro Pulse.*)*

Earth Angel

by Marilyn Kallet

Mrs. Greenfield
our huge school nurse
used to gobble up
my soggy sandwiches.
Mother slapped
Wonder bread with mayonnaise
and Dole pineapple rings.
The bread lay sopping.
Mrs. Greenfield didn't care.
She weighed 200, easy.

Why didn't I trash my lunch?
Why not pitch a fit?
"Mommy, the kids tease me!"
Six years old, what could I
use as leverage?

Years later, Mrs. Greenfield
held my retainer during lunch.
She'd open her hand—
I'd plop the pink plastic
saliva-soaked device
into her palm.

Bless you,
Mrs. Greenfield,
priestess of leftovers
and oral fixtures
for your ample fields
of flesh.

Did your husband
savor fragrant pineapple
on your breath?
Did your Hawaiian fingers
strum his appetite?
Was he anorexic
toward your love?

Forty years later
I'm the mother
wondering about you, Mrs. G.
In my kitchen I would listen
and feed you well,
dear ravenous little girl.

Cull

by Amy Unsworth

Let me be the one
black rock in the pinto beans
picked over and soaked all night
at the bottom of the pan.

Unyielding to onion
and salty water, rattled against steel
as the pot boils dry, smoothed
with drippings of a long-dead hog.

Clatter me in the veined porcelain bowl,
to hide on the spoon, hard against
your teeth, pressed between
tongue and lip. Let me be in the palm
of your hand, unscathed.

First Fig

by Donna Doyle

We take what we do not know and ask for metaphors.
Fragile fruit too ripe for peeling,
sticky uncertain fingers,
first fresh fig inspiring questions
only our tongues can answer.
You are right to tell me
they cannot be compared to anything.
When the day grows
quiet enough to hear figs falling,
my lifelong longing has a name:
sweet taste of what hovers beyond comparison.
How will I sleep
knowing the burden of trees
bearing more fruit than can be eaten?
Tell me, now that I know my heart's desire,
how will I fall?

From Béchamel to Boiled Mutton Fat

by Emily Dewhirst

The glob of boiled mutton fat on my plate stared back at me. I couldn't eat it, but I didn't want to risk offending my Kazakh host. Mutton fat, one of the beloved specialties of the people of Kazakhstan, was a far cry from my eating experiences of sixty-three years.

At nineteen I had been a university student in Paris, wondering how, with meager funds, I could afford to eat at least one good meal a week. I had come to the Sorbonne in 1950 ready for frugal living, but a steady diet of lentils at the government student cafeteria? Ridiculous! The thought came to me that I should enroll in a French cooking school so I could not only learn to make a true French meal, but enjoy the bonus of eating my work at each lesson's end. The *École Superieur des Arts Ménagers Familials* was not a glamorous preparatory school for chefs, but an inexpensive institution for young ladies. We learned to make basic sauces, doughs, pastries, entrées and garnishes, not by recipe, but by consistency, look, touch, and taste. It was exciting to be introduced to this new world, for I had been brought up by upper middle class women of Anglo-Saxon ancestry whose cooking was definitely of uninspired English origin. French meals had flair, artistry, and I reveled in the experience.

Slowly, through my lessons at the school, I became a real gourmet. I developed a finer palate, an understanding of why foods were presented in a prescribed order, why a certain wine enhanced a particular dish, why one spice worked well while another did not. I became a lover of fine wines, apéritifs, digestifs, delicate soufflés, strong-flavored coffee, and all the other aspects of dining well. My taste buds sharpened, and my waistline became more defined even though crusty French bread became a mainstay of my diet, along with cheeses I had not dreamed existed. I imitated the French by practicing moderation, avoiding snacks between meals, and promoting good conversation and graciousness during dining.

My taste buds, still classically French, underwent a drastic shock in my sixties when I moved to Kazakhstan for two and a half years as a Peace Corps volunteer working with a specialized English school. Kazakhstan is in the heart of Central Asia, west of Mongolia and east of the Caspian Sea. It is larger than all of Western Europe. Until the Russians, then the Soviets, extended their reach far to the south, it was a land of nomads wandering the vast steppes.

I looked forward to living in Kentau, a small city in southern Kazakhstan near the Uzbek border, and to the encounter with unfamiliar groceries and the challenge of new culinary experiences. I had received warnings about a severe shortage of food in 1994. Despite it all, I was blissfully unaware of how this would affect me.

The first winter, even staples were lacking, and I discovered how it felt to starve. Thinking that it would be painful, I was surprised that after a few days of craving food, going without was not difficult for me. Apathy set in. I lost my desire to eat. Twenty-seven pounds melted away, and I regained the tiny waist and shapely hips of my youth.

By spring, a limited supply of food appeared in the bazaar, but I had no appetite. My friends worried about my not eating, plying me with *shubat* (fermented camel milk) and *kumiss* (fermented mare's milk). These fermented liquids were thick and sour and tasted like barnyard smells. I decided I would rather risk ill health.

My apartment, in a five-story Soviet creation of crumbling cement, was on the top floor of one of four buildings. There was a courtyard in the center where, among broken vodka bottles, children played in the dirt, and sheep, cows and dogs fed at garbage piled high in one corner. As I entered my building, I often had to step over sheep, dead and alive, that Kazakh families were slaughtering for a festive meal. I was fascinated by the skill of the Kazakhs in slitting the sheep's throat and skinning the animal. I was not so thrilled when the insides came out, but loved watching the women, squatting around an open fire, roasting the sheep's head on a stick. I always begged for the horns to decorate my apartment. One day, on my way to school, I found a long, curly horn in the dirt. Parfina, the young Greek girl who washed the school floors between classes, put it in her supply closet for me, and when I retrieved it at the end of the day, it was crawling with maggots. For days I dug out all the live and dead matter in the horn. It still graces my dresser.

Grocery stores did not exist in town, so everything had to be purchased at the bazaar. It was in an open field, hot, full of flies and blowing sand in the summer, freezing cold and empty of all but carrots, onions and potatoes in the winter, and knee-deep in mud during the rainy season. I missed my French bakeries and the neighborhood shops of *pâtés* and *saucisses,* but the Kentau bazaar had its own flavor.

Finding the unexpected was one of the few predictables at the bazaar. There was always a crowd of women pushing baby carriages. Each carriage contained, not a baby, but a baby blanket covering stacks of *nan,* the wonderful golden crisp rounds of flat bread, soft and chewy on the inside and pricked with a design on top. Delicious! *Nan* was my mainstay, my comfort when my stomach rebelled against all else. Sometimes the rounds of *nan* were baked in a normal oven, other times on the curved side of a *taba,* an outdoor pot-like oven with coals at the bottom.

Other women in the bazaar squatted on the ground selling their wares: vegetables, old pots and pans, odd eating utensils, crocheted baby booties, an ice cube tray. On tables, mounds of butter, open to dust and sand, emitted a spectrum of color from sickly pale yellow to artificial bronze gold. Sugar harmonized in colors from yellow and gray to brilliant white. When purchased, the sugar was ladled onto a sheet of newsprint, and after coming in contact with the oily ink, it all turned into a drab color. White sugar, more expensive and sweeter, came from China, but it often harbored shards of broken glass, as did the rice that was available. After cutting my mouth several times, I became an expert at picking out even the tiniest of pieces. Canned goods were nonexistent, and fresh vegetables and fruit were available only in summer.

Meat was the most interesting commodity in the bazaar. It appeared as large, stringy globs, lying on a sheet of newspaper or plastic on the ground, never revealing its origin or the part of the animal it represented. After buying a chunk and carrying it home, one cooked it the same way all meat was cooked, washed thoroughly and boiled in a pot for hours. In a large bazaar, heads of cows, horses and sheep—dead eyes glazed, and tongues lolling out the side of the mouth—were strewn on a table, blood dripping on the ground below. No wonder I almost became a vegetarian while in Kazakhstan.

One Saturday I courageously stepped forward, and, in my halting Kazakh, indicated I wanted the butcher to cut a small piece of meat for me. A friend behind me said, "Why, I didn't know Americans like camel meat!" I didn't, and I still don't.

Buying chickens was difficult. There were a few scrawny live ones in the bazaar, but I've always been squeamish about wringing necks, plucking and drawing. The dead ones had probably been so for a long time. But I did eat eggs. A tall, gaunt Uzbek woman with bright stainless steel teeth and a red flowered kerchief sold them at school. She held down two full-time jobs, janitor at school and worker in a chicken factory. Since the chicken factory had no money, she was paid in eggs. Fresh would not be the right word to use, but her eggs were somewhat better than those in the bazaar.

The horn signaling the arrival of the milk truck had a high, tinny sound, and when you heard it you had to hurry with your container to line up at its back door. If you were lucky, the milk did not run out before your turn. Otherwise, it was a week's wait for more. The driver ladled a thin bluish liquid into your pot. You took it home, strained it carefully to remove the bits of manure and straw, and boiled it. When I was a child, I was always disgusted with the crinkly scum on top of boiled milk. In Kazakhstan, I relished eating it because butterfat might be hiding there.

In summer there was no refrigeration, so frequent bazaar visits were necessary. Neighboring Uzbekistan provided electric power, but since Kazakhstan had little money to pay for it, the electricity ran only sporadically. Stalin had manipulated the location of industries so that it would be very difficult to split up the various Soviet republics. To make matters worse, there was no gas and, in summer, no running water. Husbands went out after dark and illegally cut branches from trees so that their wives could cook. I didn't have that possibility, so my cooking efforts were as sporadic as the electricity. *École Superieur des Arts Ménagers Familials* had not prepared me for all this.

As the first American and also the first Westerner to live in Kentau, I was adopted by the inhabitants of the city as an extended family member. Kazakhs are very generous people and kept me alive by inviting me to *dasterhans* or feasts in their home. But I was also invited to every engagement party, wedding, circumcision, and funeral, frequently by people I didn't know. I was puzzled by the plethora of invitations. A friend explained that during the Soviet years, a general was always invited to a party to insure its success. Now the city of Kentau had me!

Traditional Kazakh families served at a low table, guests sitting on the floor. My knees do not bend in the same way as theirs, so it was easier for me when there were chairs and a higher table. The food was always the same: pickled vegetables grown during the summer at a *dacha,* a small country home with a garden. Having a *dacha* had been one of the perks given to those in important positions during Soviet days. *Nan* was always on the table as well as a broth (in which the meat was boiled). A sheep's head was served and frequently a joint bone with strings of meat, gristle and fat hanging from it. Sometimes a large ball of boiled mutton fat was presented as a special delicacy. Hot tea, packaged dry cookies, and perhaps hard candies and raisins followed, along with Kazakhstan's exceptionally sweet melons if the meal was in summer.

After the beginning toasts, the *dasterhan* began. The guest of honor was served the sheep's head. The portion to be eaten was determined by the gender of the guest. A man ate the eyes to see matters clearly and wisely. A woman ate the cheek or forehead, for thinking, especially if she were a teacher. The ears were reserved for children who needed to listen better. The head was then passed down the table, and each partook of an appropriate piece. If a joint bone was served, it too was offered first to the guest of honor, who picked it up in his or her hands, chewed off a piece, and, with greasy fingers, sent it down the line for other guests to do the same.

I enjoyed participating in these rituals of the table, except for a few. The ball of mutton fat was a problem for me. I could not face eating the grisly gray mass. I would pretend to take a bite, chew and swallow. Then, with all the graciousness I could muster, I would say to the hostess, "Thank you for giving me such a great honor, and because you have such beautiful, intelligent children, I would like to offer this delicious mutton fat to them in respect for their parents." It worked, and whether or not they saw my real intention, they always seemed pleased.

Another sticking point for me was gregarious alcohol consumption. Drinking vast quantities of vodka is obligatory in Kazakhstan even though Kazakhs, on the whole, claim to be Moslem, and Islam forbids alcohol. However, religiously, Kazakhs are like a layer cake with animism at the bottom, stabilizing everything. Islam is a second layer, thin to thick depending what part of the country one comes from, and, at the top, there is a very light sprinkling of Russian Orthodoxy which is now in decline as those of Russian origin move north to Russia. But the cake is soaked with the influence of Russian culture, including heavy vodka drinking.

Certainly no dinner could take place without the Russian habit of drinking numerous toasts of vodka or local brandy, the quality of which would horrify any respectable Frenchman. Glasses were filled to the brim and expected to be downed in great gulps. Even known alcoholics were pressured to drink heavily. It was always a boozy evening. I am no teetotaler, but twenty or more glasses of alcohol during a dinner were more than I could take. Mirash, my Kazakh confidante and protector, found a solution. I would request brandy, then take a small sip at each beginning toast. Mirash would then pour my remaining brandy in a potted plant when no one was looking, and fill my glass with tea, which was the same color. I always hoped my generosity didn't kill the plant.

One night I explained to the hostess that I was taking a very potent medicine and was ordered by my Peace Corps doctor to abstain from alcohol for two weeks. Everyone was aghast. Surely I would not insult my hosts by not drinking a toast to them! I persisted, and the evening was saved only when a woman across the table came over, stood behind me, took my glass and declared, "My name is Emily Dewhirst, and I drink this toast to the honor of my host and hostess."

The order for giving toasts is prescribed and often directed by an appointed person. The host offers the first toast to welcome the guests; the guest of honor gives the second; then other guests are called in order of their importance, ending with the host and hostess. The toasts play a large role in cementing the close relationships of the Kazakhs, and I found myself included as an integral part of their beloved families. The Kazakhs do not toast with a single word. The toast is composed of long, spontaneous expressions of friendship and love, of gratitude and appreciation for others. Often the work of the national poet, Abai, is recited, extolling the life of the nomads of the distant past. My toasts were mixed, but they always represented my feelings of joy at being with them and having the opportunity to work in their schools and share their lives.

Along with the toasts, the dinners were punctuated with the singing of old nomadic songs accompanied by the *dombra*, a two-stringed, long-necked instrument similar to a lute. Then everyone got up to dance, Middle Eastern style, with arms and hands held high in flowing, twisting movements, and it was back to the table for more food and more toasts. As the meal ended, the Moslem ritual of blessing was performed. Each person cupped his hands in front of him while a prayer was recited. Then, in a lovely gesture, the hands were lifted and brought down in front of the face.

Six years have gone by, and the twenty-seven lost pounds have reappeared. The American grocery stores confuse me with shelves loaded with far more than necessary, much of it frozen or pre-packaged. I no longer make French gourmet meals, nor do I go to a meat counter to ask for a ball of mutton fat or a sheep's head. I miss the bazaar with its unexpected treasures and horrors. I miss my loving, generous Kazakh friends and the camaraderie of the *dasterhans*. My experience in Kazakhstan left me with no profound thoughts about food, except that each culture believes strongly that their cuisine is the best. But the experience did give me the realization of how important it is to me to have a working refrigerator, freezer and stove. Hence, I have developed a reverence for heat and electricity. I never, ever waste a second of it.

Huckleberries

by Jane Hicks

Spread hot August on a biscuit
dark, thick, purple, and sweet,
storm clouds rolling low.

Bleached backbone of the ridge
shimmers as tin buckets
swallow plump berries.

One eye on the bush, one on the rock
lair of scaly, coiled lightning,
Granny stands guard with a hoe.

We steal the treasure,
make a getaway, untouched,
meet the storm at the head of the holler.

By night, rows of hot August
gleam purple and sweet in a Ball jar
ready for January biscuits.

Persephone Addresses the Herbs

by Connie Jordan Green

*In the fourteenth and fifteenth centuries . . . the harvesting of herbs and
vegetables was often accompanied by the chanting of verses or the muttering
of spells.* —(from *Betty Crocker's Kitchen Gardens*)

Lovage, chervil, sweet marjoram,
what has it cost you
to remain safe from winter's wrath
in your airtight jars?
Colors faded, leaves crinkly
and dry as old skin,
still you punctuate our dinner,
give back summer's flavor,
essence of meals almost forgotten.
You awaken memory of sun's long journey.

Here in underground's Stygian gloom
let us praise perennials—
mint, sage, rosemary, tarragon, thyme,
hearty souls who outlast snow, ice,
freezing rain, who endure
while our eyes close on dreams
of pale lavender blooms,
gaiety of chamomile flowers.
Blessings upon generous biennials—
angelica and frilly parsley
who hallow our planting
with an extra year of growth.

Soon spring and tender basil,
sweet bay, garden cress,
and may our spirits rise
like green tips of chives
long held prisoner
where darkness marks eternal night.

Every Man Receives a Measure of Faith

by Jack Rentfro

No hamburger from an ordinary eatery held me in its sway.

The Spot was a hole-in-the-wall lunch counter on Ocoee street, a mere hallway niched into one of the blocks formed by the intersection of two state highways in downtown Cleveland. The crossroads had been the nexus of commerce for the biggest town between Chattanooga and Knoxville, now a deteriorating, redbrick backwater of Interstate 75.

With the bleak ecstasy of a junkie back in his old neighborhood, I surrendered. It wasn't what I came home for. But, as I parked my car, the aroma of saturated fat molecules roiling around the corner of Inman and Ocoee Streets became irresistible.

Grease-laden delicacies from the Spot were clotted with local attitudes, local politics and local religion, all combined into a sutra of civil religion. Pilgrimages to this humble grill for its renowned hamburger had more to do with answering to the mystic realms of circadian and ultradian actualization than filling the belly. It was about knowing God. It was more Eucharistic than the ordinary comestible. It didn't digest; it transubstantiated.

Inhaling deeply of the burnt stink from the sizzling grill was enough to spike one's blood cholesterol level. Habitués of the joint claimed this atmospheric miasma was detectable to the naked eye, as if there were an airborne plume of animal fat globules gushing from the double doorway onto the street and flowing along the sidewalk like an invisible river in the streets, kept aloft by the oven-baked air of a summer afternoon. Transients and dogs in the shade of the band shell in the park occupying another quadrant of the old town square could smell it and dream.

I remember my brother and his friends riffing: 'Spot hamburgers are so good, you can even taste the seeds in the slice of tomato,' they chortled.

At the time, I was too young to realize Larry and his beatnik clique were enjoying the kind of minutiae that marijuana smokers found amusing, the Spot being a favored haunt for munchie-crazed potheads. Larry had also claimed that service at the Spot was so prompt that it wasn't unusual for Ulys Odom, the cashier, to meet you on the street with your change *before you even got to the place.*

I rounded the corner. The oily redolence wafting out the open doorway ahead intensified, smacking me in the face as I crossed the threshold.

Ulys Odom still manned his post behind the cash register hard on the left. My arrival registered in Odom's bespectacled gaze as his sleepy lizard eyes glowered at traffic passing along Ocoee Street. An instant later, I confirmed that the second of the Spot's humbly famous staff also remained on duty: Freeman Stubbs' elbows pumped as he jockeyed at the grill down at the far end of the long, narrow corridor.

The long and lanky half of the Mutt 'n Jeff team, Ulys Odom dressed year-round in the same costume, beginning with a white, long-sleeved button-down shirt, sleeves rolled up to the elbows. And below Odom's begrimed, white apron were the black slacks, black brogans and white socks that rounded out his workday ensemble. Odom never lost that thousand-yard stare except as he rang up the bill or scooped the soft-swirl shakes known as Frosties from the freezer mounted in the wall behind his station.

Freeman Stubbs may have had on the very same sweat-soaked, cigarette-burn-holed undershirt and apron with their palette of obscene brown stains that he wore the last time I came home. And the same scuffed cowboy boots and filthy jeans as when I made every other lemming run to the Spot in the 30 years since I left the town where I was born in an ancient redbrick hospital that once occupied a corner on the other side of this block.

Odom had skeletal arms and a gaunt, sallow face jaundiced from a life as a chain-smoking workingman who had maybe caught on too late to a joke about how he would spend his entire life as point man for a greasy spoon diner. In contrast, Stubbs seemed to be the recipient of some kind of hillbilly satori, as if he needed nothing more than his iconic griddle and the endless customers lined up in homage. Stubbs was dark-eyed and olive-complexioned like Odom, but short and brawny, a pot-gutted, swaybacked, insulting caricature of a Cherokee Elvis. His backswept mountain of hair shone as if the cantilevered marvel of its swirling, organic architecture were indeed held together by a pomade of burgerfat, as was speculated. Odom's

Brylcreemed pompadour was far less dramatic. Only the fenders of gray in both men's hair suggested the passage of decades.

I found a stool at the far end of the counter directly behind the wizard of the griddle. Another bit of Spot lore came to mind: how Cleveland youths were solemnly informed at some point in their lives of the way Spot hamburger patties got their unique size and shape. Stubbs, my brother assured me, formed the patties by inserting hamburger meat under his blubbery armpits. As a boy, I had imagined Stubbs in the morning, frantically squeezing out patty after patty in preparation for the lunch rush.

While working the grill, Stubbs reached into the industrial fridge plugged into the wall to his right—the very end of the Spot—for the eggs, bacon, sausage, ground beef, lettuce and mayonnaise that went into the makings of the dozen sandwiches he had going at any time. Armpit story notwithstanding, I watched as Stubbs clawed raw wads of ground beef from a stainless steel basin. Balls of red and white marbled beef splatted against the dull surface of the griddle—sloped for grease drainage—with such force that they barely needed additional flattening with a spatula.

The offal-blackened griddle was seasoned with fame. Every few years or so, it had been deemed a fit subject for a feature story in the Cleveland *Daily Banner*. Each was a puffy rehashing of Odom's acquisition of the electric griddle from a junk store, which meant it was even older than the Spot itself with its half-century of existence. Odom and his partner, Stubbs, a distant relative, had signed their first lease on the former candy shop location and thrown open the double-doored entrance to the Spot the year after World War II ended.

The antique kitchen equipment was linked to an America that was still on the side of the angels. Whatever danger accrued as a result of eating off something not scrubbed well since the war turned this into an act of faith. No GI in the Ardennes or the fetid swamps of Guadalcanal worried about whether his bacon was credentialed with perfect sanitation at every point of its distribution. War and want undoubtedly tinctured the griddle with the tiny Spot hamburger's transcendent flavor.

No one asks the priest where his hands have been when he hands out the holy cracker. The Spot proudly displayed a "C" restaurant rating on the wall at the far end where most eateries would have had rest rooms.

The Spot was divided down its length by a Formica counter. Between diners' elbows, this countertop was landscaped with chromium condiment racks that held matching knobby glass salt and pepper shakers, the former

always half-full of rice to absorb the humidity; red and yellow plastic ketchup and mustard squeeze bottles; and a freestanding paper napkin dispenser, half a wad of tissues wastefully protruding.

Miniature jukebox consoles were installed atop the counter, one Select-O-Matic module for each pair of stools. Song titles were tabulated on moveable panels that could be flipped with knobs extending through the top of the plastic bubble where the coin drop was located. At the bottom of the unit were parallel banks of numbered and lettered selection buttons. "Lonely Feeling" by the Guess Who was the most current listing.

The jukebox had never worked, it seemed to me. In such a cramped space, canned music was irrelevant, a texture not called for among the amplified townsfolk chitchat and guffawing, Stubbs and Odom's call-and-response order-taking and mutual cursing, the constant clattering of cookware, the intermittent roaring of the Hamilton Beach malted milk machine, and the rumbling of passing cars a few steps out the open door.

At the base of the counter, an elevated banquette provided a footrest for those seated along the row of twelve stools. The red vinyl seats themselves were invariably splitting, repairs made hastily with duct tape and something similar to bicycle-tire patching. Thereupon no jury was ever assembled with such random perfection. No disciples ever broke such bread: the nuances of mayo and beef grease syncretizing cheap white bread into an ineffable *prana*.

Well-coiffed and prosperous individuals bumped elbows with besmudged millworkers. Shirtless thugs shared napkin dispensers with children and lovely young secretaries daintily working flat wooden spoons into their Frosties, all in shoulder-to-shoulder proximity to the Spot's steady courthouse influx of jail trustees, cops, commissioners and lawyers, plus the town's leading bankers, bums and freaks. One and all pawed and gummed their burgers and egg sandwiches and slurped down the Spot's uniquely explosive configuration of meat and tomato by-products that was called chili though it had no beans and was palatable only when diluted with a fistful of oyster crackers.

Eavesdropping was unavoidable in the Spot: everyone had to shout to be heard above the sizzle and clatter. A casual listener munching his hamburger and keeping to himself might pick up on a Babel of preaching, weathertalk, politicking and japery of one kind or another, mostly focusing on the tribulations of an ordinary working man muddling along in this world and hoping for a break in the next, as in: "Me, I'm just waiting for the next big thang, Lord." The quiet paradoxes expressed in such redneck koans as "You know, everything takes longer than it does," and "I feel more like I do today than I did yesterday" are the kind of one-liners any poor hungover bastard might inadvertently say to anyone listening.

Practically every third man in Cleveland is a preacher or is called "Preacher." It is a town where anyone, at any time of day, could be collared on the sidewalk by a minion of Lee or Tomlinson Bible Colleges anxious to further his evangelical mission.

Just such a jackleg religionist came in to the Spot. Even those who have been away a long time knew better than to engage Odom longer than it took to place an order or pay up. Odom wanted nothing more than to tote up the bill and get back to his basilisk oversight of town life passing outside.

"Every man receives a measure of faith," he was assuring the unflappable Odom at the point when I homed in. The veins on the preacher's gin-blossomed face stood out like earthworms on pavement after a rain. The man reached out and patted Odom's gnarled paw. It was obvious from Odom's slow burn that he wanted the man to keep his hands to himself and get out his wallet to pay for the six slaw dogs and endless cups of coffee he had enjoyed. The customer, possibly trying to get a ministerial discount, finally fished out his wallet.

"God don't use miracles when he can do things without them," the preacher chuckled as he stepped outside and wagged a finger at Odom as if he had just taught him a valuable lesson. Odom glared after him through his grease-speckled, black-framed glasses.

Suddenly I was confronted by a pair of dark, quivering jowls: "Eh, whaddyahevvin'?" Stubbs barked.

"Couple of hamburgers with everything," I answered, staring nearly cross-eyed at the long cigarette ash dangling from the ever-present filtertip in Stubbs' droopy lips. "And another to go."

"Whut-che drankin'?"

"Co-Cola."

With the fluidity of a juggler, Stubbs instantly spun back to the grill with its constant inflow of raw materials and outflow of fried foodstuffs. The short-order cook was in constant motion, taking orders from some customers without even looking up from the sizzling beef patties, the congealing mass of yellow scrambled eggs for sandwiches, cutting and flipping all with the same long, wooden-handled spatula.

Stubbs whipped a square of wax paper from a carton and slapped it on the counter in front of me. This was how the Spot served sandwiches. Only the chili and coffee were served in anything like porcelain.

Communication between the front and back of the Spot was a ululating mix of orders, curses and ribald one-liners. If Odom took a to-go order, for example, he shouted it down to Stubbs in a burst of glossolalia which only he and Stubbs could fully comprehend. "Eh, sixburgertwocheetwo-yallerdogs, eh, fourchilitwoCo-colas'n'fourcuppamud, allwalkin'!" yelled Odom, muezzin of the hashhouse, in a wondrous phonic slurry.

Stubbs, chained like Prometheus to his grill, looked up with his dark, puffy, basset hound eyes: "Eh, jewsay sixburgertwocheetwoyallerdogs, eh, fourchilitwoCo-colas'n'fourcuppamud?"

"Raht!" Odom snapped sharply. "'n a speckledogwalkin'!"

A little blond boy clambered up a stool to get a closer look at the stainless steel bathysphere-like, wall-mounted freezer behind Odom. The machine had no markings other than an arcane logo, a decal of a gaily waving, red-capped elf named Frostie. The boy wanted a half-dozen Frosties to go. He kept cutting a glance outside to the vintage car double parked on Ocoee Street, parents watching from the front seat. "We're going to freeze them to eat later!" chirped the boy, who was actually me, circa 1965.

"They're good any old way. That's what I always said!" Odom said, lighting up another Pall Mall, eyeing the boy myopically over the top of his thoroughly grimed specs. He gobbed paper cups full of the chilled, grayish, viscous substance and capped them, somehow using a behind-the-back, one-handed catch for a white paper bag full of burgers Stubbs hurled the length of the service aisle like a fast-pitch champ.

The lunchtime crowd nodded in appreciation, then resumed feeding and exchanging a stream of prosaic gems: "A workingman can't make a living anymore;" "It's them pills. Them pills they're a'takin' and thet mary-joo-wanna;" "Kids these days!" and "If you ain't a crook when you get elected, you'll be one soon enough."

My meager lunch on a piece of wax paper had cost nearly $10, about what a white-wine and potted-plant place would have charged for the same volume of foodstuff.

The past wasn't dead, it just cost more.

The effects of the Spot's sale to an Atlanta consortium were already taking place, it seemed. It was all part of an economic boom everyone was anticipating as if the copper rush were on again at Copper Hill and gold had been discovered once more at Dahlonega, providing a reason to send the Cherokee away again so as to not hinder this corner of the world's attempts at growing rich.

I stepped out to the white-hot sidewalk, to-go burger in a white paper bag already translucent from oozing grease. Time now to take my offering to the cemetery. At the corner, the readout from the Bank of Cleveland's electronic time and temperature sign malfunctioned. The digitized lettering zipped by so fast it could be understood only subliminally: "Have a Nice Day."

"Every Man Receives a Measure of Faith"* *is a compilation of impressions from a lifetime of enjoying a well-known Cleveland, Tenn., eatery that no longer exists as depicted here. While true in spirit to that particular dining experience, this story does not claim to be a journalistic account. Hyperbole has been employed and names have been changed as have some pieces of background information.*

* *Adapted from Romans 12:3 (KJV): God hath dealt to every man the measure of faith. (ALSO: New American Standard: Because every man receives a measure of faith to begin with; as God has allotted to each a measure of faith; etc.)*

Fish & Cheese Grits

by Shane Allison

Too many bones in bream,
But my mama loves it best.
I prefer mullet cuz it got more meat.
Poke at its death trance-iced eyes.
Add pepper,
Seasonin' salt.
Baptized in flour,
Laid to rest in a lake of grease.
Potta grits at the back, to the left.
Stir to prevent from sticking.
Throw in tongues of cheese.
"Come getcha some fish," Mama yells.
She's gotta voice like maple syrup.
Can't see her from the living room.
Everything smells so good.
Spoon out some butta.
Like to watch it melt.
A glass of strawberry Kool-Aid,
A fork picks out rich mullet meat.
Needle-like bones stick to greasy fingertips.
Pick 'em out for the baby.
Sit them aside on the chosen plate.
I like mustard on my fish.
Oh! These grits hot!
Blow on 'em.
Burn my tongue, roof of mouth.

Drink some Kool-Aid to put out this fire.
Bone in the throat?
Swallow some bread.
Fish sticks,
Fish cakes,
Fish . . . paste.
The skin that once glittered
Becomes coated batter.
Brittle fins.
Meat skinned clean,
Ladder vertebrae.
Think I'm gonna call Ma
Tonight & tell a I want some
Fish & cheese grits my first night back home.

Sarah Kendall / *Cornbread*

Hog Heaven: In Search of Tennessee's Best Barbeque

by Jeff Daniel Marion

Who knows where a quest begins—or ends? Perhaps life is a series of over-lapping beginnings, launching out, seeking, turning back, circling, maybe once in a while arriving. So perhaps this all began with the birth of my son, Stephen, a trip on a cold February evening in 1964 from Rogersville to Knoxville, only to be told by the doctor that we should find a place to stay the night, this baby isn't ready to arrive yet, maybe tomorrow. Time then for a late snack at Bill's Drive-In on Kingston Pike of what I believed to be the finest barbeque I had so far tasted, rivaled only by the fiery homemade concoction served up at the Dixie Queen back in Rogersville.

Whatever magic existed in that long-ago sandwich on the eve of my son's birth has surely haunted us down through the years, has marked our relationship, joined us in the common bond of barbeque brotherhood. As a boy Stephen grew up on Buddy's Barbeque, back in the days when Buddy's was take-out only, and you stood cramped in that tiny space on Kingston Pike waiting for Buddy or Lamuriel to dish out the unmistakable savor of hickory smoke. And from there to the days of Buddy's Pickin' and Grinnin' Friday and Saturday shows, bluegrass and barbeque served up with a mix that suited an array of tastes. Those lazy summer days we floated on Price's Pond, casting plastic worms for bass, drifted in the little aluminum boat Stephen had christened *Satisfied Mind,* daydreaming the ultimate feast of the gods. Heather, our Shetland sheep dog, settled in the belly of the boat, lulled by the cool waters, was soon fast asleep.

We branched from Buddy's to discover other East Tennessee possibil-ities—Johnson City, we found, had Firehouse Barbeque, a North Carolina vinegary sauce much to our liking, and not far away, outside Bluff City, was Ridgewood, an East Tennessee tradition, if not the finest barbeque around then certainly the best baked beans anywhere, period. And judging from the girth of those serving such fare, this was substantial food, the kind that would, according to my Uncle Dennie, put meat on your bones and lead in your pencil.

But it was in 1986 that the real quest began when I accepted a summer teaching appointment at the Governor's School for the Humanities in Martin, Tennessee. We had long heard of Memphis barbeque, the true Tennessee mecca for all those seeking the most succulent pork this side of paradise. So now I would be within a couple of hours of the city—plans could be made for the two of us to make the journey. But true to the nature of a quest, this was no straight line, Point A to Point B progression, for as I approached McKenzie, Tennessee, on my way to Martin, I caught a whiff of an unmistakable aroma, the one that whets the appetite and twangs the old taste buds in a salivating frenzy of anticipation—yes, hickory smoke! And there perched on a hillside along Highway 22 was a sign mounted on a twelve-foot metal pole proclaiming " od to go." In passing I caught a glimpse of what appeared to be a shack, although *shack* is far too grand a word for that contraption of a building I saw. I made a mental note to return after I was settled in Martin for a month-long stay at Governor's School.

And return I did—after a few days in Martin sampling Damron's Barbeque and finding it very good, but still I hankered for that deep-down, soul-satisfying, ultimate barbeque, the wellsprings where I would bring my son for communion. I was beginning to understand the hunger of those Indians from the days of Hernando de Soto and his exploits into this territory, bringing to the new country the first hogs, introducing the natives along the way to slow-cooked hogmeat over a pit of smoking embers. Now I had some notion of why those natives, once having had a taste of such meat, would risk having a hand chopped off for stealing de Soto's pigs, sneaking into the dark forests to fulfill the hunger that led them to such risks on their quests.

I entered what I came to know as Wood's Barbeque, a pine-slab unpainted structure with rough, slanting concrete floor, a single smoke-filled room with slab benches beside homemade tables, a potato chip rack with bags in disarray, a thin patina of ashes coating them all, counter up front with a variety of items including a small tin that read "Road-Kill Possum," a calendar on the back wall with the month's centerfold prominently displayed, a scantily clad shoat in a provocative pose. Soon a black face emerged from the even smokier pit room back of the counter, and asked, "What for you?"

"How's your barbeque?" I replied.

"It's pulled, man."

Not chopped, chipped, shredded, sliced, no: for years I've considered this answer to my question and now know what mysteries and truths are embedded within it. He did not say "Great," "Good," or "The Best." He said simply the last step of a long journey. For here the journey *is* the destination, the culmination of hog to mouth-watering succulence, a transformation by fire little short of miraculous, flesh to flesh and finally flesh to spirit. So this is the ritual: slow cooked over a pit, the hickory coals kept from reaching a flame, the meat pulled by hand.

He passed the jumbo sandwich across the counter to my waiting hands. On first bite I knew in a delicious shiver—this is the mark against which all others will be judged, great chunks of pork tender with no hint of greasiness, succulent with both the flavor and aroma of hickory, some bits of brown, crusty outer skin meat mixed in with the white. And the sauce was vinegary, just enough tomato to flavor, enough pepper to give it real zest.

Here in a room that would defy any carpenter's level, cause the floating bubble to go astray and even disappear, here I had found the shrine to the pig. When Stephen visited with me a couple of weeks later, my deep pleasure was doubled in watching him experience what I had earlier known. From that day forward we knew the best—not that we would cease our search, but that we had "home base" from which to measure, a kingdom from which to judge. Now the test was to find an equal and, who knows, just maybe one that would surprise us and actually surpass Wood's.

And a time or two over the summers we came close. Traveling to Shiloh from Martin one year, we came upon a newly opened small barbeque stand in the middle of farm country. The owner invited us back to the pit, showed us the shoulders slowly soaking up that hickory flavor, let us linger and ask questions and savor the sandwiches. We never knew his name, only remember his kindness, his delight in explaining the art and process of real barbeque. And our trips to Memphis from Martin became standard parts of the visit: we sampled Topps and found it good; relished the visits to Rendezvous, but knew the pursuit of barbeque ribs was another quest altogether, found their complimentary red beans and rice a favorite; were disappointed by Gridley's. So far nothing surpassed Wood's and it was here that we brought friends and colleagues, made barbeque dinner runs between classes and plenary sessions at Governor's School, hauled carloads of Yankees in the hope of converting them, trying to show them at least one solid reason for not crossing the Mason-Dixon line in a northerly direction. At one point, Danny, the pit man at Wood's, after seeing how many folks we had brought to sample their wares, exclaimed, "You boys sho do like barbeque." Many, many others shared our taste in Wood's, for it grew from the primitive shack to a huge barn-like structure complete with banquet room. And, to our amazement and delight, the quality of the barbeque remained the same.

Year after year, from 1986 to 1994, we made our trek to Wood's, a month in summer and two days in February. Mid-February was time to read applications for Governor's School and I was a lucky one, chosen as a reader. One February, Stephen, Ernest Lee, and I made our way to Martin following an ice storm, dodging trees fallen across Interstate 40, arriving at Wood's to find the lights out, the pig weathervane on the roof frozen in a sheet of ice. But Colonel Wood himself was there, served us the last barbeque sandwiches before closing due to the weather. We have photographs of us sitting in the car chowing down on those last barbeque sandwiches. Arriving home from that trip I decided to write my friend and Governor's School colleague Keith Daniel in Yankee Massachusetts about those last sandwiches. I had saved one of the wrappers, even smeared a bit of sauce on it, and thought I would tease his taste buds. I began the letter, but what evolved was the following poem:

Song for Wood's Barbeque Shack
in McKenzie, Tennessee

Here in mid-winter let us begin
to lift our voices in the pine woods:

O sing praise to the pig
who in the season of first frost
gave his tender hams and succulent shoulders
to our appetite:

praise to the hickory embers
for the sweetest smoke
a man is ever to smell,
its incense a savor
of time bone deep:

praise for Colonel Wood and all his workers
in the dark hours who keep watch

in this turning of flesh
to the delight of our taste:

praise to the sauce—vinegar, pepper, tomato—
sprinkled for the tang of second fire:

Praise we say now for mudwallow, hog grunt and pig squeal,
snorkel snout ringing bubbles of swill in the trough,
each slurp a sloppy vowel of hunger,
jowl and hock, fatback and sowbelly, root dirt and pure
piggishness of sow, boar, and barrow.

Those mid-winter sandwiches proved apocryphal, for a year later in the summer when we arrived at Wood's parking lot we noticed with a sinking feeling that the place looked abandoned, weeds growing wildly everywhere. Only later were we to learn of the Colonel's death, the closing of his business, no one in the family to continue the tradition. We were forced, then, to try a spot just down the road from Wood's, a little nondescript block building that announced simply *Mayo's*. We sat inside and talked with Mr. Mayo, then an elderly man who told us of Wood's death. Mayo's barbeque was *nearly* as good as Wood's, but within a year, Mayo too was gone, his business dying with him.

So on we traveled, following tips of special places in Memphis, discovering Interstate Barbeque and finding it mighty fine, but Memory is an unforgiving mistress, will allow few if any contenders. In a moment of great sadness at the loss of Wood's and simultaneously a moment of sheer delight in remembering the place and its food, I asked our friend John Egerton, food writer and critic, if he had ever eaten at Wood's. When he said "no," I went on to describe the barbeque to him.

"You need to go to Bozo's," he said. "And here's how you get there. . . ." So it was on another trip to Memphis that we found Mason, Tennessee, a wide space in the road that boasts both Bozo's Barbeque and Gus's World Famous Fried Chicken. Yes, Bozo's is as good as Wood's, but the sauce at Wood's still seems better, just the right edge of pepper and vinegar (begrudging Memory again!). On our annual southern pilgrimage this May, Stephen and I stopped again at Bozo's, declared the barbeque sandwiches as good as ever. As we were about to leave, I asked the waitress about a particularly delicious-looking chocolate pie behind her. "Oh, that's German chocolate pie," she said. "It's so good it'll make you want to slap somebody." Whereupon another customer standing in line said, "I always heard it's so good it'll make you want to slap your mama." We laughed and agreed that wouldn't be advisable, but we both knew the joy of finding something so good it's almost inexpressible, so powerfully fine you are set into motion, so moved you speak in the most elemental gestures. And so with quests: something stirs deeply within, occasioned by season or weather, and we're off; as Geoffrey Chaucer long ago noted, "folks long to go on pilgrimages." Whatever, come spring expect to see Stephen and me on the road southward, still searching, loving every step of the journey.

Never give a child an artichoke

by Jenine Holmes

Never give a child an artichoke to eat.
Never.
In their limited time on earth
they can never know what lies
within its folds.

Never give a child an artichoke to dine on.
They do not look upon the new with intrigue
but fear.
The prickly bits designed to keep them out
do.

Never give a child an artichoke to feast upon.
They'll never get past the choke.
Its frightful, slender, funny bits
will scare them for sure.

But if they are brave
they quickly learn it all falls away.
So easy.
Here the softest
sweetest bits
wait for the man who
takes mouth tender flesh over tongue
teeth
rolling sweet warm butter
only
to call out for more.
And that man is the luckiest bastard in the land.

Food

by Matthew W. Schmeer

On a six-thirty train
between St. Louis and Chicago
there is too much flat farmland
outside the windows and the
grain does not wave with the
regularity of wind
but flails in the turbulence
of passing trains.

There are cows on the tracks
between Springfield and Joliet;
slaughterhouse heifers being led
to the kitchen table.
I've heard that hogs scream when they're slit
from ear to ear and only
the hardest of men
do not mind.

I am removed from my dinner plate;
I do not pluck chickens or draw the
blade across the calf's throat.
I do not labor in the fields to
bring in this year's corn crop
or pluck pole beans by hand in
the delta sun.

I have on occasion gutted the trout
or pan-fish after sport, but there is no
work in what we deem relaxation.
I do not pull carrots and potatoes
from the ground or beat the wheat

against the earth to separate the
hull from the chaff and grind it into flour
after milking the cows and churning the butter, nor
do I worry about swarms of locusts and weevils or
fret about too much or too little rain; there is no worry
in driving to the store in the pouring rain other than getting
a little wet putting the groceries in the trunk of the car.

It is all there in the supermarket:
obscene stockpiles of fresh frozen chickens
and hamburger patties, cans of peas and pineapple
from harvests two years gone,
heads of iceberg lettuce picked by Mexican hands
in the fields outside Phoenix,
oranges and lemons from the thousand-acre orchards
of Florida and California, bushels of Washington apples,
d'anjou pears, artichokes, asparagus, radishes and
cantaloupes—what do they do with the wilting and rotten, the
squashed and the bruised?

The farmer's market, the butcher shops, the Italian bakeries,
the Vietnamese restaurant on the corner of Grand and Chippewa—
they are all the same.
I do not work for what is on my dinner plate.

I have read that we
are still living
our hunter-gatherer past,
adapting the skills of the veldt
to the trappings of life
found in the city.
If you find me
chasing the buffalo
or stalking the antelope
during rush hour traffic
on I-70, do not interfere;
for it is meat, and you do
not want to do the job
yourself.

Killing Chickens

by Bill Brown

We hung out on Aunt Black's
back porch, sipped sweet tea
and waited for her to kill
another chicken.
The dumb-clucks knew
something was wrong,
but when she scattered
new feed, they'd scurry
from under the porch to
the hardscrabble yard
behind the kitchen. Black
would grab her choice
by the neck and wind its
body in the air like a
cowboy roping a calf.
We wanted to cheer but
her side-glance let us know
death wasn't funny business.
She killed two when Preacher
Beard was due for dinner;
enough legs, livers and gizzards
for us, breasts and thighs
for him. He talked hell so much,

we were glad to eye our food,
thankful for anything.
The only event better than
eating Black's chicken was
watching the killing. The "death-
flop," my father called it. We'd
learn quick enough, Aunt Black
warned: a short headless flight,
flapping jumps, nothing left
but the shivers.

Margaret Scanlan / **Beef Plate**

I'm Still a Vegetarian

by Jim Eastin

I hope it would make you happy to know
That I'm still a vegetarian
Even in this place
Where people think asparagus
Is a kind of pasta

I miss your sweet potato pirogues
I miss your cashew surprise
I miss your special couscous
That whole new world of foods
You introduced me to

But you did ruin me for the thousands of restaurants
Where they can't spell words bigger than "cow" or "pig"
And for my brother's grill where the choices are always rare or burned
And where-oh-where can I find the drive-thru window
Serving roasted red peppers and portabella mushrooms on a
    sesame seed bun?

Most of all I miss the one who created the food
And served it so elegantly
Who blushed when I said how lovely it was
Who made even the simplest meal special
Because you held my hand when we said grace.

Meet Me at Long's

by Flossie McNabb

In the 1950s and early '60s my family drove our Pontiac up and down Kingston Pike like one of those plastic convertibles on the board game of *Life,* where you traveled from real estate boom to the Poor Farm at the mercy of the dice. My sister and I were two pink pegs plugged unbuckled into the backseats. Thank heavens we never landed in the Poor Farm or in a ditch along the road, but we did strike it rich by making frequent stops at Long's Drugstore. Along with the Blue Circle Drive-In and Zesto Ice Cream, Long's was one of our favorite destinations. While Mother was getting a prescription filled or looking for the right shade of red lipstick, my sister and I would make a beeline for the comics stand, grab an *Archie* and *Veronica* or a *Superman,* head to the lunch counter and order cherry Cokes. Sometimes we would just sit at one of the tables by the huge glass windows with our soda pop and watch the world go by on Kingston Pike. We loved to play "Every 10th Car Is Ours," a game we'd made up, and giggle if the 10th was an ice truck or a jalopy. A few years later, after getting off the school bus, I would be sitting at that same table at Long's with my friends. We'd order plates of fries and Coke after Coke, pretending to study but really waiting for our latest "crush" to walk through the door. Since its beginning in 1956, Long's has been the best place to meet or accidentally-on-purpose meet people.

Just as I can't imagine driving a car without seatbelts, I can't imagine Knoxville without Long's. The other day I was sitting at one of the tables by the window having a BLT (with burnt bacon, as requested) when I remembered a girl who once rode her horse to Long's. (When someone wants to get to Long's, they get there!) In the early '60s there was a girl in my neighborhood called Miss Pat (her father's name was Pat, too). Being three or four years older than I, she could do no wrong in my eyes. One day a bunch of us were galloping around the neighborhood as Roy Rogers and

Trigger and the Lone Ranger and Silver. Miss Pat sat on the grassy hill close by observing our play. Late in the afternoon we heard the loud bell from Miss Pat's house ringing her home to dinner. Before she got halfway up her driveway, she turned and called out to us. "I'll be riding a real horse tomorrow." She waved goodbye and added, "Meet me at Long's after school." Well, no one believed her. She lived way up on the hill, and we'd never seen a dog up there, much less a horse. But, if she was telling the truth, I thought later that night, I wasn't about to miss it. The next day I talked my mother into leaving me at Long's after school while she went grocery shopping. I sat at the counter with a stack of comics and a chocolate soda. I had finished my soda and comics and was about to give up when Miss Pat walked in and sat down at the counter a ways up from me. She ordered a chocolate soda from Maybelle and slurped it down in a hurry. Before I could get her attention she was up and running toward the door. I quickly followed, just in time to see her swing up on a chocolate-colored horse in front of the barbershop. The horse was at least a head higher than the roofs of the two Pontiacs he stood between, one belonging to my mother still down at The White Store. Miss Pat smiled at me with a chocolate mustache, and waved as she rode off at a trot down Old Kingston Pike toward home about a mile away. I told my mother about Miss Pat and the horse on our way home but she only smiled. At dinner that night my father confirmed my story when he reported the horse droppings he'd seen on Scenic Drive on his way home from work. I was very relieved. I'd been wondering whether my afternoon story of a horse at Long's was going to be just another one of my tall tales.

Speaking of tales: these days, some forty years after Miss Pat's ride to Long's, if I'm not going there to eat or have a prescription filled or buy a magazine or cash a check, I'll just go there for entertainment. The other day a customer and one of the waitresses were having a grand time insulting each other. The customer was winning in the insult skirmish but, a few minutes later, while making her victorious exit, she accidentally left a small package on the counter. The waitress saw her chance; she grabbed the package and called out the customer's name loudly just before she reached the door, waved the package high in the air, and announced in front of the whole lunch crowd that she'd forgotten her "butt cream."

I'm still driving around Knoxville on my own little board game of life, and I hope to make frequent stops at Long's for years to come. Long's is a walk back, or a trot back, I should say, in time where the counter stools still topple, the waitresses are all characters, and the banter is refreshingly familiar. If everyone who works there doesn't know your name, they at least know your face and whether you like your bacon burnt or your prescriptions delivered or whether your daughter is about to graduate from college. Long's is one of those places which still means home to many people. Long's may never be on the historic preservation list, but I imagine the line of people protesting its demise would stretch to town and back, half of them being under the age of ten and over the age of seventy. We don't know what our energy sources will be in thirty years. We probably won't be riding horses to Long's, but we may be scooting there in battery-powered wheelchairs. For those who are accustomed to the friendliness and comfort of Long's, it will definitely take more than an energy shortage to keep us away. Whether or not I arrive there with my seatbelt on will depend on the mode of transportation.

Starving in Kroger's

by Deborah Scaperoth

Women go around hungry all the time;
no wonder Eve took the first bite.
We hunger for chocolate and cheesecake,
bread, thick with butter, salty nuts and chips.
We walk down grocery aisles, apprising,
how many calories, how much fat?
The quantifying reminds us of deeper hungers;
talcum scent on the neck of a baby
born at our discretion,
the deepest sleep in the softest bed,
a dozen roses from a secret lover,
the kiss of one true love.
Things we can't have.
Most of us learned our lessons from
sister Eve who, after the fall,
grew uneasy in her naked skin.
But, really, we'd all love to wake up
without the guilt—simply fat and satisfied,
knowing that the sturdiest bodies
rest on ample thighs.

New York Embarrasses Me

An excerpt from the unpublished novel *Oh, Jimmy, I Hate Your Death*

by Jennifer Spiegel

At the Pancake Piazza on Lexington, one has the option of ordering silver dollar pancakes, standard pigs in a blanket, a variety of French crepes, Belgian waffles, buckwheat and buttermilk batters with a miscellany of fruit and chocolate and nuts, or potato latkes.

Then there's the Epic Proportion Pancake Plate, which carries with it no caveat.

In truth, the pancakes on the Epic Proportion Pancake Plate are the size of manholes—too big for Goliath, just right for the Jolly Green Giant. They're jokes for pancakes: decadent, opulent, improper, and tasty. They come in the same varieties as the others, only *bigger*.

Generally speaking, whenever I coerce people into ordering them, there's laughter, a deluge of hot maple, a slathering of real butter, and a doggy bag for when the fun is over. Sure, there may be guilt, forced elimination, and bouts of self-hatred, but the pancakes are well worth it.

I always say, "I'll never do it again." I do it about four or five times a year.

So, when Maggie arrives, fresh from Middle America, I figure we'll go nuts. We'll be outrageous! We'll break world records! We'll eat flapjacks of shocking, scandalous, *indecent* proportions!

Maggie is visiting New York for the first time; she wants to see a *Saturday Night Live* taping, pose for pictures with Sirajul and Mujibar from *The David Letterman Show,* go to the Hard Rock Café, and maybe find a few squirrels in Central Park.

Maggie, arriving at JFK, takes the shuttle to Grand Central—when I see her for the first time since our cousin's wedding in Idaho, she's straddling her suitcase protectively. On the subway to my place, she whispers, "Should I keep my money in my sock?"

I make excuses for the sound of the train vibrating my walls. "The rent is only six-hundred and fifty. All my friends pay *much, much* more."

Leaning against the kitchen counter and strategically placing my hand over the century-old water stains that make the place historic, I tell her, "Just down the road, Dylan Thomas drank himself to death. There's *a lot* of history around here."

When Maggie showers, I stand outside the curtain, ready—at a moment's notice—to turn the dial from hot to cold. The water makes swift temperature changes at the most unforeseen times. "This is something new. I'm sure my landlord will get right on it."

I read Maggie's thoughts: Is Jennifer aware that all her friends have recently bought new Saturns? Should I tell her our student loans are paid for?

She wants Ray's Pizza, having heard so much about it. It's a good thing any old Ray's will do.

We walk around Greenwich Village. Pretty scary stuff. All those freaks.

She wants to see the Statue of Liberty. I flat-out refuse. "The lines are too long. Have I shown you the Church of the Exquisite Panic? Incorporated?"

Three solid days of burgers at Planet Hollywood, cheesecake at Carnegie Deli, hot pretzels on the street. Since she tends not to substitute food for love, these aren't quite the experiences I hoped they would be. Rather, we're just spending a lot of money on a lot of calories, taking half-hearted advantage of photo opportunities.

"You walk too fast," she complains.

"But I always have someplace to go," I explain.

And there's this point, this one moment in time, when we sit at a table at Dean and Deluca on Rockefeller, sipping drinks and taking a breather. It's raining and we have standby tickets for *Saturday Night Live*. We're uneasy. She wants to see the show; I need Maggie to love New York. She *has* to love it. I sip my coffee and look out at the *Window on the World* of the *The Today Show*. The AP rattles off headlines. I read the headlines, one after the other, a tickertape of doom, a garland of true epic proportions, streamers of another kind. And the latest news is that people are dead around the world. They just keep dying. I turn to Maggie, moving slowly as if the air were thick, and I wonder—I really do—if I'll survive the night, if I'll make it through. I want to ask her, "But do you *love* New York?"

On the last day, we go to Pancake Piazza. Having considered the options, Maggie closes her menu. "I'm getting blueberry silver dollar pancakes with syrup on the side."

"Did you just say *blueberry?*" I cock my head.

Maggie, who doesn't even drink coffee, spoons an ice cube out of her water glass. "Yes. Blueberry."

Oh. My. God. I lower my menu onto my chest, which is experiencing uneven palpitations. I plead. I beg. "Maggie, this is what they're known for. Big, fucking pancakes. Why do you think we came here?" Do it, Maggie! Be outrageous! Be a sport!

"I can't eat all that," she says.

Understand, my life is on the line. "You don't do it because you're going to *eat* them, Maggie. You do it just to *do* it." She stares at me; I stare at her. "You take them home with you. You roll them up into little pancake balls and play catch with the neighbor's dog. You keep them in the fridge till you have company and then you bring them out as a conversation piece. You don't have to *eat* them."

She folds her arms over her chest. "What do *you* do with them?" she asks.

"Well," I hem and haw, clearing my throat. "I eat them." Then I quickly add, "Over the course of several days."

And so Maggie has blueberry silver dollar pancakes with syrup on the side. The sadness, the disillusionment, the stark reality hits me like the sensation of standing on a street corner waiting for a lover who's just not going to make it, never was going to, didn't even plan on it.

When she leaves, I eat her leftover blueberry pancakes. I'm like an Israelite wandering the wilderness, begging for meat. I eat pancakes till they come out of my nostrils. I wish things with Maggie had been different. Maybe if I lived some other place—some other place that didn't take on a life of its own. A place which I could impose myself on instead of the other way around. I wouldn't need to explain why I live in a basement or why I risk getting scorched in the shower.

I want to tell her things. *Eat pancakes, Maggie.* They're a deal—just like my rent. Break out of the pizza-or-Chinese chains that bind you. That's what we *do* here. We walk fast and eat a lot. I want you to eat those epic proportion apple and cranberry pancakes and, when you're done, you'll eat some of my banana and coconut ones, too. I want you to eat and eat until you're so damn bloated you'll need a good long walk to work it off because then, by God, you'll appreciate my life.

And, over and over, the question pierces my head like a migraine: But *do you love New York?* 🍵

Love Feast

by Catherine Crawley

Beginnings

Hearty wild mushroom polenta, saffron-infused New Zealand mussels, crawfish rolls with sesame drizzle—each can tap into cravings one never even knew one had. If, as they say, food is like love and the act of eating a truly sensual experience, then good first courses must do exactly as they're intended—whet the appetite.

The tender two-inch bundles of mozzarella and tomato perched delicately in a semicircle and rested quietly on the leaf of basil. Rebecca knew each morsel would go down well. First, a burst of balsamic vinegar followed by the smooth creaminess of the mozzarella, rounded off by the hearty tartness of the sweet summer tomato. The temptation was too much to bear. She dived in.

Rebecca's companion for the evening was Doug, whom she'd met a few weeks ago in the parking lot of the tennis club. New to Los Angeles, Rebecca had decided to join the club as a way to meet people and hopefully to find a connection to some kind of community in this seemingly disconnected city of millions. It was the best she could do, having arrived fresh out of graduate school from a small town in Virginia.

In the tennis club parking lot that day, she'd found Doug in a rather surprising condition as she rounded the corner of a car—bare-chested with his shorts skirting his ankles. Seeing her coming, he rushed to scoop them off the ground.

"Excuse me," he said quickly, blushing slightly in the glare of the sun.

"No. Excuse me," Rebecca replied, also slightly reddening at the sight of this man in only his underpants. "Men's changing rooms closed? Or let me guess, you don't believe in indoor changing," she queried, sounding more condescending than she'd intended.

"I'm sorry," he said, pulling a clean shirt over his head. "I'm not normally this much of a naturalist, but I forgot my change of clothes in the car today. And I'm in a bit of a rush."

Rebecca admitted to herself that she was somewhat disappointed that he'd now covered up his tautly muscled chest. He'd obviously just come off the tennis court, and she had caught him in a vulnerable moment. Suddenly, she wanted to change her earlier tone to a friendlier one.

Doug made it easy for her by introducing himself first and again apologizing if he'd scared her. His match had gone longer than he'd expected and he had to get across town to visit his parents and his brother for dinner. He was already running late. "One of my only vices," she remembered him saying as he got into his car.

They'd exchanged info, and before long, they were exchanging e-mails during the day, spending evenings talking on the phone, and making plans for the weekend. And now here they sat across from one another at their favorite West Hollywood eatery, both happy to plunge into another culinary adventure.

This was in the beginning.

Rebecca eyed the rest of her mozzarella and tomato salad. It was slowly diminishing and yet she just couldn't get enough.

The Middle

Over dinner one evening, they planned a going-away weekend in Montecito. Between mouthfuls of blackened noodles and plump, juicy Gulf shrimp, Rebecca listened while Doug recited his long list of activities for each day.

"On Saturday morning," he said eagerly, after gulping a bite of his hazelnut-encrusted sea bass, "if we get up by eight, we can make the brunch at the Aubergine. Then, we'll be able to make it to the winery by noon. In the afternoon, we can rent kayaks and hit the beach."

Hmm, Rebecca thought, twirling a noodle engorged with garlic and butter. Does that mean we will actually go kayaking or hit the beach, as in loll peacefully in the sun? Doug's tendency toward over-planning and over-organizing was beginning to grate against her preferred unhurried and less structured mode, which in her mind allowed for more spontaneous discoveries.

Rebecca remembered an earlier time when their lovemaking was sweet and spontaneous—a time when together they seemed to move with the moment—at times frenetic and impatient and at others, sensuous in their play and touch. She yearned for that softer time.

Now the edges were more defined, and for Rebecca, the picture was beginning to come into focus. No longer the wispy form Rebecca fell in love with in the beginning, Doug sliced into the rest of his fish.

"So, what do you think?" he asked, cocking his head a bit too cheerfully.

"About what?" she said, swimming out of her thoughts.

"About the weekend?" he said.

"Oh. Yes. Right." She set down her fork. Already she was feeling full and thought perhaps she'd overdone it on the olive oil and sourdough that came with this course. Inhaling deeply, she shut her eyes for a moment before speaking.

"Doug," she said softly. "Do you remember when we spent the Sunday just reading papers on the porch, drinking coffee? Finally, by about three, we decided to make something to eat. Well, as I recall we ended cooking up other things in the kitchen . . . do you remember?" She said, pausing again and smiling. "I miss that."

Rebecca was sure Doug's eyebrows began to sag at the edges. He didn't say anything. Not encouraging, Rebecca thought.

She forged ahead anyway. "Can we have that sort of day while we're away?"

"I guess we can," he said finally. "But I just thought it would be the best use of our time."

Not to put too fine a point on it, added Rebecca. Right. If you over-schedule us with all kinds of activities, they'll be no time for intimate moments.

On the other hand, her thinking continued, if I desire a more intimate time, perhaps that indicates I'm not ready for the reality of official humdrum couple-dom?

Well, she'd thought enough—said enough. He'd too said enough. They'd eaten enough. The satiated couple.

The plates were cleared. It was time for dessert.

The End

Wasn't that the fourth time Doug had looked at his watch in the last half-hour? Not that Rebecca was keeping track. She couldn't help it—there were other things that caught her attention in the restaurant on that late evening as well.

Over glasses of red wine, the elderly couple in the corner smiled conspiratorially at each other as though they'd just shared a private joke. Next to them sat a much younger couple, eyeing their menus as eagerly as they eyed each other. Across the room in front of plates of roasted lamb and chicken, a husband and wife appeared to be deep in one of those mysterious conversations that seem to take place only between married couples.

Doug and Rebecca sat quietly, resigned to their mugs of coffee as they waited for dessert.

Rebecca noticed the red stain on the tablecloth from the pasta dish she'd sampled this evening. She tried a new topic of conversation. "You know that play we went to a few weeks ago. Well, I heard the director has decided to stage another play by the same playwright."

"Oh really. That's interesting" was Doug's meager response. He began drumming his fingers on the ceramic.

"Please don't do that," Rebecca said, trying hard to disguise the note of irritation creeping into her voice.

"Sorry," Doug mumbled, cupping his hands back around the mug.

Rebecca shifted in her seat and began to survey the restaurant again.

Now it was Doug's turn to steer the conversation. "What's the play about?" he said, as though he'd remembered something he'd forgotten to ask from some distant conversation.

"It's about the end of an affair," Rebecca said reluctantly, now wishing she'd thought of a different topic. "The main character is a chef. He leaves his lover—apparently, she's fiercely obsessed with his cooking, more than she is with him."

"It's meant to be some sort of tragi-comedy," she added, hoping he'd understand the humor it in better than she.

The waiter's abrupt appearance halted this back-and-forth. He placed the house specialty, banana bread pudding, on the table between Doug and Rebecca, adding two bright, clean forks on the side. This was a sign that they'd be sharing, even though Rebecca had ordered the dessert and Doug had chosen against it this evening.

Doug sat like a pudding. He didn't rush to get a fork. He let out a grand sigh. "Rebecca," he said haltingly. "This isn't working, is it?"

"What? You mean the bread pudding?" Rebecca said, ignoring the obvious question. "Actually, I think it's working just fine," she said, stuffing another sticky bite.

But they both knew what this was about. Doug waited, eerily silent. Resigned to the inevitable, Rebecca decided to devour every last bite of her pudding. She would enjoy every morsel while it lasted. Each bittersweet mouthful, however, became harder and harder to swallow.

Finally, she was finished. Triumphant, she set down her fork.

Friendship, they said, would be the answer. They would continue to be friends—often the death knell solution to any relationship.

Later, Rebecca would recall this fleeting romance with the tennis star what-was-his-name. Was it really that they weren't truly compatible? Isn't that always the excuse? Perhaps it was just as it should be—a beginning, a middle and an end—a sweet summertime diversion and a momentary anchor while she searched for a mooring in her new city.

As time went on, the details began to blur. Still, around the edges lingered a sharper memory—of summertime tomatoes, basil, mozzarella, a drizzle of balsamic and other grander beginnings. ☕

Harvest

by Ted Olson

My crops grew up
without my help;
harvest's coming.

Walked so far today,
hardly breathing, I

remove my boots,
pants, shirt,
bathe in the river;

as dirt washes off me
a coon robs my food;

I don't care,
I'm heading homeward,
going to lay

my vagrant body
in her bed . . . .

I'm still alone, clothed
in pain—though I'll rest
at my road's end:

she'll feed me meat,
beans, cornbread;

I'll be there
soon, if
I'm not dead—

she'll shuck
me then.

In My Blue Kitchen

by Kay Newton

In my blue kitchen
I chop onions with a vengeance,
never mind the tears.

In my blue kitchen
I chant hexes over chicken soup,
weave spells with bay and barley.

In my blue kitchen
raw spaghetti strings
become the *I Ching*.

In my blue kitchen
I sing hymns
and slice cucumbers lengthwise,
pit ripe olives.

In my blue kitchen
I brew hot black tea
and hide the leaves
that tell me you will never be
in my blue kitchen.

My Fortune

by Jo Ann Pantanizopoulos

Ekei pou klaney e Aleppou . . . I proudly recited before my new husband's family and relatives. I was the new American bride, stiff and embarrassed before my new Greek family. Moments before, my mother-in-law had just taught me a children's nursery rhyme in Greek. "My pronunciation must be pretty good," I thought. Everyone burst out laughing and clapped their hands. Pride engulfed my red face until my husband, Yianni, leaned over to whisper what I had said. "There where the fox farts . . ." he began. "She taught me to say that?" I asked him. "Mamá is *kati allo* (something else), *Iosifina mou.*" My mother-in-law indeed has been *kati allo* for me during the thirty years I have known and loved her. I often dwell on what an influence this rotund, five-foot-tall woman has been on me.

Vera Saoulidou walked with her parents, Eva and Dimitri, over two thousand miles from the *Pontos* region of the Black Sea to Odessa, Russia and on to northern Greece—at the age of three. A large Greek population, although located in the former Soviet Union, inhabited the Odessa area. In 1917 during the Bolshevik Revolution most of the Greeks left and returned to their homeland, Greece. I never tire of hearing stories about her life. When she tells me of the gypsy woman who stole her during the long trek from Russia to Greece, a brief question of, "How could she remember from such a young age?" skitters across the logical side of my mind, but I refuse to allow it to remain. Sometimes the gypsy woman, who had no children and took very good care of little Vera, keeps her for two days and sometimes I hear it is three days before Eva and Dimitri call her name and she runs outside to greet them.

Mamá Vera went to school through the third grade. In her youth it wasn't necessary to educate girls, but Yianni and two of his sisters are university educated. Her letters to me are simple, often misspelled, and always empty of any of the five stress marks required in formal written Greek. It's funny how my letters to her are simple, often misspelled, and always empty of any of the same stress marks. Recently the Greek government legislated out of existence four of those five marks so Mamá and I are among the new age literates. Although she speaks no English, she knows a few words in Turkish, Russian and the Pontian dialect of Greek as well as the Lord's Prayer in Armenian.

We share a common bond besides the one that unites mothers of three girls and one son. She says I saved her life once and I say she's saved mine in many little ways. When she visited us in Pittsburgh, her first visit to the U.S., she came down with pneumonia and was hospitalized for eight days, during which time I (five months pregnant with my third child) stayed with her during the day to translate her wants and the nurse's directions. She probably caught pneumonia during the 45-minute rush to the hospital the week before when her cardiologist wanted to witness the krisis, one of a series of unexpected arrhythmia attacks that we all wanted to see ended, but which still plagues her. It was a memorable ride that night. Because Yianni was out of town on business, I grabbed my two little girls, Antigone, age 2, and Vera, age 5, in their pajamas and put them in the back seat with a blanket. Mamá and I rode through the 2 a.m. rainstorm to the hospital, but during such an attack it was common for her to pass copious amounts of fluid. Winding through Pittsburgh's dark, dirty steel mill streets, I could find no gas station or even a sheltered tree for her to sit behind. Finally, under an overpass she squatted outside the car door and became drenched. We often laugh about that picture, but at the time I was scared of many things—boogey men, the night, the rain, my unborn, her sudden death. She tells her friends I was brave and confident.

It probably wasn't easy for her to accept that her only son would marry a chubby American with no dowry, but she never once showed me that she disapproved. Since then she told me her philosophy was, "If Yianni wants her, then I want her." I remember the time when I was going to make a *pastitsio,* a Greek version of lasagna, for my father-in-law. My husband told his mother to let me do it all by myself, and she agreed. She called in a neighbor friend and together they squatted in the doorway watching my every move like an audience at a tennis match to see exactly how an American makes *pastitsio.* Mamá, who has made enough Greek coffees in her lifetime to keep entire armies awake, tells her friends that I taught her how to make Greek coffee. I measured the coffee cups of water into the pot before I added the coffee and sugar. This brilliant feat of mine, she says, changed forever the way she used to measure the water with her eye.

I've probably broken her heart many times by my misunderstandings of her way of life, food, or language, but she has opened my eyes and my heart consistently. Yianni and I married in Thessaloniki, Greece, in 1970. Before we left the U.S. she had written to us that she would make my wedding dress after we arrived there. My own mother and I searched for patterns for days until I found the style I wanted, but when I arrived Mamá brought out a wedding dress covered with silver embroidery, which she had been working on all year. When I first saw the dress, I began to cry because it wasn't the dress I had envisioned myself wearing, but I told Yianni to tell her that I was only crying because it was so beautiful. I didn't want to hurt her feelings. After I had my own children, I understood the thrill she must have experienced embroidering those silver flowers every night thinking of her son's wedding. My daughters, Vera, Antigone, and Alexia have all asked to wear that wedding dress someday. Her embroidery and handwork are seen throughout my home. My coffee table is covered by a crocheted scarf consisting of small patterned circles of eggshell cotton. Another small table is graced by an embroidered table scarf with blue Byzantine peacocks and clusters of blood red roses, each petal separated by tiny stitches in gold thread. My linen closet is full of tablecloths and doilies and table scarves she made for me and for my daughters' dowries.

When I was living in Greece and was pregnant with my second child, my husband returned to America to begin his U.S. citizenship papers. My three-year-old daughter and I went to stay with my parents-in-law for forty-five days. It was winter, and I had a head cold that wouldn't end. I was homesick and lonely and she knew it. To take my mind off myself, Mamá taught me how to make unusual culinary delights such as *yemista,* a dill, liver and rice mixture wrapped and baked in paper-thin sheep stomach's lining. She taught me how to crochet, which enabled me to make a little jacket for my new baby. To make me laugh, she taught me dirty jokes and every dirty word possible in the Greek language. Crocheting and cursing became very useful tools in clothing my babies and arguing with taxi drivers. It was during these forty-five days when Yianni was away that I realized she loved me unconditionally. Besides a head cold, I became ill with flu and was sick "at both ends," which she cheerfully cleaned up. In addition, she rubbed my pregnant tummy with lemon-scented cologne water to rid my body of the *grippe.* She took little Vera and me to a Turkish *hamam,* a communal steam bath where women sit on marble stools around a large sink of hot water. It was a divine repetition of pour and soap, pour and soap. Since I wasn't allowed to take medicine, she showed me her home remedies that worked even better than aspirin. For a headache Mamá placed cotton wadding soaked in alcohol and sprinkled generously with pepper in a man's handkerchief folded lengthwise. The poultice was then placed around my neck with the peppered cotton wadding at the base of the skull. The cold-hot sensation was soothing and soon enough my headache was gone. For a fever, she again folded a man's handkerchief lengthwise and placed three slices of raw potato in the center. This was tied on the forehead with the potato slices next to my skin drawing out the fever. Unlike a wet washcloth, the potato slices remained cool to my fevered forehead. Mamá dosed me with chamomile tea—that universal medicine for the old and young.

Vera Saoulidou Pantanizopoulos has not had an easy life. Her father was a stove maker in a village where everyone already had a stove that lasted a lifetime. He died a few days after her engagement to Niko, when Vera was only seventeen. A few years after their marriage, World War II broke out and the Italians and Germans invaded Greece. Niko became a Resistance fighter in the mountains, leaving her with three young children; the youngest was Yianni, born in 1939. During the German occupation, a strict curfew was in place. All civilians on the streets after nine p.m. were to be shot. One day she received word that Niko was coming home from the mountains to see her. The day and evening passed and still her husband had not appeared. Shortly before nine p.m. she heard gunfire outside her home and seconds later a loud banging on the door. They had come to tell her that her husband had been shot. As she tells this story, she is smiling, nodding her head, and a tear falls from her eyes. "It was not Niko after all. They had shot someone else!" she whispers.

Every year on the feast day of the Elevation of the Cross, September 14, my mother-in-law goes to church and lights candles for the Virgin Mary to thank her for saving her and her three little ones from being shot. In the village of Yiannitsá, where Vera and her children lived then, the Germans discovered one of their officers dead. To find the killer, all the villagers were rounded up and told to stand around the edge of a freshly dug pit. Vera held little Yianni on her hip with Iro and Kaiti whining at her skirts. "Who did it? Tell us or you will all be shot and fall into your grave now!" the Germans shouted. As my mother-in-law tells it, just as the German soldiers lifted their rifles to their shoulders, another German ran from the village with news that the Greek saboteur had been found. Knowing that the

Germans almost decided her fate has not embittered Vera to Germans. Her youngest daughter Dimitra, born after the war, majored in German at the University of Thessaloniki. Mamá often talks fondly about the German doctor's wife who took over the house next door during the war. Recently my daughters learned how to make the German potato salad that their *yiayia* learned to make from her former neighbor.

Once, when I was helping her clean her house, I found an old rag placed on the balcony rail to dry. When I picked it up and began to fold it into a square to finish my cleaning, I noticed English words printed on it. It read, "___t from the people of the United States of Am___" When I asked her about the cloth, she told me it was just an old rag, but later Yianni told me it was a piece of a cornmeal sack that people received just after World War II when many Greeks were on the brink of starving. Although cornbread was not a Greek dish, *bobota* was a staple in their diets during the Greek Civil War until wheat fields could be planted and harvested. Many Greeks, including my husband Yianni, dislike cornbread because they had to eat it in difficult times.

Besides the fact that we each have four children, my mother-in-law and I have a special feeling for each other. Mamá knows when something is wrong and when something good will happen to me because she reads coffee cups. Greek coffee* is brewed with pulverized coffee so that when the liquid is drunk, a fine dark brown silt is left in the bottom of each cup. When the cup is gently shaken and turned over to drain, fine lines and

* In a *briki,* or small Greek coffee pot with a long handle, add 1 demitasse cup of water, 1 teaspoon of sugar, and 1 heaping teaspoon of pulverized coffee per person. Bring just to a boil, letting a few bubbles come to the surface. Remove from the heat and pour a small amount of the thick foam to each cup and continue pouring a little into each cup until full. It would be a bad sign if you hand someone a cup without at least a few *fouskas,* or bubbles, showing! After drinking the coffee, swish around the grounds and some leftover liquid. Pour into the accompanying saucer making sure to coat most of the cup's inside. Place on a napkin upside down to dry a little. With a calm bravado, begin to read your own fortune. (Only the first-born daughter of a woman who reads *flitzania* can have the knowledge handed down to her to read the cups of others.) Within your cup, you might be able to see some of these common signs:

peacock, bird, turtle, rabbit, deer = good news/fortune
cat = bad
2 dogs fighting = bad
road with/without obstacles
round-faced person with a gift
a number = in "4" hours/days/years something good/
significant will happen
a letter = someone whose name begins with that letter is
thinking of you (or is an enemy of yours)
tiny bubbles on the cup's lip = mail or packages (count them)

patterns are formed. Mamá has fine-tuned this *flitzani* reading throughout her life. By reading your coffee cup, she can tell you how many letters you will get today, if your friend got her engagement ring yet, if your unborn is a boy or a girl, if you will soon be taking a long journey, but if there is a *big* blob in the bottom of your cup, she will tell you that you are having *big* problems and you had better tell her about it.

During a visit to her home one summer before our fourth child was born, I wasn't feeling well, particularly in the morning hours, and I refused to eat her mussel pilaf, a family favorite. Often I would catch her looking at me with a little grin on her round face. When my lethargy continued, she asked me point blank, "Are you sure you're not pregnant?" "Of course not, Mamá. I would tell you, wouldn't I?" I blustered, feeling caught in a lie because I did have "that feeling" again. When she suggested I go with her to her bi-weekly blood test for diabetes, I agreed to a urine test just to, hopefully, prove she was wrong. Later in the day when the doctor telephoned her with her blood sugar results and I heard her say, *"Efharisto, yiatre!* Thank you, doctor. This will make ten grandchildren for us!" I knew she knew even when I didn't know.

I've thought lately about how I will feel when she passes on. Like many older Greek women, Mamá talks about death especially after an exhausting arrhythmia attack. During a recent visit, I gave her a new white slip and, when we were dressing to go out for dinner, I asked her to wear it so I could be sure it fit her. Tears grew in her eyes and she said she'd set that slip aside for later. "What later, Mamá? If it doesn't fit I can take it back and mail you another size." "Eh, *pethi mou,* my child, I will need that slip soon and I don't want to burden my other daughters to rush out and buy me one." Still not understanding, I asked her why they would have to buy her a new one. She continued, "It's a custom to dress the dead in new clothes for their burial and I want to wear that slip then." I turned away trying to understand, not wanting to accept her reason. She quietly refolded the new slip and put it back in the closet. Then she smiled at me. ** 🍵

** Mamá died in her sleep on January 29, 2000, four days before her 85th birthday.

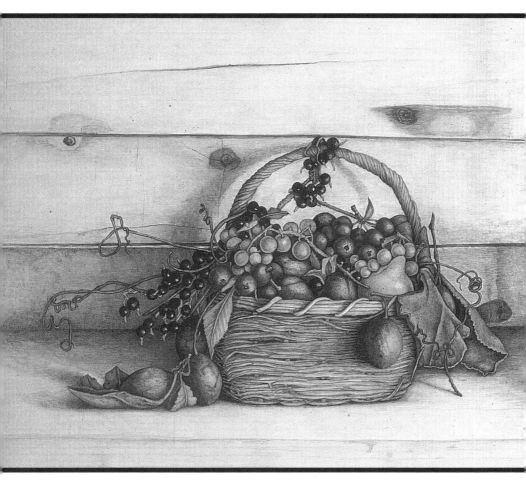

Sarah McCarty / **Basket of Fruit**

Portabella Prince

by Carly Sachs

The worst advice I ever got was
if you're looking for love,
try the produce section at your local grocery.
I've been a vegetarian for two years
and I've never taken a romantic stroll
down the lettuce aisle.
I'm alone from romaine to rapine.
Week after week I dream of my prince.
He'll be wearing faded jeans and a button-down shirt,
preferably periwinkle, and he'll have on sandals,
either Tevas or Birks, I can't decide.
He'll be holding a bouquet of broccoli
and a shy smile will tip-toe across his face
as he approaches me. *"It's my favorite,"* he'll say.
"Mine too."
Then he'll slip his arm around me
and we'll fill our buggy with corn and tomatoes,
eggplant and bok choy. Anything that grows
out of earth's belly will be fair game.
We'll measure the days in corn stalks and potato peels
and I'll wear dresses the color of *habenero* and summer squash.
At our wedding I'll carry a nosegay of cilantro and basil.
We'll push that shopping cart around the aisles,
pointing out produce as if we were on a gondola in Venice.
The sign on the back will read, *Just Cookin'.*

Portabella Prince Gets a Make-Over

by Carly Sachs

No one finds Mr. Right at Gristede's.
Who am I kidding, Ramona thinks.
Mr. Right doesn't have time to buy radicchio,
that's ridiculous.
He's not going to woo me with broccoli.
Men in this city aren't like that.
They are into the greens,
but it's the benjamins and not the beans.
Ramona sighs thinking of her Portabella Prince.
He's probably at some Acme or Giant Eagle in Jersey.
"You're not going to find love in with the lettuce anyway"
advises Lucy. "You're like an ostrich.
You've got your head in the cheese case.
You need to get out there for Christ sake.
Everyone goes out in New York.
Why don't you go to a restaurant every once in a while?"
Ramona can almost see it, bumping elbows in
a crowded café, or better yet, sharing a table
with a perfect stranger.
He'll know how to order wine, be courteous
to the wait staff, and never ever use his cell phone
at the dinner table. She can almost taste the tiramisu
they'll share and the kiss afterwards, and of course
he'll always be in the mood to eat out.
They'll take taxis to Thai and Vietnamese restaurants.

No taste will be too exotic, no price too large to pay
for Ethiopian or Cantonese, no hour too late
for *carpaccio* or caviar. He'll whisper sweet nothings
across the table, feed her forkfuls of his fettuccine,
and swear utter devotion over crème brulee.
For days Ramona fantasizes about her new *Bon Appétit* beau.
Lucy is right, she says to herself, the grocery scene is long gone.
If I'm going to find Mr. Right in this city,
I need a new strategy.

Mango Salsa

by Leo Williams

My girlfriend created a mango salsa shortly after we began dating.

The salsa was almost an afterthought. Kate was doing a shrimp recipe she had gotten from a friend of a friend, and she was clearly looking forward to it. Her green eyes gleamed with confidence as she strung the shrimp on bamboo skewers.

"I think you might enjoy this," she said as she placed the skewers on the charcoal grill. It's called 'Trinidad Shrimp.' Or maybe 'Tobago Shrimp.' Anyway, it's good. Mango, chilies. Ha cha cha!"

She said that last little bit as the last skewer went on the grill. She raised her hands over her head, started snapping her fingers, and danced in a little circle in front of the barbecue. It was sexy as hell. Her long, red hair danced behind her as she undulated. I couldn't tell if she was dancing for me or for the shrimp. It didn't really matter.

She was right: I was already enjoying it very much. I was enjoying the warm summer evening on her back porch. I was enjoying the pleasure she took from being the maestro. And I was enjoying the opportunity to just sit there and watch her dance, to stare without guilt. I have to admit I was feeling smug at the thought of getting involved with this smart, irreverent, artistic woman. Kate was a teacher, passing her love of art to high school seniors, while I was spending my days with suits, business types who were neither irreverent nor artistic. I've never quite decided if they're smart.

In our years together, I've witnessed Kate's artistry in the kitchen as well, and I know that the shrimp would have been every bit as good as she was letting on. But fate was not her friend that evening and, just as she put them on the grill, she got a phone call.

She spoke in an undertone as she took the call, and I sat there like an idiot watching her try to hide from me the anger she felt over being called right then. "Hello? What? Look, Mr. Johnson, I'm sorry you feel that way, but can't this wait until tomorrow?"

Apparently it couldn't wait. Kate ducked inside to be out of earshot, and by the time she got back to the grill, the shrimp were beyond redemption. She pulled them off, and we both tried one just to make sure. They were pure rubber.

You'd think I might have saved the day. I'm a passable cook, and God knows I've been victimized by overcooked shrimp. But I was having too much fun watching to think about going to the grill and being helpful. It didn't dawn on me that I could have salvaged dinner until she gave me a badly disguised look of disgust.

"Well, I guess we'll have to do something else," she said, standing there and looking down at me. With a jolt of recognition, I realized that I was largely to blame for the disaster. I must have turned red. I know my ears were burning. I wanted to hide, but all I could do was mutter, "Um, yeah, that'd be OK." Smooth.

Kate is nothing if not a resourceful woman. She had a mango and a handful of fresh mint that had been intended for the shrimp, and she had a Scotch Bonnet chili in her refrigerator. I followed her into the kitchen, hoping to be helpful. "Can I do anything?" I asked. "Nah," she said, "just relax." Well, I'd shown I was good at that.

She stood there chopping things for what must have been about five minutes, although it seemed like an eternity as I waited uncomfortably. Once she had everything together in a bowl, she threw in some salt and pepper, tossed the whole mess a couple of times, and set it on the counter.

When she turned to me, she was smiling, but there was still fire in her eyes. I was forgiven, but there would be a price to pay.

"Hey, Buddy," she said, "go get me some chips."

The command took me off guard. For one thing, my name isn't "Buddy," but this was no time to argue. I managed to stammer, "What?"

"I said, 'Go get me some chips.'"

"Um, OK." I fished in my pocket for car keys. "I guess I'll be back in a few minutes."

She looked at me for several seconds, hiding a grin and enjoying herself. Finally, she said, "They're in there," and nodded up at a cabinet she could have easily reached without taking a step.

I was a puppet in her show, but I was enjoying it. She didn't move when I walked over to open the cabinet. Just as she had said, there was a bag of unopened tortilla chips in the cabinet. As I pulled them down, we were nose to nose. I kissed her. She kissed back. It was good.

The salsa was good, too, delicious, exotic and dangerously spicy, qualities I quickly learned to associate with Kate herself. And so a tradition was born. The salsa became a regular thing. Kate seemed happiest when she was chopping things for the salsa. It was her respite from the battles of the classroom, or rather her battles at school. As we spent time together, she made it clear to me that teachers, as well as suits, live with bureaucracy, and she complained about it up until the time she began chopping.

But once she started in on the salsa, she had a singleness of purpose. She told me it was her "Zen," and it was during these times that I discovered her terrible, wonderful sense of humor.

"Hey, Buddy!" she called out of the kitchen one night. "What are the most exciting three words you can hear while you're making love. 'Honey, I'm home!'" She roared with laughter, waving the knife helplessly through the air as she struggled to catch her breath. I learned early on not to stand in the kitchen while she was making salsa.

Kate didn't care a bit if I groaned as much as I laughed when she told these jokes. She also didn't care who heard them. Kate had a warped genius for telling just the wrong joke at the wrong time. The night we invited our neighbors Mike and Jennifer to dinner has since become legend. Mike was a minister at a little country church about ten miles down the road. Jennifer was, as far as I could tell, the perfect minister's wife, all smiles and small talk. They were nice people, but they didn't share Kate's sense of humor.

They showed up just as I was getting home. As soon as I shut the door, Kate called out from the kitchen, "Hey, Buddy! This guy walks into a doctor's office complaining of a splitting headache and a ringing in his ears. The doctor says, 'Have you been masturbating recently?' The guy looks worried and says, 'Yeah.' Then the doctor says, 'me too. Isn't it great?'"

I could hear screams of laughter coming from the kitchen as Mike and Jennifer smiled weakly and pretended they hadn't heard. They didn't even last until dinner. Mike suddenly remembered a sick parishioner he needed to see right away, and they were gone. They haven't been back.

Unfortunately, the salsa wasn't our only ritual. We had one more: mystery telephone calls. The scene that first week seemed to play out regularly over the coming months. Kate would pick up the telephone, and she would change, becoming angry or fearful, timid or defensive. Invariably, the woman I was coming to know would disappear while she held the phone. As much as she tried to hide these calls from me, I had her end of the conversation memorized: "Hello? Look, I'm sorry, but I can't talk about this right now. No, I'm not trying to ignore you, but I can't talk right now. No, I don't think I did a terrible thing, but I can't talk right now."

At first, I was able to ignore these calls, but they quickly grew worrisome. At first, I asked Kate what the calls were about, but she told me "nothing" in a manner that made it clear she didn't appreciate the question.

Despite the calls, though, we seemed to be getting closer and closer, and the mango salsa evolved with the relationship. Over time, Kate and I learned to trust as well as enjoy one another, to share comfort as well as excitement. During that time, the salsa gained chopped onion and garlic and cilantro.

"Look at this," she said one evening, setting a watercolor painting in front of me and a bowl of salsa off to the side. I stared at the painting. I could make out what looked like a medieval knight holding a lance. Off to the side was what looked like a mushroom cloud. In the middle was someone who looked sort of like the president.

"What is it?" I asked.

"It's by one of my students."

"I don't get it."

"It's abstract, Buddy, you're not supposed to get it."

"Then I think it's great."

She looked at me with mixed exasperation and amusement. "Take my advice, Buddy. Don't become an art critic. Now go get me some chips."

Kate knew I was undiscerning, but she kept showing me her high school masterpieces. I brought my work to her as well, but in comparison it was decidedly unromantic and unrewarding. Office politics, that sort of thing.

Kate would listen to me whine, and then she would invariably say the same thing: "Take the long view, Buddy. When you're on your deathbed, you're not going to be worrying about how high you made it on the org chart. Now go get me some chips."

Kate and the salsa became unbreakably connected in my mind. I couldn't even see a photo of salsa without thinking of her. Standing in the kitchen, chopping. Lying in my arms watching TV. Lying naked in bed, thighs spread, wearing a smile that was far raunchier than her posture. Offending strangers. And talking on the phone.

When we had been seeing each other for about four months, the calls seemed to get worse: not more frequent, just worse. I could feel her fear even as she took the phone farther and farther away from me to tell someone she couldn't talk right then. I could feel her fear when she came back into the room, no longer able to slough off whatever reality the calls represented.

We spent a lot of time lying quietly together in those days. We spent very little time eating mango salsa.

And then, one day I walked into her house to find that she had been crying. In the time I'd known Kate, I'd never known her to cry. At first, I'd seen her sharp and irreverent. Then I'd seen her anxious and frightened. But I'd never seen her cry.

She was lying on her couch, eyes red, with a hand on her forehead.

"What's the matter?" I asked.

"Nothing, God damn it!"

That was also a first. In the time I'd known Kate, she had never cursed at me in anger. In the early days, she would take a break from calling me "Buddy" to call me "Asshole," but she always said it with a grin. It was a pet name, a term of endearment.

I sat down on the couch with her. "Bullshit," I said. "Something's been wrong since I met you. Tell me."

"I just got canned." She said it in a whisper.

"Shit!" I said. "How did that happen?"

"They don't like the way I teach."

"What do you mean, they don't like the way you teach?"

"I said, 'They don't like the way I teach.' Can we just leave it at that?"

I wasn't ready to let it go. "Come on. Please. Just tell me."

She opened her eyes and looked at me. "All right. Fine. It was last semester, just before we met. We were talking in class about nudes. I can't let the kids draw nudes, but I thought we should at least talk about them. It was an art class, for God's sake. Some kid asked me what was the difference between art and pornography. I told him, 'If you get a hard-on, then it's pornography.'"

"I thought it was funny. The parents didn't. They've been calling me at work, at home, anytime, anywhere. They've also been calling the school board and my administration. Right now, I'm on 'administrative leave' until the board can fire me officially."

"You told him *what?*"

It was the wrong thing for me to say. Her eyes narrowed, and she said softly, "You heard me."

"Sorry. But don't you think that was kind of dumb?"

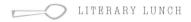

"Go to hell!" she said more loudly this time. "I've been getting this morality crap for the last six months. I really don't need to hear you join the chorus right now. Why don't you take a hike. I'm tired."

I'm not really a master of the sensitive moment, and I knew I'd blown the hell out of this one. "Look, I'm sorry," I said.

"Just leave," she said. "Go away."

She turned away from me, and I stood up and left. Whatever I might have said, the time had passed.

We didn't see one another during the next two weeks, although we spoke on the phone several times. We spoke, but we didn't say anything. We didn't talk about her job, and we didn't talk about us. Looking back, all I can remember talking about was the weather and horse racing. Neither of us follows horse racing, but the Kentucky Derby ran during this time, and we knew just enough about it to help fill the silence.

She called the night before the hearing and asked me to come over the next night. "Are you sure you want me?" I asked. She replied, "Well, I've got to have someone to share my doom with."

I knocked when I got to her door the next night. I hadn't knocked since that first week, but I didn't dare just walk in. When she got to the door, she said, "Come on in, I'll be out in a minute." We didn't kiss. We barely made eye contact.

Kate walked into the kitchen, but I didn't follow her. I sat at her dining table, feeling uncomfortable.

Finally, I said, "How did it go?"

"I'm history," she called out without emotion.

I felt sick. "Do you know what you're going to do?" I asked.

"No, I don't."

I sat there for a moment that seemed very long. Then I said, "God, Kate. I'm sorry. I'm sorry that you're going through this, and I'm sorry I haven't been any help."

"Yeah, well. Them's the breaks."

She was silent for another minute or so. Then she said, "Hell, you might even have been right. I don't know."

I said, "I don't know, either."

Just as I said it, she walked into the room and set a bowl of mango salsa in front of me. Then she sat down and said, "Hey, Buddy, get me some chips?" 🍵

The Milkmaid by Vermeer

by Judy Loest

She wore her good dress,
the indigo apron pulled to the side,
sleeves pushed above her elbows.
Although her arms must have tired
holding the earthenware pitcher so long
controlling the thin stream of milk,
she is serene, transcending the implied
drudgery, her stout, plain-faced body.

I envy how she has stood
in that porcelain light pouring
milk for over three hundred years,
unchanged and unchanging,
innocent in the concentrated reverence
she brings to the task, as if the objects
before her are sacred proofs
of God's providential care.

But there is no denying the light
already fading, the broken bread
on the bare table, the exposed white skin
of her forearm, reminders that beyond
the window lie the immense, perishing fields,
that this bone-white, luminous room
is like every calculated shrine, pretending
to give us what we need then taking it away.

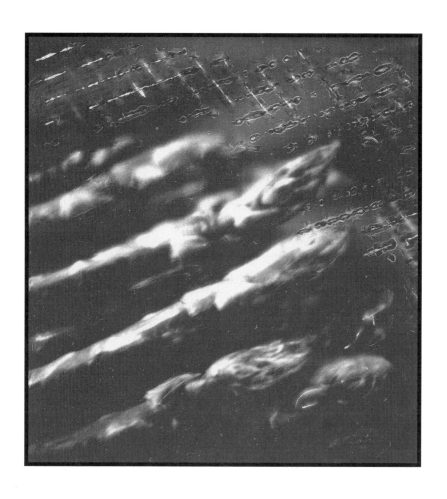

Lindsay Kromer / *Asparagus*

Refuge

by Lisa Collett

Cooking has been my passion and my pain.
Grandma's shiny silver pots,
the infinite teaspoons and measuring cups—
they caught my eye when I was just a boy.
The neighborhood kids had fists for people like me.
I didn't spend my summer at the ballpark
flexing my muscles and chewing tobacco.
My pale, scrawny fingers never felt the wood of a bat,
but they knew each fiber of the wooden spoon.
I tossed color onto my black skillet like Monet to his palette.
The sizzle of butter, the scent of fresh spices,
the oven's warm exhale—they wrapped me
in their art and carried me to my own piece of world
where cuts and teary eyes came only from
the careless slip of a knife and onion fumes.
The glimmer of the kitchen light was my refuge
if only for the span of a batch of cookies.

Homelands

by Leslie McGrath

He'd sniff my skin like a dog
when I came home from work,
licking scabs of powdered sugar
from my arms before I showered
off the bakery smell, his
foreignness an aphrodisiac. We'd
unwrap each other like a picnic,
savoring the delicacies first of his
homeland, then of mine, beads
of moisture littering the bed's bright
tablecloth like crumbs. Afterward,
the slow goodbye: his hand atop
the table of my hip, slipping
as his breathing eased; his sex
still reddened, pointing homeward like a thumb.

Rendezvous, Neither First Nor Last

by Emily Dziuban

Peanut butter. Omnipresent in my memory. I don't recall our first date, our first separation when I traveled, our first official affair after I married Knut. In my baby book my mother has written "Adores Peanut Butter!" next to the One Year entry on the Favorite Foods page. Frankly, I'm surprised my mother and father exposed me to such a powerful force so young. The strong possibility of seduction must have been clear to them. True, millions of children are able to spend years with peanut butter then forget him completely, probably why he's never been questioned about the appropriateness of his many relationships. I certainly could not make an accusation, bring the truth to light as they say, because then he would disappear from the shelves, my unsatisfied need ruining me.

The thing is, I just don't feel like a victim. I feel touched by God. Those children, those millions, now they praise steak and potatoes, chocolate cake, even beer with enthusiasm, but without the light. Without the glow indicative of being truly loved. Knut would tell you he loves me, and so he does. I'm at the top of his list and will be forever, even if we do decide to have a child. After me, Knut's love list, should he put it on paper, would read, in order: Mom, Nephew Jake, Dog Ripken, Brother Charlie, Sailing, Dad. Herein lies the problem. Peanut butter's list reads thus (I've seen it): Liz, Late Nights with Liz, Weekends Alone with Liz, Surprise Meetings with Liz, Liz's Lips, ad infinitum. To my mind, this level of devotion justifies my beginning my first romantic relationship before I could speak. Perhaps my parents were progressive rather than naïve. Perhaps they knew precisely what my reaction might be to that smooth, sticky manhood and decided to reject modern ideology attempting to desexualize children.

"When I first met you, I just thought friends. You were awfully cute," peanut butter says, reading my thoughts as I stand in the kitchen talking to him.

"I'm envious of your memory. Of your ability to place before against after." He's thick silk on my tongue.

"What before? Only you."

"What about the others? I still see you with them."

"Cover, *mi amore.*"

I've heard this before; I'm suspicious, but I let it stand. I don't want to talk now as the pleasure heightens. He's difficult in my mouth, a challenge, as with most physical pleasure. Knut comes in. I lick the back of the spoon, calling a noncommittal look to my eyes, and promise a later rendezvous as I close peanut butter's cupboard door.

"Want anything special for dinner?" Knut asks.

"Nah, I'm really not that hungry."

"I wonder why." Knut complements this statement with an eye roll. I walk out of the kitchen thinking about the man Knut will never be.

Knut's breathing does not transition into a light snore until after one-thirty that morning. I will be tired at work, which is really of no consequence. Knut must wake before me, so I sleep next to the wall. The bed, relatively new, squeaks little, but the challenge of getting out without reversing the light snore back to deep breathing builds more tension. As with any illicit affair, this tension only reinforces desire, but unlike a twenty-something meeting a married forty-something in a cross-town hotel, peanut butter and I will last. We role-play that Knut might wake up and stop us. Or, that we are strangers meeting for the first time at a sandwich shop hoping that my husband is delayed as we touch under the table. Or, my favorite, that he is my college literature professor and Knut my twenty-year-old boyfriend waiting for me in the parking lot. Yet, the joy of role-play, as you remember, stems from its safe boundaries. If Knut were to wake, come to the kitchen and suggest that I return to bed or roll his eyes at me spoiling my breakfast, I would look at him clearly and say, voice unwavering, "After I finish with peanut butter." Knut always retreats.

Tonight Knut lies on his side, which is smaller than his stomach and easier to traverse. Just as in my school age years, I have memorized the foot placements needed to reach the kitchen *sans* squeaks. I walk slowly, visualizing him in the cupboard. He's awake but patient. Our trust in each other is of the kind frequently written about in women's magazines, enigmatic to ninety-eight percent of those in relationships. Enigmatic to Knut. Peanut butter's red cap is screwed on tightly for protection. His shirt, a tunic, really, as it covers the bulk of his hard, round body, is a bit colorful for my taste.

He wears it to attract attention, but I've always argued that a simple solid color, even white, would bring out his eyes.

When I reach the kitchen, I also reach a new emotional plane. If Knut were going to move, he would have mumbled something as I left. The kitchen is a neutral zone, a safety area on the edge of danger. It's the hotel lobby before you've checked in, so the chance to present a plausible excuse when your husband shows still remains. Peanut butter knows I'm there even when I don't announce my presence. He feels me, straightens his tunic.

Tonight, my pace slows as I cross to the cabinet where he lives. On a hill, our house reaches above some smog and most streetlights. The moon, with an accompaniment of stars, provides the requisite romantic glow. I soak this glow into my skin so that when he sees me, he'll mistake me for the moon. I place my hand flat on the outside of his cabinet, where it grows hot. My throat, hot as well, calls for a longer delay. Milk out first. While sexy, Milk's never been able to reach peanut butter. Milk has accepted his position as catalyst, serving to sustain and elongate my time with my lover because it allows him to be near me. I shouldn't encourage Milk by placing my lips directly on him; I should use a glass, but this makes the delay too long. I unscrew Milk's cap, readying him and, finally, reach for my love.

"You've made me wait tonight," he says.

"I'm here now."

"You look like the moon," he says.

It is after three when I return to bed.

Sappho Dessert

by Eve Rifkah

peel the mahogany surface
from Anjou pears
hold the peeler so it traces
the curve from narrow bell top
to round ass bottom
pale firm flesh lies bare undressed

then poach the pears
in burgundy until as dark as
the shed skin
cut in half then in thin slivers
the outer edge curved the inner straight
arrange in radiating circles
on the prepared pizza dough
drizzle a bittersweet dark
chocolate sauce over the rounded
slices of dark-edged pale soft flesh
bake until crust lightly browned
and the sauce runs between
ass and breast
eat very slowly
preferably with someone you love
if that is not possible
then dream a good dream
let the tastes of dark chocolate
blend with tender pear
and yeasty dough to
merge into a celebration
of sweet endings
and more beginnings

A Delectable Debriefing

by Don Williams

"So what did she say?" Katrina asked.

"About what?" Forrest hedged.

"About the job."

"Well—"

"Did you get my message to pick up steaks for Saturday?"

"Um—"

"I need you to look at my car."

"Sure."

"So . . . " Katrina stood at the stove, ladling barbecue sauce over the puckered skin of a baked hen. A warm, spicy aroma rose from this feast of the week, as she called it, a break from carry-outs and snacks they and their son Davy subsisted on most workdays. "So what did Mary say?"

"About what?"

"About the job."

"Oh, it was all very speculative," Forrest hedged again. He walked to the refrigerator, brought out a beer and twisted off the lid.

"So speculate."

He ran his tongue around the bottle's cold rim, savoring not so much the touch of cold glass, but rather the way it rearranged his face. For months, when he looked in the mirror he had beheld the same bitter expression, lips compressed in a sour, pinched grimace. Now, with a glimmer of good news on the horizon, he felt the muscles in his face relaxing. It was good to be home, away from the limestone-gray walls of his carrel. He peered into the den, a habitual reflex, to see if the way was clear to the plush easy chair beside the bay window, where he could read the paper or watch CNN. Good, Davy hadn't claimed dominion yet; must still be at soccer.

Katrina turned to him, blocking the way, holding her wooden spoon upright like a club. His eyes roved down to her stockinged toes. She had shed her shoes already, and her feet and ankles were shapely in cinnamon

hosiery—their alluring rusty tint extending to the hem of his denim shirt she
had thrown on to protect her silk blouse. Her stylishly uneven hair bushed out
from the shirt's collar like plumage on some exotic bird—auburn plumage
that set off twin emerald points of inquisitiveness in her eyes. Such eyes.

"Didn't you hear me?" she was asking. "So speculate."

"Well," he resumed, "she made vague references to certain opportunities." He took another sip of good bitter beer.

"Forrest, what did Mary *say?*"

"She asked if I'd had enough of Product Development." The way she
had pursed her lips on *product development* there in the conference room
had been distracting, given their history, so that he'd had a hard time concentrating on literal meanings.

"So what'd *you* say?"

"Well, I—"

"What'd *she* say?"

"Oh, just—"

"Did she offer you the job?"

"She said to think about what I'd like to be doing five years from
now."

"Five years? What'd she mean five years?"

"She said Myers would ask me that if he offered the promotion. Kind
of a test."

"Really? So there's already been talk of moving you up?"

"It was nothing that concrete—"

"Are we talking management here or what?"

Forrest felt dizzy from the barrage of questions. He hated to calcu-
late, to presume, to feint and lurch toward tantalizing possibilities the way
Katrina did. Still, she had a right to know that Millennial Toys seemed high
on his potential . . . .

It was the Seascope that had caught management's eye. Just a simple
transparent tube with a magnifying-glass bottom and twin waterproof
flashlights attached to the sides that doubled as handles, fully immersible.
With Seascopes, kids could spy on all the primordial creatures skittering
along bottoms of rivers and lakes and oceans. The gadgets would be sold
for $9.95 in every surf and bait shop from Nantucket to Key West, from
every sports shop and Wal-Mart in America. Kids would love them and so
would their mothers. He already knew.

"So would you be flying a lot?" Katrina asked.

You will be flying a lot, Mary Simmons had informed him, before asking, *Do you like to fly?* Her eyes had seemed to widen, then narrow as if closely reading his reaction. Had there been a double entendre there? She had shifted her legs toward him—*whisper of nylons*—had leaned forward in her chair—*whiff of ambrosia*—as if everything hinged on his answer.

Sure, he'd said, *I like to fly,* just enough mystery in his voice to keep her off-balance.

"So would you?" Katrina asked as she opened the oven and placed the cooked bird back inside. Heat wafted up from the oven and Forrest's mouth watered again as he took in the curve of her thigh and the hollow he sometimes kissed behind her knee when they made love.

She turned and looked at him, blushing as she licked a drop of rusty sauce from a forefinger.

"Maybe," he evaded.

"That's concise," Katrina said. "Chicken's almost ready. I took the drapes from the den to be cleaned on my way to work this morning. The Thompsons will be coming Saturday. I think they want us to be godparents for Traci. Davy's at soccer practice but Janice will be dropping him off. There was a boy at school today with a gun, but it turned out to be one of those handgun look-alike BB thingies. So what do you think? Would you be flying?"

He actually liked to fly. He liked the way Montview Estates looked from the air. His little kingdom. All the trees, the neatly tucked away cul-de-sacs, the new sidewalks growing like vines along all the roads. He liked stepping off airplanes to find himself in exotic cities. He liked the costumes people wore when they traveled. The sense of pent passion lurking behind bored masks of pretty women in stylish clothes.

"When would you start?"

"Christ, Kat," he said, suddenly. "What is this?"

"This is *talking,*" she said.

"Well I'm not in the mood for talk."

"You never are, you like to go around all secretive and sullen, like none of this matters. Like your little conference with Mary what's-her-name has no repercussions for this *family.*" She gestured towards the table with her spoon, as if the table were filled by The Waltons or The Brady Bunch, though their only child was Davy, still at soccer practice.

"I prefer to let events take their course," he said.

"But that's how good solid information gets lost," Katrina said, "the kind I need to plan our lives."

"I don't want you planning my life."

"Too late, Buster."

"Is that what all this is? All these questions you ask every damn day?"

"Somebody has to retrieve all that information. Otherwise your brain is like a . . . a black hole, sucking everything into it without letting anything back out, not even light. I know you think of me as a flighty chatterbox, Hon'." She stood leaning against the oven door. "You read all those pop psychology articles about how men and women are different, like this woman I heard on the radio yesterday. She said it goes back to the Stone Age, when men would be out in the woods all day. This woman—this psychologist—was saying how you men used to have to be quiet all day in order to catch game for the stewpots, while the women were home taking care of babies and sick old people, so *they* got in the habit of talking a lot and comparing notes about what they'd gleaned from their mates. Those tendencies make you guys seem stolid or solid or . . . *something* but it makes me look like a chatterbox."

She's right, Forrest thought. That's how I have her pegged, and me too, but when did she get that out of me?

"But that's total bullshit." Katrina was waving her wooden spoon again, upright, like a club. He shook his head to avoid being mesmerized. "Total bullshit," she repeated. She put the spoon down, knelt, pulled three potatoes from a bag under the counter and tossed them at him in rapid succession.

"Wash these." He held them under the tap, located the scrubber and scrubbed them down. He remembered digging in the dirt for potatoes as a youngster. The look of satisfaction on his father's face as he smiled down the handle of a spade that had turned up a cluster of six, seven new white potatoes at once, hanging from the subterranean vines in clusters, like giant pale grapes. He placed the three plump tubers in the microwave and set it for ten minutes.

"But those psychologists have it all wrong. I'll tell you what this is," Katrina said. "What this is, is a debriefing."

"A what?"

"A debriefing. You know, like what NASA did when the astronauts would come back from the moon? Or the way the CIA questions spies after missions to make sure no crucial intelligence gets lost." Katrina handed him a florid bowl, opened the refrigerator and passed a plastic bag of pre-cut salad to him. "I'm debriefing you. Just like women have done through the ages."

"But that implies you're in control."

"Shhh, don't tell anybody," she said, holding the wooden spoon—its thick end still covered with barbecue sauce—to her lips. She touched her tongue to it experimentally, then put it down and wiped her slender hands on a towel draped over the lip of the sink. "You see, even Og the Cave Girl knew that if you didn't ask Ug *specifically* whether he had seen a saber-toothed tiger during the day that Ug would sit on the information and get drunk on . . . mead . . . or . . . or . . . fermented potatoes . . . and not mention that he had *even seen* a saber-toothed tiger, and it would be Og's little rump that got chewed off next day down at the waterhole. All this talk is merely a survival reflex, that's all."

"That's a pretty view of nature," Forrest said, but he loved the lilting way her full lips had formed the words *little rump*. Her hair was beginning to wilt. A strand had fallen over her left eye and she blew at it.

"Well, it's like Woody Allen said, it's just one big restaurant out there, and we women learned a long time ago to watch out."

"Damn," he murmured, "you've revised the entire field of gender relations." He felt sudden tenderness for her as he reached over and pushed errant auburn strands from her eyes. He knew her tough talk disguised a vast well of insecurity, as did his reticence.

She parried his gesture, pushing a salad bowl at his chest. He took it, opened the plastic bag and dumped the lettuce, flecked with purple cabbage and orange chips of carrots. He remembered his father's plump heads of lettuce, his gnarly carrots coming out of the still-clinging earth.

"So what'd she say, really?" Katrina asked again.

"Look, can't we just drop it for a while?"

"She put the move on you, didn't she?"

"Wha-hot?" he asked, sounding a little too surprised he realized too late.

"Don't wha-hot me, buster. I knew there was a reason you weren't talking. By the way, my front end's been making a funny noise lately, I was wondering if you could have Clyde take a look at it tomorrow?"

"Huh?"

"So are you two having an affair?"

"Me and Clyde?" She didn't laugh at his joke. "No she didn't come on to me. God, Kat, you jump from subject to subject so fast I hardly—."

"I have to. A woman's work is never done." She took off his denim shirt, plucked her skirt from a chair and wriggled into it, then moved two tapered candles from the buffet cabinet to the table. Forrest pulled out a lighter he carried for no reason he could think of and lit them. They stood for a moment savoring the magic now in the room.

"So are you?" She was pouring red wine into long-stemmed glasses.

"What?"

"Getting it on with Mary Simmons—why do you carry that lighter, anyway—or are you just tiptoeing up to an affair?"

"No—I don't know—and no," he said. "Anything else?" It had been a mistake, he realized, to tell her about the office Christmas party. How Eli Myers, the CEO, had started telling some story about the early days of the company, *"when we were young and hungry and flew by the seat of our pants,"* and there had been a scramble for chairs and it was as if a puppet master had placed him beside Mary, sitting there in her red Christmas tights and her Santa hat with its white puff ball tickling his nose as they had shared her drink and her red-clad knees had rubbed against him in the crowded space and then, later, at the copying machine, how her forefinger had lingered on his wrist and how he had kissed her, although he hadn't told that part to Kat and neither he nor Mary had ever mentioned it again.

"So if you have this affair and get the promotion, will it make us rich and famous?"

"Rich at least," he said, taking the mirth in her eyes as permission to lighten up. "I'll bring home tiger skins and jewels from exotic kingdoms." He plucked a brown morsel of fallen thigh from the platter, tasted its warm sustenance, fed her the rest, and she licked the sauce from his finger.

"Sit down," she said.

"Should we wait on Davy?"

"No. I'm ravenous. He'd just as soon eat alone."

And they had dug in then, excited by hunger and glimmerings of possibilities.

Davy arrived in the middle of dinner. Forrest saw their friend Janice's arched neck and inquiring face as she drove off, peering from her minivan into their dining room windows. Davy emerged from behind the van running, his long legs so like his mother's, propelling him lightly across the lawn. He jumped the border of the flowerbed, bestowing youthful glory on sidewalk and lawn. Then he was in the house, breathing hard, a fine mist of sweat across his forehead. His face was so much like Kat's it was eerie, but his genes had picked up Forrest's jutting chin and big ears, bestowing perfect replicas on Davy.

"Who won, champ?" Katrina queried.

"It was only practice, Mom."

"Were the Thompsons there?"

"Yep."

"Did you remind them about Saturday?"

"Yep."

"Were they driving the convertible?"

"Yep."

"How'd you do?"

"Great."

"You going to start Saturday?"

"Yep."

"That's wonderful, champ. Come give Mama a hug."

He went to her and laid his face, relaxed now, on her shoulder. He held the beatific pose several seconds, one arm crooked around her neck, then released her and reached to take a fleshy dark wedge from her plate. His tongue—a copy of Katrina's—darted out to snap it in.

"Go wash your hands," Katrina said.

He stood there chewing. "You know what? I'm third best scorer on the team, just two back from Jason."

"Mighty hunter, mighty fighter," Katrina trumpeted as Davy headed for the bathroom.

She smiled at Forrest, her gaze locked onto his, and they entered freefall like binary stars burning silently through space, devouring one another in slow embrace.

We're in this together, her eyes stated.

Yes we are, his responded.

We're pretty wonderful.

Yes we are, and he wondered if he would ever leave her or even have an affair. This gathering of questions she presented him with every night would make it much too complicated. He could think of them as bouquets—tokens of love presented at the door each evening, these questions: *How did it go? Who did you see? What do you know? How are we?* It would always be this way. She constantly advancing, devouring. He always holding back. Only not now.

He took her hand and stood up, prompting her to rise. The wine was going to his head. *I know how to make you hush.* It would be his last calculated thought of the day, for the glint in her own wide eyes as she stood told him she was ready to devour his body's appetites with her own. He felt a thrill surge coursing through the room itself as his right foot pushed his chair back to clear it away. There would be other evenings to dine with Davy. They heard his shower running. Such a driven boy. Where did he get that? They left the chicken out for him. 🍵

Chocolate Pills

By Alison Condie Jaenicke

Once upon a time
when we were just friends,
you knew that my being dumped by an asshole boyfriend
would leave me sick to my stomach
would make me ache until
all I could do was bend double in the shower
letting hot water scald my back.
You knew to come to the echoey house
where I was alone, bring me chicken soup in a can,
feed me small round noodles,
pearls slipping over my tongue.
You knew to bring a sleeping bag,
stand watch all night on the couch,
chasing away my demons.
You knew when to take me out of the house
into the bracing cold to watch *The Princess Bride*
in which the hero chases his kidnapped lover
over rough seas, through dark swampy woods, past burly castle guards.
Even as he lies on a torture rack, near death,
he swallows a chocolate pill concocted by a magician
and revives, whispers the words "true love"
and drags himself off to rescue his bride-to-be.

What about now? Imprisoned in a tower,
nothing to eat but bitterness,
I cannot see how to save myself, do not think you can save me.
I stand washing dishes at the kitchen sink,

hearing our children whimper for this or that,
and sense your weariness.
There are moments like this,
when I think I will starve, fall off the edge,
but I don't.
You bring me from the brink
with a marguerita, with homemade mac 'n cheese, with a memory:
languorous nights at The Dancing Crab
face-to-face, between us nothing
but a pile of blue crabs turned orange by steam
and pitchers of cold, cheap beer.
Fingers spiced with Old Bay,
we would lift the sweating mugs with the heels of our hands.
I could eat the longest, picking crabs relentlessly,
feeding a hunger that never seemed satisfied.

Sarah Kendall / **Pickled Shrimp**

Dinner

by Janet A. Zimmerman

Carbonnade Flamande

She is caramelizing onions for *carbonnade flamande;* he leans against the refrigerator telling her about the time he and his fraternity brothers tried to steal the bell from the roof of the Taco Bell in Dallas. She has a searing, oppressive vision of being old, eighty-five or ninety, in a rocking chair on a nursing home porch, listening to him tell this same story again, or one of the others: the lost-in-the-desert story, the Mexican customs story, or, she shudders, the cow-tipping story.

As children raised Catholic, she and her sister would offer up small penances to shorten their stay in purgatory. Sleeping without a pillow or going without dessert would count for a day less before they could get into heaven. If she were still capable of belief, she thinks, this would count for months. Years.

"Thump thump thump," she thinks, despite her resolve to ignore him.

"So all the sudden I hear this 'thump thump thump' from the roof," he says. She tunes out, tries to concentrate on her onions, but has limited success.

"No, wait, this is the best part. Two cops walk in and start to talk to me." Here he affects a southern drawl, not a good one, but it's better than the rest of his accents, which generally sound like a cross between Anwar Sadat and Sean Connery.

This is new, this invasion of her kitchen. He usually avoids the room while she's cooking; he says he feels in the way. She's glad, although she didn't start out like that, never used to think of the house in terms of his and her territory.

When the onions are dark amber, she spoons them over the seared beef, inhaling deeply. The scent, sweet and pungent, brings a fleeting moment of something near contentment.

She opens a bottle of porter to deglaze the pan. As the beer hits the hot pan, thick yeasty steam envelops her. She adds salt and mustard, tastes the resulting pan sauce and pours it over the meat and onions. Adds more beer. Drinks the rest, tilting back her head.

"You're not listening," he accuses her.

"Of course I'm not listening. I have listened to this story and every story about you and your stupid fraternity and your moron friends so many times I know them by heart. You've been out of college for almost ten years; can't you talk about something current? And why don't you ever listen to my stories? Why is it that I never get more than a sentence or two into a story before you interrupt? Answer me that one." That is what she would like to say, what she swears she will someday say.

But not this time. She merely answers, "I'm sorry. I am listening, but I'm busy. I have to get this in the oven."

"Is this the same recipe as last time?" he asks.

"Yes," she lies. She finds it impossible to follow a recipe exactly; it would be like painting the same scene over and over again. He likes consistency, though, and she pretends to acquiesce.

"It tastes different."

"How?" she asks.

He screws up his nose, concentrating. "I'm not sure. I mean, it tastes fine. But I think it was better last time." He always seems to prefer memories of meals to the food on his plate.

Take-out

"How about we go down to Garden Thai for dinner?" she asks, deceptively casual.

He looks up from the program he's watching; something with a close-up of beetles. She cringes, looks away. "I thought we were having pork chops," he says, turning back to the screen.

"I know, but I forgot to take them out of the freezer. Besides, I think I'm coming down with a cold," she lies, "and I feel like soup."

"But I don't want to go out; I'm tired. I had a bad day."

She bites her lower lip. "Well, I really don't want to cook tonight. I'm tired too."

When they first started dating, they ate out frequently, and even after they moved in together, they still went out at least once a week. He especially liked Thai food, so they made the rounds of the many Thai

places in the neighborhood. He'd bought her a Thai cookbook for Christmas a few years earlier, but she'd studiously avoided learning how to cook anything in it, knowing instinctively that if she did it would mean the end of their dinners out.

She stands by the sofa until he looks up. "I said I don't want to go out," he repeats. "But you go ahead and go. I'll just make myself a sandwich."

"I don't like going by myself," she says. "You know that."

He glances up again, shrugs.

"Okay," she says, breathing deeply, "how about if we order something and I go pick it up?" It is not what she wants, but it is what she will settle for.

He sighs. "Whatever," he says. She knows the end of the conversation, plays it out anyway. "What should I get?" she asks.

"It was your idea. You decide."

"Soup? Green curry? Pad Thai? Chicken with cashews and basil?" She names his favorites.

He is seriously annoyed now, or acts it. "I don't care. I wanted pork chops."

Linguine di Mare

"Hey, you know what day it is?" he asks as he sits down. He doesn't wait for an answer. "Five years ago today was our first date. Happy anniversary, sweetie." He sets down a small box.

It's not the right date, she knows. The actual anniversary isn't for another three days, but he's gotten it into his memory bank that today's the day; no use trying to set him straight. Besides, he's so pleased to have remembered, she doesn't want to spoil the mood.

She opens the box. Inside is a thin bracelet inset with mother of pearl. She's touched by the gesture, even though she hardly ever wears bracelets.

"Thanks." She tries it on.

"I got it from a street vendor for two bucks. Not bad, eh?"

She forces a smile. "Yeah, great," she says.

"So what are we having?" he asks as she brings out their plates. "Spaghetti? What's in it?"

Linguine, she corrects mentally. Aloud, she says, "Just shrimp and some of that leftover salmon. In a sherry cream sauce; you know, I've made it before."

"Looks good. Hey, let's celebrate. Want some wine?"

She eats in silence while he tells her about his day, the unfamiliar bracelet clinking against her plate occasionally. Suddenly he stops, grabs his napkin and holds it to his lips, spitting out his mouthful of food. "What's wrong?" she asks.

"A bone. In the salmon," he says. "I hate that."

"I thought I got them all," she says. "Sorry." She looked over the salmon carefully, knowing of his fish-bone phobia, but of course if she missed one, it would end up in his serving. He breaks apart the remaining salmon, looking closely and suspiciously at his plate.

"C'mon," she says, "I thought you liked it. I'm sure the rest is fine."

"But there was a bone in it. I could have choked."

She sighs. "Well, just eat around the salmon, then," she says.

He pushes the linguine around on his plate for a minute, picks at a shrimp, then sits back.

"You want something else?" she asks.

"No, I guess I'm not hungry anymore," he answers. "It's okay; it's not your fault, really." That's how he thinks, in terms of blame and fault, as if nothing bad could ever just happen by chance.

She gazes at him, long and searchingly, as if trying to place him, trying to recall who it was she once loved. She reaches across the table, takes his plate, and stands as if to carry it to the kitchen. Instead, she throws it at the wall, high, as hard as she can. The plate breaks and the pieces fall to the floor.

She reseats herself and takes off the bracelet. Picking up her fork, she resumes her meal. The shrimp swim slowly down the wall, following the path of the cream river. Clumps of linguine and salmon hang momentarily, before gravity takes over and they tumble down. 🍵

Paprika

by Susan Rich

Here we are in her kitchen. Here
in between her toaster and Mix-master,

by her silver grill and rotisserie.
I am four, learning to hula my hips

as she cuts the crusts off Wonder Bread,
her body closed tight as she rolls out slice

after slice, tears the bread into flat, raw pieces.
Lemon Tree plays low on the radio

but the fruit of the poor lemon
is impossible to eat.

The pastry board, the emptied tin,
the rolling pin's red handles

she touches in a way she will
never touch me. Still, I am here

in my fire engine patterned pajamas,
clean flannel consoling my cheek.

And when Mother layers the bread:
mushrooms and next, bleu cheese,

then tastes her favorite hors d'oeuvre—
she adds paprika and smiles just past me.

How the heart double-speaks
as it crisscrosses forty years—

how I remain locked
in this false fluorescent air.

Emily Taylor / *Yearning*

Happiness

by Caroline P. Norris

So much and yet not very much of what I know
will fill my heart with joy and overflow—
glimpse of robin perking through the grasses;
mouthful of cookie thick with raisins and molasses;
lilt of Schubert on a cloudy afternoon;
vision of one escaped bright balloon
against a blue-bright summer sky;
echo at sundown of a nightjar's cry;
whiff of honeysuckle tangled by the shed;
touch of your shoulder late at night, in bed
under the rain-stroked roof, the sweet night breeze—
surely no joys are needed beyond these,
and I am stuffed, exuberant with this
great feast of senses, gluttony of bliss.

Breakfast Analogies

by Jane Sasser

To him
she is a bowl of oatmeal:
warm, nutritious, filling,
predictable, and yet
there remains this vague
dissatisfaction,
and he finds that he longs
for the exotic taste
of Eggs Benedict,
the sleek lightness
of crepes in raspberry sauce,
the heavy stupor
of fried ham with red-eye gravy,
or even the gritty sweetness
of a bowl of Cap'n Crunch.

Chamomile: tea of choice for gods and newborn babies

by Jo Ann Pantanizopoulos

Having grown up in Roswell, New Mexico, before New Age teas of every herb became common, I knew only the standard black tea that my elderly disabled neighbor across the street made me in her fancy pink and gold cup after I vacuumed her house. I was twelve years old. Mrs. Bickford served it to me with a little pitcher of milk and some sugar cubes on the side and told me how to hold my pinkie finger when I lifted the cup. I thought she and the tea in such a fancy cup were the height of sophistication. But I grew up and found other teas.

The best tea came from a Greek god. A couple of months after meeting this god, I came down with intestinal flu. I was a freshman in college a thousand miles from home and sick on my own for the first time. My roommate called my god, and told him I was sick. He told her to stand by the side door of our all-female dormitory, and he would meet her in ten minutes. She soon came to my side with a thermos of hot chamomile tea and a bag of yellow lemons. Chamomile to soothe my tummy, and a lemon to suck on after my nausea attacks. The lesson to my daughters will remain: don't marry him unless he brings you lemons and chamomile. Then you'll know he's the right one.

After the god and I moved to Greece to live happily ever after, I discovered more about chamomile tea. This small plant with tiny daisy-like flowers grows in a dry sandy soil. On our walks in the countryside with my mother-in-law, we often picked chamomile to take home. She placed the flowers between her cupped fingers and pulled off only the flower heads. She spread them out on a white sheet and placed them on a sunny tin roof to dry. After they dried, we put them in a white cloth bag with a drawstring. Before zipper-lock plastic bags, women made cloth bags from worn sheets or pillowcases to store herbs. To make the tea, she placed two large tablespoons of the dried chamomile flower heads in a little wire strainer and poured boiling water over the flowers, letting the strainer sit in the water a bit. A fragrant dark yellow brew emerged.

I soon became a true believer in chamomile as a universal healer, soother of tummies, wounds, and bruised souls. When our second daughter, Antigone, was born in Athens, Greece, at Elenas Hospital, the midwives-in-training gave her sugared chamomile tea between breast feedings. Chamomile is given to newborn and colicky babies as a calming addition to mother's milk. Shortly after she and I returned home, Antigone developed thrush. My pediatrician told me to make a strong chamomile tea and, with a clean gauze pad, wipe out her mouth after each breast feeding. The thrush soon disappeared.

A Greek friend of mine used chamomile as a feminine douche. Another friend rinsed her natural blonde hair in chamomile after every shampoo to enhance the blonde highlights. When my son Niko was a toddler, he fell on the corner of our coffee table cutting a slash clear through his earlobe. Fearing a permanent scar, I took him immediately to our pediatrician. Instead of a stitch, he told me to make a strong chamomile tea and bathe his earlobe with the dark yellow liquid 3-4 times a day. Healing occurred with no scar. Chamomile doesn't sting like alcohol, iodine, mercurochrome, or hydrogen peroxide when touching sensitive cuts and scrapes. Alexia fell on her bike, scraping the underside of her arm—quick, make some chamomile tea. Vera fell on the gravel and punctured her knee—out came the chamomile tea. When we feel a cold or flu approaching, we brew a cup of chamomile. The amber elixir soothes nerves at the end of a hectic day and serves as a natural sedative, much like warm milk before bedtime.

I cannot find chamomile growing in East Tennessee, and the white cloth bags my mother-in-law gave me are lying empty and folded in my kitchen drawer. But in our kitchen we always keep boxes of store-bought chamomile tea bags . . . and fresh lemons. 🍵

Preserves

by Steve Sparks

Spring nights we listened to bluegrass,
notes like whirly-birding maple seeds,
Comfort and Coke, and toast
lavished with blueberry preserves
bought from the mustached lady
at the farmers' market. Her meager
booth festooned with jeweled jars
of tomatoes, relishes, and jellies.
Black marker on masking tape
like Xs on calendar days—
Blackberry '00, Pear & Pepper '01.

You said: *Preserves— that's
a funny thing to call them when
there's nothing of real blueberries
preserved at all. Too much sugar.*

You were my sticky-sweet
savior—the one who plucked
me from the thicket of empty nights.
I tell no one of the dingy foam
skimmed off the top and discarded;
how in our last season your
kisses were like quinces—
prickly and so bitter they burned
the back of my throat;
how the last three months
your flesh rippled in hesitation
at the approach of my cool touch.

Now it's October and fat deer wander
through corn stalks in wood smoke,
gorging on forgotten ears of Indian corn,
anticipating the hoarfrost of hunger
winter scatters on the drowsing land.
Once I slathered you across my bed,
crammed as much of you as I could hold,
sickened myself on the excess of desire.
Now I preserve you with indigo ink,
across bread-white paper, these notes
of tempered sweetness mark
our sour seasons together. Displayed
on shelves of memory, I hope
there's enough to last the cold:
Valentines '98, Winter '99.

Never Enough

by Donnell King

Most of my friends had parents who said, "Eat your supper, there are starving children in IndiaChinaAfricaSomewhereElse, so don't waste it."

I never had the luxury of dismissing this as a hypothetical hyperbole concocted by parents just to shame kids into eating. I always heard, "Don't waste your food, your father almost starved, 16 months in World War II German prisons getting one cup of potato soup a day with worms he'd eat for the protein."

The war left Dad unable to leave food on a plate—on anyone's plate. I used to worry he would notice people leaving perfectly good uneaten food at another restaurant table and feel compelled to finish it. I prayed for fast, efficient bus service.

Holiday family gatherings clearly demonstrated the difference in my parents' food philosophies. Competing family obligations often led us to share two huge meals around Christmas, one with each set of grandparents.

Mom always arranged everything on her plate just so, striving for a balance of color and visual weight with a little tableau of food cleanly segregated, set upon a level table so the various juices wouldn't intermingle. Her parents and aunts all practiced similar culinary artistry, admiring the plates and commenting on the visual appeal and the colors and the balance before delicately navigating bite-by-bite through a meal seasoned by polite conversation and occasional gossip. Her father, true enough, held himself aloof from all this, but he didn't interfere with it either. He ate quietly, leaving the ladies to their sculpting and social deconstruction, though occasionally lobbing in a comment that caused them to scatter in outrage.

Dad practiced a style and appreciation of food diametrically opposite. He piled his food together on the plate in a promiscuous mingling of starch and protein and plant fiber. No matter what was served, he always ate stew. He considered it serious business, too, with casual conversation as welcome and expected as it would be at an autopsy. His family likewise passed the plates and cups and utensils as if passing out weapons, sent the serving dishes around like trucks of ammunition ("Take plenty, men, you don't want to run out"), and then settled into a concentrated campaign of consumption, accompanied by the slurps and gulps associated with stocking up for the next big famine. It left little room for dinner conversation. If you shouldn't talk with your mouth full, you couldn't converse in that setting at all.

Mom once told me she was "horrified" the first time she ate a meal with Dad's family.

War didn't make him that way, but it certainly amplified his genetic and socialized tendencies. He seemed extreme in his relationship with food, but I discovered he was far from unique. Once I went with him to a meeting of The American Ex-Prisoners of War. This particular group always met, spouses in tow, at a restaurant with a buffet. The POWs all shared in the horrific experience of wartime imprisonment, a psychological and physical battering that affected over 130,000 people (mostly male) and their families, and robbed them of the ability to uncritically expect to receive their next meal. Over 16 million wore American uniforms during that war, just about 11 percent of the entire American population from those years. All of them, from the shipyards at home to the Bataan Death March in the South Pacific, came back scarred to one degree or another. The POWs came back with a special scar, born out of months of living between life and death, a scar they mostly learned to hide from scrutiny.

Their families generally know relatively little about their experiences. They know some factual material, some statistics and dates. They know that the man who carried a passion away to war—perhaps a hot temper or a love of baseball—returned in body but maybe not in spirit. They know that, with the exception of unexplained and overheated outbursts at inanimate objects or confused relatives, the formerly imprisoned soldiers display very little emotion.

That day in the restaurant, in the safety of strangers closer than brothers who shared a private kind of hell, they laughed, swapped stories and figured out whom they knew in common, and took off their shells for a few moments. Sometimes they got quiet, traveling together back half a century to the muddy, miserable sheds they had shared. Their eyes focused together on something I could not see. They paused, one of those pauses in which the entire universe stops moving for a moment, and then they sighed and moved on.

They took care of business like electing the next commander and announcing where the next reunion would be. They brought old, worn photos culled from wallets and newspapers and even torn from books. They compared issues of *Ex-POW Bulletin,* turning first to the obituaries and then to the column in which people try to find old buddies.

And then they cleaned their plates. They left not one scrap of food, not even a potato peel, on any plate in the room.

Now Dad lives in a retirement home, surrounded by other men watching life from within their own shells, and by women who just think he's hungry, unable to explain his reality to anyone who has not shared it. My mother now has a steady source of complaint fodder, a continuous supply of "below-standard" food, food they nevertheless spend between four and five hours a day dealing with.

They go from their apartment to the dining room at least a half-hour before each scheduled meal to get a "good table." Servers bring out soup or salad and serve the entire room before starting on the main course. Dessert follows the meal in its own stately way. The servers work quickly, but there are a lot of people to serve, and many need hugs along with the cornbread muffins. The scene replays itself three times daily: Dad clears his plate, Mom transfers some of hers to his, and he sets his jaw and commences to clean his plate again. At varying times during each meal women come from other tables to bring him their oatmeal, whole baby carrots, buttermilk pie and baseball-sized globes of vanilla ice cream.

He laughs, shakes his head, and crinkles his eyes. Then he takes a deep breath and loosens his belt while complaining about his "Dunlap disease" ("my belly done lapped over my belt" he tells anyone who will listen). Because he has congestive heart failure, he literally gets out of breath from eating. He knows he should not eat so much, certainly not the kinds of things they bring him. Far from overweight because of the nervous energy with which he burns away the old demons, he still struggles with being heavier than he has ever been.

But the food must be taken care of. It is sacrificed to unknown gods to stave off famine and war and starvation. He can't help it. After all, as he seems to think in his bones: you never know whether you'll get the next meal. If you can just eat enough now, maybe it will finally, truly be enough. ☕

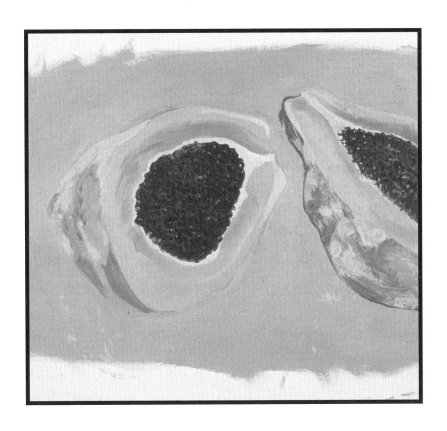

Emily Taylor / *Packed Papaya*

Malabsorption Syndrome

by Marianne Worthington

In the end, she starved to death;
the food she had savored and craved
her long life stopped nourishing her.

*If I only had a green dollar for every garden
I've worked and raised,* she would say.
All those truck patches teeming
with greens and beans,
potatoes, beets and okra, cabbage,
tomatoes, squash, peppers, peas
and cukes, carrots, pumpkins and melons,
leafy lettuce and little spring onions.

Beyond the vegetable earth she knew
orchards and trees dripping fruit,
her applesauce and canned peaches were legend.
She relished cooking every part of a pig,
could kill a chicken fast and neat,
have it plucked, cleaned and fried
in time for weekday dinner.
Her favorite supper of corn dodgers
and sweet milk was all she could eat
at the last, though none of us could fry
the hoecakes to suit her. Even coffee turned

on her, the daily drink she took strong
and black with one saccharine tablet fished
from her jeweled pillbox, dropping
in the tiny white pellet to sweeten the heat.

From her nursing home bed
hollow-cheeked and hungry for death
she dreams of her lilac sunbonnet
and racing her brothers to the garden,
the flat-bottomed harvest basket swinging
empty from her stocky arm.

Eggs Goldenrod

by Laura Still

Easter evening the eggs
were gathered (those that survived),
their finery removed over the sink,
kaleidoscope shards swirling
down the disposal.
Slicing through naked whites
to gold hearts,
she collected a bowl of treasure
to be sifted by a fork
in a dimpled toddler's fist.

Butter sizzled in the saucepan,
she stirred in salt, milk, flour,
parings of albumen;
sauce thickened while bread browned.
The toaster's *ding!* called everyone
to the kitchen to fill their plates
with mounds of crisp toast
slathered in dense white froth,
powdered with pollen-yellow yolks—
hungry revelers in the creamy comfort
of love, the taste of Mom.

Bulimia

by Jennifer Polhemus

Avocados, baklava, cupcakes.
Diet, eat, famish, gorge.
How insidiously
jambalaya karma
lacerates my nights.
Oreos, pancakes, quesadillas.
Remember, sustenance thrives
under vomit; wounded,
xeroplastic, yet
zealous.

Still Life, with Orange

by Marybeth Boyanton

"Size and subject are of no object," the little man
had said, but the raisin eyes had sparkled when he added,
"It may be small, but must also be significant. It needs to
hold the gaze awhile." "Of course," the artist sighed, thoughts
glued only on what, at last, the promised francs would buy.

In his kitchen, the girl was scrubbing pots with lemon rind
and salt. He wondered at her industry, there had been so little
to fill them with of late. But the copper caught his eye—it
gleamed like marmalade. In the glowing bain-marie, the porcelain
liner sat like heavy cream. Aha! What was so significant as food?

At first light, the market. He did not send the girl this time, but
went himself. His senses perked at the cacophony and stirred-
up stew of smells, but he kept his vision only for the things
he sought: the roundest loaf, a blue-finned fish with eye so clear
it seemed to meet his own, oh, to follow! But . . . a single orange,

or two? Favoring the odd number and unable to afford
a third, he chose the one most nearly perfect sphere
and held it to his nose. More than with the fragrance
of the bread, his mouth watered with this scent of sunshine
caught within the vivid globe, and he reined his thought

to color. War, the occupation in the north, made pigments
scarce, but sales, too, were hard to come by. For months
he had confined his musings to the cuttlefish's ink, vine
charcoal he had burned himself—yes, the remainders
of his colors should be enough for this important work.

Busy at his set-up, he did not notice precisely when the
morning haze was gone, but felt instead the warm butter
light that had replaced it. On the studio table, the red-and-white
cloth seemed trite to him, but the blue-and-yellow would
require his dear cerulean. "The girl could cook the fish," he

thought, "and I would save what blue'd be spent on its bright
scales. Then she could make the stock into what can pass
for lunch!" The red pigment in its jar, besides, distracted
in its suggestion of rare roast meat, and so he had decided.
While she cooked, he arranged and rearranged the bread,

a silver pitcher and the orange the blue set off so well.
With his handling of the smooth brown loaf its scent
escaped and mingled with what wafted from the kitchen;
he tore off a chunk and tasted it. "It would be better
warm," he thought, picked up the loaf and went downstairs.

After, in the studio, he was about to weep for his mistake:
fresh-orange stickiness still stained his fingertips. But no!
A crust of bread, reflected in the little silver ewer, made
him see a different *nature morte*. "What indeed," he
cried, "could be of more significance than food!"

Finally finished, the canvas hung in his cool foyer and
the little man was there. "You've done it," he remarked, gaze
fixed upon the perfect rendering: the crumb, the twisted peel,
the fish's bones all bound in melting golden light but seen
only on the creamer's curving side as it sat upon the cloth.

"Surely—a masterpiece," the man exclaimed. "I cannot
express exactly what it makes me feel, but it is tense. I
must have it, and will pay you well for it. It does so
command the moment!" "Yes," the artist pleasantly
agreed, then said (winking at the girl), "like hunger."

Emily Taylor / *First Melon*

Hunger in the Swamp: Runaways in Waterland— September 1862

An excerpt from the novel, *Tehano,*

by Allen Wier

They followed a narrow channel of water that cut through the grass and, judged against the sun, ran southwest widening as it flowed. A hawk gliding overhead dropped from the sky like something killed. It dimpled the water's surface and rose again, a fish flashed silver, caught in the bird's talons. "I wish I had a fishing pole, Elizabeth. That hawk's got a fish supper, and all we've got is half a yam and some cornbread."

"Lets us eat what we got, Knobby. I'm starved to death."

"We might as well carry it inside as outside."

Elizabeth stepped onto the shorter grass; it sank, and she slid away from him.

"Knobby, it's moving, the ground is moving."

He jumped after her, grabbing her hand, and they held onto one another, the grass beneath them drifting slowly toward the edge of the lake. *Dear God, don't let us drown.*

"Knobby, is we in some dream? I ain't never walked on no floating grass before."

His foot went right through the grass, through the sod beneath, plunged into the water. His wiggling toes and kicking foot felt nothing solid. Writhing-snake, spider-web, dark-night terror raced up his leg to his groin and iced up his belly and chest. He came out of the grass the way the hawk had come off the lake, and his sunken shin and foot came free, shiny with mud. The half a sweet potato shot from his overalls like ball from cannon, rocketed a good twenty feet and plopped into the water. Close to tears, Knobby searched for a ring where the potato had sunk.

"Look what I've done, Elizabeth. Look what I've done."

"We still got the bread."

Water bubbled up in the hole Knobby's leg left, the smell of a struck match rising from the floating grass. They ate the cornbread except for one small piece Knobby hid deep in his pocket, something to give Elizabeth in the morning. At least they weren't going to die of thirst.

Several times the grass underfoot moved, and they learned to recognize the greener grass that grew on the floating islands and keep to firmer footing. Elizabeth stopped where marsh grass gave way to a wide pool of water and held to his shoulder. Finger to her lips, she nodded to the edge of the pool. A turtle the size of a big skillet sat in the sun. Mossy green, his head bobbed, mouth open like a singing bird, a red blotch on each side of his head. Knobby knelt and drew Elizabeth down beside him. "Unwind some twine off of that feedsack dress," he whispered.

"What you going to do?"

"Just unravel your hem."

Knobby drew the square of saved cornbread from his pocket and looped the end of the thick thread Elizabeth gave him. He wrapped the bread with several loops. He gave Elizabeth a *stay-close* tug and a nod, and they duck-walked toward the turtle. Knobby pitched the bread out beside the green shell, but Turtle didn't take notice. Knobby tried again. Turtle didn't even twitch. Elizabeth pinched Knobby's arm. She took the line and flipped the bread onto the water so it floated past Turtle, and he took a look. Elizabeth gave a twitch. Turtle scrabbled after. Inch by inch, Elizabeth twitched the bread closer. Turtle followed. Knobby got between Turtle and the pothole. When Elizabeth had Ole Turtle in the grass, she let him catch the bread. Time he bit down, Knobby pounced and grabbed his shell. Turtle head jerked sideways, beak snapping hard. Hissed like a snake. Knobby held the shell on the sides where neither the hissing beak nor the clawing feet could get him, and in a blink Ole Turtle jerked head, tail, and feet in under his shell.

"I've got him, Elizabeth, or he's got me. I don't know which. This damn country doesn't have any rocks or limbs lying about that a man can use for hitting or clubbing."

"I'm bout hungry enough to eat him live," Elizabeth said, with no trace of a smile.

Knobby swung the turtle down and brought his knee up hard, like he was breaking a limb, and he cracked the yellow bottom of the shell. Turtle's head and feet all came out at once and Knobby dropped him on his back. Dodging the hissing, snapping mouth and the clawing feet, Knobby brought his bare heel down again and again, crushing in the bottom of the shell.

"Where's your little toe?" Elizabeth said. In spite of himself, Knobby counted his toes. Elizabeth chuckled down deep in her chest, sounded like Grandfather Samuel storytelling.

Knobby gutted and dressed the turtle with his bare hands, tossing entrails into the water and rinsing away blood and yellow balls of fat. What he wouldn't give for a knife, and for a match and firewood. Elizabeth chewed the raw flesh with her eyes closed, chewed fast and swallowed fast. They ate all the meat Knobby could pull loose. For the first time in days his stomach felt full, and he lay back and tried to empty his mind.

When the wide sky pinkened with sunset, they rose and continued west across the wide marsh. Knobby carried the turtle's top shell at his side like a stiff-brimmed hat.

"What you going to do with that?" Elizabeth said.

"We can dip water and drink from it."

"Knobby Cotton, just cause I's hungry enough to eat raw turtle don't mean I got to drink from that nasty shell. My own hands will do me just fine."

Still Knobby toted the shell.

"Woods ahead," he said. "We won't have to sleep lying in this wetness."

"Good, I don't want to get as pruney all over as my wet feet are."

The channel they had followed all afternoon widened into a bayou separating them from the trees. They looked across at willows and oaks and tall cypress. The bayou was freckled with rings and kissing smacks filled the air as fish dimpled the surface feeding on swarming insects.

"I ain't swimmin' that snakey-lookin' water, 'specially not in the devil's darkness."

"Elizabeth, we've got to cross."

"I done put up with enough. Bout time I rethink fallin' in love with you, Knobby Cotton. God his Ownself'd have trouble gettin' me out in that swamp water." Even as she railed Knobby, Elizabeth was walking toward the bayou. At the edge, Knobby took her hand and they squished down into the soft bottom. A few inches down, the muck was firm. Every few steps Elizabeth looked Knobby in the eyes and said there was no way she would ever cross this wide water. Even in the very middle, Knobby was surprised the bayou was only chest-deep. Elizabeth waved her hands, swatting at mosquitoes thick beneath the brim of her bonnet. Knobby breathed in a mouthful, felt them catch in his throat, dry and prickly. He breathed them out and they continued jerking and humming, tiny, winged Jonahs out of Knobby's whale-mouth. He fanned them away with the turtle shell, and Elizabeth shook her head, but she didn't complain when he fanned air up under her bonnet. From the woods on the other side, tree frogs filled the night with hollow, clicking songs—ghosts beating sticks against limbs. Knobby slapped at mosquitoes, and his hand slid down his arm, slick with blood. Elizabeth was on her knees laving mud on her exposed skin.

"No moon to see by, we can't walk these black woods," she said. "Must be a whole army of water moccasins and lizards and who knows what other critters of the devil crawlin' those swampy woods. But sleeping *here* we'd just feed the skeeters."

They found an open swale of grass between the bayou and the trees where the marsh breezes kept most of the mosquitoes away. Knobby drew Elizabeth against him and softly kissed her lips, surprised that she did not resist. Beneath her touchous ways there was some slight give. Soft, her lips; a taste of mud and a faint sulphur smell. His thigh pressed between her legs, warm through her dress and his overalls, and a different kind of emptiness pulled at his belly, not the tugging of starved for food, but the hunger of desire. He moved his hand up Elizabeth's thigh, over her hip to her waist, her ribcage to nest in the feathery hair of her armpit. He pressed his lips to hers again and drew his hand forward to hold her breast. He rose on an elbow and looked down at her closed eyes. Her lips were slightly parted, her breath soft and steady. She was deep asleep, the bonnet still on her head. Knobby put his fingers against her throat—life pulsed there. He kissed her chin and snuggled against her, and the stars went out like extinguished lamps.

An animal from the woods, dark and small, a weasel—no, a wild pig, bigger even, poked hard at Knobby's swollen foot. *Po, yi,* the creature snorted, *Po, yi.*

"*Po, yi, Negre.*"

Knobby sat up, his mind struggling to reconcile the wild pig of his dream with the short, wiry old man who looked down at him from a gray cloud from which poked the long barrel of a gun. The man jerked his chin toward Elizabeth who stirred, restless in her sleep, but had not waked up. Knobby rubbed her shoulder wondering what he had gotten them into now.

"What is it, Knobby?"

"*Mais,* what is it, I want to know this, me, too," the man said.

"Oh Knobby, it's that ole ghost been ridin' me. Get off, Ghost, get off, please."

"He's no ghost, Elizabeth." Knobby rubbed Elizabeth's shaking shoulders and spoke to the odd-talking man. "We are travelers, sir, just passing through on our way to Texas." *Jesus, help me know what to say.* Knobby stood up into a swirl of early morning fog that surrounded them.

"Texas? *Non, non,* that I don't believe."

Knobby started talking faster than he could think what he was going to say. The man was small, not much over five feet tall, his skin as weathered and dark as a leather bridle. His long nose hooked down over the middle of his lips. His cheeks sunk in on both sides as if he were sucking on a bone, trying to get the marrow out. His stubble beard was grizzled, black and silver, as was his hair, which looked to have been hacked unevenly with an ax. He wore brogans weighted with black mud and what looked like moss or fungus covering the toes. His brown twill britches were patched with hide at the knees and covered halfway down his thighs by a long blouse that had many flap pockets down its front, most of which pockets bulged secretively. One eye squinted—the man still aimed the gun at Knobby—but with his open eye he was listening. Knobby heard the story he was telling as if *he* were his listener, and he added to the story as his listening ears demanded. "I work all the stables for Noble Plantation, Sir. My master freed me and made me a hired man. While he is off fighting in the war, he has sent me to Texas to buy horses so he will be well set-up after the war is ended."

"*Non.* Me, I think no man come to this marshland to find Texas, no, and no man bring a woman out here. I read about some slaves uprise down to Tabadieville, down near Thibodaux. Me, I think you runaway slaves, you."

"I'm a freedman. Highwaymen fell upon us and robbed me of my Master's money. We ran in the dark and got ourselves lost."

Elizabeth reached two fingers inside her dress and removed the paper the slave Joseph had given them. "Here," she said, "This paper say we free."

The man studied the paper, neither speaking nor moving his lips. Knobby could not tell whether the man could read.

"We been tryin' to find the road but was afraid soldiers might shoot us," Elizabeth said.

"*Non,* no soldier boys. This is *Monsieur* Etienne's trap line, no war comes here."

"Who is this *Monsieur* Etienne?" Knobby said.

"Me. I am *Monsieur* Etienne." He lowered the gun. "Who are you, *Negre?*"

Knobby stuck to his story. *Monsieur* Etienne grinned at every word. But the strange talking trapper did not care about runaway slave or the *Americains'* war with the Confederates.

"Here is *Acadienne,* me and this country, from the *bois,* woods, to *la fourche,* the fork"—Etienne spread his first two fingers into a fork—*"des grosse* bayou"—Etienne spread his arms wide, "as far south as *Pointe Chevreuil,* this is the trapline of Etienne, yes."

"If it's not too much trouble, Mr. Etienne, could you point us in the direction of the Sabine Pass and Texas?" Knobby said.

"It's a long way, *Negre,* take you two, three week, *if* you know how you go. Go north, maybe you run into soldier boys. *Aux vases,* all the swamps is safe; war don't come here, no."

"Will you show us the way to go?" Knobby said.

"Maybe I do that, me, I don't know. You hungry, no, you woman and you?" He gave them strips of dried meat. *"Boeuf,"* he said. "Better and more we eat later, yes."

Etienne led them through the fog to a long, dugout boat he called a "pee-roe," made of a huge cypress log, with carved prow in front and back. There were no seats in the long, narrow *pirogue,* which was piled with heavy spring traps. Another long-barreled musket, like the one Etienne carried, lay beside the traps, and, next to the musket, a knife Knobby would call a short sword. Etienne pitched Knobby's turtle shell into the grass. He had Knobby sit in the front of the *pirogue,* Elizabeth beside the traps in the middle. The narrow boat wobbled when they climbed in, but even with their added weight did not ride low in the water. Etienne pushed off and stood in the back where he wielded a long pushpole, poling them through the shallow water.

The feedsack dress tightened across Elizabeth's hips and rode up above her knees. Knobby could lose himself in the stretched places of the poor dress. He imagined how Elizabeth looked to a man alone in this swampland. He wanted a blanket to throw over her, to hide her from the man's hawk eyes. Knobby had never before felt jealous. But did his jealousy mean he was thinking of Elizabeth as a thing he owned, as the Master had owned them both?

Beneath tall cypress and scrub oak thick with Spanish moss, Etienne pointed out other inhabitants of his marshland, *terre bonne,* he called it. He showed them the heads of otter pups sticking like small stumps from the fog-shrouded water. A serpentine movement across the bayou that made Elizabeth tremble for fear of a snake, Etienne said was a mink, prized for its pelt. "Look up, there," Etienne said. High in a cedar, a marsh hawk watched them with yellow-circled eyes. Lining the water's edge were bushes Etienne named *roseaux,* and impaled on the purple thorns of the *roseaux* stems were small snakes and lizards that he said the black-beaked butcherbird had hung out to cure. "Come the winter, when the snake and liz-zard hide away, the butcherbird eat his dried kill, him." When the grass grew thick across the narrow path of water Etienne hacked it away with the sword he called a cane blade. Mosquitoes rose like smoke from the cut brush and Etienne gave Elizabeth and Knobby a salve to rub on their skin. *"Le M'decin,"* he said. The oily paste smelled faintly of polecat, but it not only soothed the itch and sting of bites but also kept away the mosquitoes that hovered over the bayou.

They came suddenly into a large clearing, and Knobby and Elizabeth blinked at a bright streak of orange where the sun was about to rise. *"Lac a La Hache—"* Etienne whispered, chopping his hand down like the axe the lake was shaped like. With a finger to his lips he pointed up, where a cluster of dark specks slowly became an angled line of birds. *"Canard noir,"* Etienne whispered. Knobby just stared blankly, and Etienne said, "Ducks. *Poule d'eau.* Good to eat, him." The ducks circled the lake, getting closer as they flew—gray ducks, brown ducks, black ducks, ducks with bright green heads. *"Dos-gris,"* Etienne said softly, speaking to himself or to the musket he lifted toward the sky. Though Knobby knew it was coming, the explosion made him jump, the muzzle flare as orange as the streak of dawn. The boom came back from the water's surface like a wave slapping the side of the *pirogue,* and a brown duck dropped like a leaf and suddenly became a rock. Before the gunshot stopped ringing, Etienne had lain the fired musket in the boat and raised and shot the second gun. This time one of the green-headed ducks hit the water, wings splashing in a brief flurry. Etienne poled them out into the lake. He reached the green-headed duck first, its wings still, but when Etienne touched the duck it came to life and thrashed in his hand. He grabbed its head and twisted the neck with a soft *snap-snap.* The brown duck was fatter than the green-head. *"Ma-mere* and *Pa-pere,"* he said. "Drake and hen."

Etienne plucked the ducks, saving the feathers and down in a cotton bag he pulled from one of the many pockets of his blouse. Knobby had not seen the sheath at Etienne's ankle from which he slipped a narrow-bladed knife, slit open the ducks, and pulled constricted entrails from the carcasses. In the cool fog, steam rose from the glistening offal in Etienne's hand before he flung it out into the water where it disappeared in a furor of brown bubbles. He rinsed his hands, wrapped the cleaned ducks in wet blades of grass, and laid them in the bottom of the *pirogue.*

He showed them mounds of mud and grass that rose from the floating grass islands—muskrat homes. Along the edges of Ax lake he showed them wild rice growing. He poled them through the grass, the floating islands pushed away by the flush points of the *pirogue.* Etienne pushed the set of his pole and the *pirogue* wouldn't budge. Etienne hopped out onto the firm grass. *"Trainerant,"* he named the grassy passageway over which they dragged the boat until they came to a pothole that led to another pothole, forming a watery trail through the grass. Mullet swarmed at the surface of these watery holes and tiny shrimp fed in duckweed around the edges. He lifted cane sticks they thought were growing and revealed the anchor to a steel trap that held a muskrat, pink-white flesh showing through the fur where it had pulled against the trap's teeth. The animal hissed and bared its teeth. Etienne lifted a heavy stick from the *pirogue* and with one practiced motion crushed the furred skull. By the time he opened the trap, humming blue-green flies covered the animal's wound.

They left the string of small lakes and entered another dark bayou amongst cypresses and mossy oaks, the bottom of the *pirogue* piled with muskrat, rabbits, and a fox. These traps Etienne had not re-baited, but had collected and added to the pile in the boat. "You look strong, *Negre,*" he said. *"Mais,* I hold in my head, me, all the trails and trap lines from way up *de arc des Fausse Riviere,* the bend at False River, down to *L'anse Atchafalaya,* Atchafalaya Bay, and all the way west to *Lac Calcasieu.* Next after *Calcasieu* the *Bayou Negre* he finds Sabine Pass. I think, me, with these ways I keep in my head and with my *pirogue,* I bait you to help me."

"What help do you need?"

"Me, I show you. First, we eat, us, yes?"

Etienne poled over to a *roseaux* bush where a dark blue strip of cloth marked a limb. He lifted the thick twine of trotline and gave an upward tug, nodded, and knelt in the boat, pulling up the line, working the *pirogue* diagonally across the bayou. Some of the hooks were bare, the bait stolen by something that had dodged the hook. The catch was mostly catfish, eight to ten pounders judging by their trunk in the bottom of the *pirogue,* a couple of perch Etienne seemed to prize, a copper-colored fish he called Buffalofish, and one long, sharp-toothed creature Elizabeth thought was an alligator. Etienne said he almost was; he was alligator gar, and he grew near as big as a gator. The last line, closest to the bank, was jerking hard, and Knobby reached for it, thinking this would be the biggest fish of all. Etienne stopped him and slid his push pole down to lift the line. A green fish head was on the hook, but the rest of the fish disappeared into the wide-hinged mouth of a huge, gray snake. Impossibly, the snake, four or five inches in diameter, was swallowing the larger fish which bulged from inside the snake's body. Knobby picked up the cane knife and would have chopped the snake in half, but Etienne stopped him again. "Cotton mouth hungry, too. Perch, he dead already and fill with venom. To kill the snake, it make you feel safer, but me, I feel safer to let him live so I remember how many he is out here with me." He cut up the gar, who was about three feet long, and used his meat and muskrat entrails to re-bait all the hooks but the one at which the water moccasin still dined.

By the time Etienne poled them down the bayou to his tree house—a small plank box built high between three enormous cypresses—the fog had burned off and the sun beamed through the dense foliage. Etienne pulled up the *pirogue* at a weathered plank shack that suddenly appeared between tree trunks. He unloaded his traps and the day's catch, then turned the boat upside down. He took a coiled rope from a hollow tree and with the authority of repetition tossed it up against his shack where two pegs hooked a wide loop and the rope unfurled as a climbing ladder.

The shack was maybe ten by ten, the board floor covered with deer-skins, and two windows hung with burlap that let in air but not insects. Etienne lighted a candle and took two iron pots from a shelf. He put Elizabeth to work chopping cloves of garlic big as Knobby's knuckles, and red peppers and pungent wild onions. The candle threw a nimbus of light around Elizabeth and cast her head's shape large on the board wall. The sound of her chopping and the scent of burning wax comforted Knobby with security, a sense of civilization.

Outside, Etienne tossed Knobby a knife and one of the muskrats from his traps. Knobby watched him gut and dress three muskrats in the time it took him to imitate and get one critter cleaned. Knobby held up the pink-white body, mangled by his untrained hands. Etienne laughed. *"Mais,"* he said, "I don't care, me, no."

Sitting on a short, curved bench, Etienne used a heavy knife blade with no handle to scrape pearlescent flesh from the underside of a pelt. The

meat gave up the hide with a wet, kissing noise. Up and back Etienne deftly drew the blade—no wasted motion. Finished, he fitted the pelt over a wooden stretcher. He took longer with the fox. When the hides were stretched, he nodded to Knobby to help him gather them up. Knobby followed him to a shed thirty yards away. Knobby's nose told him why the shed was distanced from the house. The small, rancid-smelling building was warm, and more hides dangled from its ceiling. Etienne hung the stretchers from bent nails and built up a fire from coals that glowed red in a cast-iron stove in the room.

"The furs they dry, *Negre,* a month, yes."

Knobby was pleased to show that he knew how to gut and skin a catfish. They put the fillets over a fire outside. The two cleaned ducks Etienne surrounded with wild rice in an iron pot, the pot he buried in the coals. He added Elizabeth's pile of chopped garlic, peppers and onions to a stewpot he'd loaded with chunks of rabbit, muskrat and venison, and that he put to simmer on a small stove inside his house. The fish was ready first, and Elizabeth burned her fingers she was in such a hurry to get the meat to her mouth. Bowls full of the spicy stew followed. When Etienne finally dug the pot out of the coals, the duck flesh had swelled and come off the bones. The tender meat was smoky and sweet, and Knobby sucked the bones and gnawed them to slivers. When they had eaten their fill and more, Etienne poured cups full from a crock of whiskey. The Master had never allowed his slaves to have strong drink; Knobby had never tasted spirits. Brown as the bayou water, the whiskey was innocent looking. On his tongue the first sip pricked all the places the garlic, peppers, and onions had missed, and it flamed up behind his face, warming his cheeks and stinging his eyes to tears. The heat spread into his chest and heated his stomach. Elizabeth drank her cup down without coming up for air, her Adam's apple bobbed, no tears in her eyes. Knobby was full for the first time in days, and the whiskey made him feel like he gave off light like Etienne's candle.

Margaret Scanlan / *He's a Wolf—He Likes to Eat*

The Cat-Head-Biscuit Woman

by Lynn Veach Sadler

I was like to send us under,
for I could not break her spell.
When she made her cat-head biscuits,
she was the snake,
with me the baby chick,
and all the farm could go asunder.
I could not break her spell.

She never measured anything,
just bent, then scooped
from out the flour bin
with her mother's big tin scoop.
She would sift as hard as sin,
laugh as flour dust
put spells about the house (and me).
I'd run, stumbling in my eagerness,
to our spring house, fetch her home
the home-churned buttermilk
that magically appeared.
I'd pull out the bucket of our lard,
set it on the green-checked
oil-cloth table cloth for her,
prize off the lid, and hold my breath
while she reached in to scoop out
with her hand one glob
that must be walnut-sized.
She'd hold her special earthenware bowl,
sent down mother to daughter,
just so beneath an arm,
reach in with her three middle fingers

to twist the dough and twist again.
She never used a spoon,
had contempt for spoons
and all who used them.

Other men bragged of
wives' apple butter,
watermelon rind preserves,
spoonbread soppers,
any manner of such truck.
I was bewitched by
my Cat-Head-Biscuit Woman,
her cat-head biscuit wares.

But then there came
a dainty teacher into our valley,
a flatlander unlike my wife.
She made tea cakes
and small provender,
looking with pitying eye
upon my woman's cat-head biscuits.
And soon the other women
and all the men but me
made fun upon the sly
of such elephant-sized vittles.
Still, I hung fire,
though no longer tethered to
my Cat-Head-Biscuit Woman
with quite the golden chain of once.

And when the dainty teacher
swept the prizes with her
fancy, light, fantastic delicacies,
my wife walked our going-home alone,
stuffed herself with
cold cat-head biscuits.
By the time I reeled on home,
my Cat-Head-Biscuit Woman
had choked and was
as cold as stone.

Summer Corn

by Linda Seals Talbert

I had not been back to my childhood home since the previous Christmas, although our commune was less than 20 miles away. And while the summer wind blew sweet with wild honeysuckle and Daddy's roses, it dodged in and out of the beech, white ash, and laurel and never found, on that mountainside, a clear path—a place to run full-force and true.

But our wind rushed through Moshawn Valley—lifting our long hair and longer skirts, tickling the fringe on the leather vests of the men, rattling the wind chimes of Indian brass, carrying the scents of home-grown herbs, candle wax, and musk so strong the deer, the bear, the mountain panther paced the periphery of our land, looking curious and confused.

I stood by my older sister, Wallis, and listened to the wind stutter through the woods, waiting for Daddy to bring the load of Seneca Chief corn up from the two-acre garden he shared with his brother and two neighbors.

"How's Dean?" I asked, staring down the mountain road, watching for a flash of the red truck, thinking I'd start with something safe—her husband, the son of the local Independent Presbyterian minister. Surely, no offense would lie in that.

"Fine," she said. She busied herself by arranging the paraphernalia of the day's work—a lard stand for the shucks; worn, hard-bristled toothbrushes for the silking; steel-bladed knives sharpened thin on Daddy's whetstone; 12-inch cast-iron skillets, bottoms blackened and crusted by heat and age; white plastic scoops for filling the cartons; the quart-sized freezer cartons themselves, their lids of lightest liquid blue.

"Here, Wallis, Dale." Mama stepped from the kitchen onto the back porch with full-dress aprons hanging from her arms. "That corn milk'll be all over the place. Usually washes out pretty easy, but no sense in messing up your clothes with no need."

"I go by 'Anne' now, Mama," I reminded her. She had taken my first name from a singing cowgirl while my sister bore the name of the Duchess of Windsor. When we villagers had chosen new names in the valley, I had honored my own teenage wish to be called by my middle name, a name of queens and prophets.

"Very well, Anne," Mama said, and the skin around Wallis' eyes tightened.

"At least 'Dale's' a girl's name as well," Wallis said in Mama's direction. "Maybe I should start calling myself something else, too."

Mama flapped her hand at Wallis and then lifted my ash brown hair to put the apron strings around my neck. She started to tie the waist strings.

"I'll do it." I adjusted my peasant blouse of thin imported paisley cotton and tied the strings loosely around the waist of my jeans. I had split the seams of my jeans' legs from knee to hem and inserted triangles of another paisley fabric. The denim brushed my bare toes, which peeked out through leather sandals.

Wallis allowed Mama to adjust the apron over her clothes. Wallis' finely textured hair was nearly the yellow of the corn kernels and was longer than mine, but Mama didn't have to lift it, for Wallis had it in a high ponytail, pulled back tightly from her face, not a tendril escaping. She looked downright regal. Her sleeveless, white cotton shirt was starched and ironed and tucked into her dungarees, which were also starched and ironed, sharp creases bisecting each of her long legs. She wore navy blue Keds with startlingly white socks.

I looked at myself, short and pudgy, with breasts too large and heavy for twenty. I was conscious of my tummy, bulging from too much freshly baked bread, pushing against the zipper of my jeans. Wallis was willowy, her abdomen concave, her breasts small and neat, her back straight and unyielding as a cornstalk.

And she's the one who hates me, I thought, as I gathered my hair into my leather hair ornament and pushed the pointed stick through the holes, gouging my scalp as I did. And she did hate me; I knew that. I had once assumed it was because I had chosen such a different lifestyle. But at Christmas, during a moment when Mama, Daddy, and I had our heads together, laughing over some childhood Christmas antic of mine, I looked up to see her eyes narrowed in contempt, and I knew then: she hated me because they didn't.

Why I was back on that mountain, I didn't know, except that Mama's voice had sounded tiny and yearning when she called to ask me to help put up the corn. I had thought of years of late-summer days on that back porch I loved, looking into the tangle of the forest, shucking and silking as a little girl, cutting off and blanching as I grew up. I thought of the incomparable taste of the corn on a cold February day with cornbread, pinto beans cooked with fatback, and a wilted spinach salad.

I had thought of how close Wallis and I had been during those years. I heard Daddy's old truck rumbling up the road.

We were deep into the ritual now. Daddy sat in the rocker, stripping off the husks, checking for worms, snapping off brown tips where worms had been—seemingly in a single motion. His eyes were so keen, his hands so deft, he made my job easy. I was relegated to my childhood job of silking. We were few in number that year—no cousins, neighbors, friends on that particular Saturday, so Wallis and I would trade off silking and cutting off while Mama blanched and filled containers. We sisters would take on Mama's job later because we knew her hands were unpredictable with arthritis, and when tired, they frequently gave out on her.

"Remember the first year I blanched and dropped the skillet on the kitchen floor?" I threw out for anyone to answer. I still had slick patches of pink scars on my lower left leg, not too bad, but, still, I was glad to wear the long, flaring pants legs.

"Scared us to death," Mama said. "Do your scars ever bother you now, Honey?"

"Not really. Occasionally they itch. That's about all."

Wallis cut off half of the tops of several rows of kernels, flipped the knife with speed and dexterity, and scraped the milk and falling kernels into the skillet. "Daddy had to replace all the linoleum. I remember it well."

I suspended the toothbrush above the ear of corn and studied her. Her face was set on her work.

"Why, you ought to remember it," Mama said. "You were just six-teen, and Dr. Ross had to give you five days' worth of Valium. You were so upset—yelling at me that I never should have let Dale, er, Anne—well, it was 'Dale' then—cook the corn, that she was too young." She grinned. "I needed a Valium by the time you's through with me."

Wallis glanced my way and back to her business. "She was too young. She's always been uncoordinated."

I rose from my stool, plopped my pan of silked corn on the table where Wallis worked, and went into the house. On the way to the bathroom, I stopped by our old room. The twin beds were still covered with white eyelet. The two walls beside Wallis' bed were spring lavender and the two beside my bed, deep crimson. Mama's adroit and diplomatic sewing showed throughout. She had drawn the color scheme together with a fabric of lilacs and red roses she found on sale at Ben Franklin's. She fashioned vanity skirts, pillow shams, even picture-frame covers from that floral chintz. Wallis and I laughed about it then, but we appreciated her respect for our differences in tastes.

We'd always been different; I knew that. Only a year apart, but as different as that creamed corn would be from store-bought canned corn. And I wasn't sure which of us was hearty and sweet and which was runny and tasteless.

But until my move to Moshawn, we'd seemed to have a sisterly respect for those differences. I looked at the room again, saw Wallis' poms-poms and my Beatles posters. I closed the door softly and walked down the hall.

When I came back through the kitchen, Mama had two skillets of corn steaming on the burners.

"These ready to pack, Mama? If they are, I'll do that. You go sit and silk for a while. Rest your legs."

"I believe they're ready." She wiped her forehead with her apron skirt. "I could silk a while, I guess. But be extra careful, Anne."

I watched her walk out the screen door, older than her forty-five years. Of course, I had not helped that. I removed the bubbling corn from the stove and positioned my equipment so I could see from the kitchen table to the porch. I saw Wallis' profile—upturned nose, pulled-back hair still constrained despite the climbing heat.

I heard Mama tell the story of the boys, the way she did nearly every year. "Remember when you were fourteen and Dale was thirteen? We were putting up the corn and Rita and Sally were here and those four boys came snooping around."

"How could I forget?" Rita and Sally were our first cousins who spent most of their summers, despite all the work on that mountain, with us.

"Let's see, there was Lester and Ray from Pine Grove and those two brothers from Redfield."

"Neil and Bill."

"That's them. They were twins. Anyway, they all come slithering up here, thinking they's gonna spend the day courting, drinking Sally's lemonade and eating your fudge and maybe getting a walk in the woods or a swim in the creek with you girls."

"Yeah, Ma." Wallis stared intently at the corn, but I saw the corner of her mouth smooth out and lift a bit.

"When we put them to shucking and toting the pressure cooker and lifting those jars out of that boiling water, I thought they'd run off. But they didn't. They stuck with it." Mama's laugh was high and gay. "They had sweat pouring in their eyes and, by day's end, blisters on their thumbs from breaking the base of the corn."

"I know." Wallis smiled. "They could hardly stand up straight; their backs hurt so bad. And when you asked them to dinner and mentioned that we might need some help with the dishes afterward . . . "

"Yeah, they made some excuse about work at home." I heard Mama slapping her hand against her knee. She got such a kick out of the tale of those frustrated boys. "I don't reckon any of them ever came up here again, although Neil kept company with Sally for a while—in the dead of winter!"

Wallis' laugh was deep like Daddy's. "Yeah, they were highly perturbed when they didn't get so much as a wade in the creek with us. Dale and I laughed over that for days." She glanced my way, and I wondered if she could see my grin through the smoky screen. "We joked that if we ever had a suitor we wanted to get rid of, we'd bring him up at corn harvesting time."

"They didn't get what they came for." Daddy's voice was coarse, but full of mirth. "That's for sure!"

I had filled the containers and stepped back on the porch to help with cutting off. Wallis' face sobered slightly when I took my place beside her.

Sweat and corn milk were in my eyes, and I lost a lot of time wiping my brow. I was practiced, but slow, at cutting the kernels just so and scraping them close to the cob, but not too close. (Mama cautioned, as always, against scraping too hard. "It'll taste cobby.") My hair clasp had slipped down my neck, and my jeans felt tighter than ever. Wallis was pink-faced, but dry. Jeez, didn't this girl ever sweat? But I noticed a few liberated curls at her temples.

We cut and scraped, cut and scraped, my tempo about three-quarters of hers. Occasionally, our bare arms touched. Sometimes, she would move over. Sometimes, she didn't; maybe she was tired.

"Daddy, do you still use that packaged fertilizer on the plants? In the valley we make our own compost. It's a lot healthier."

"Well, are the kernels in the valley," Wallis said sarcastically, "as big as knuckles?" She exaggerated, of course, but some were the size of my pinkie knuckle. Daddy didn't answer.

A nice breeze slid through the porch, and it bore the portent of coming rain. The decaying smells of the forest floor—leaves, needles, black earth—rode on the wind. A blue jay squawked from a nearby poplar, and I heard the knock-knocking of a woodpecker and the murmur of the creek.

"No, Wallis, our corn's not this big and thick." I left it at that.

Mama led the conversation and we talked about Wallis' job at the bank, Daddy's tobacco crop and how hard it was to find someone to help work it, Dean's accounting job at the electric company, and how many jars of strawberry jam, peach preserves, and plum jelly Mama had put up, and she *still* had quarts and quarts of fruit in the freezer, she said.

"You knew about Rita's twins, Dale. Born three weeks ago?" I did. "Skinny as she is, she's nursing both those boys. I'm afraid she's gonna go down." She stood up and stretched her back. "Course, I nursed both of y'all at once, and it didn't hurt me. But I was a mite heftier than Rita."

"For God's sake, Mama." Wallis pointed in the air with her knife. "Let's not talk about breast-feeding, especially breast-feeding us."

I put my knife on the table and turned to Wallis. "Breast-feeding is perfectly natural. Two women in the commune are breast-feeding now, and it's a beautiful thing."

"It may be, but it's not a thing you talk about while you're working corn, *Anne,* in polite company, *Anne,* especially when you're talking to the people involved."

Mama put her silking brush down and headed for the kitchen. "Somebody's gotta see about this corn on the stove before it scorches."

I stared at Wallis, who stared at Mama. I picked up my knife. We both resumed cutting.

When Mama was inside the kitchen, Daddy, who spoke rarely and even more rarely of private matters, said, "Your mama almost died when Wallis was born."

Wallis and I looked at each other, our lower lips dropped down, foreheads crinkled.

"Daddy, what are you talking about?" Wallis asked.

"We never told you 'cause we didn't want you to feel bad about the way you came into the world." He tore husks off of four ears before he continued. "They couldn't stop the bleeding. Took 'em a long time." He husked four more ears. "Something I felt bad about for years, never told your mother." I had to strain to hear him. "I was in the nursery holding you, Wallis—your tiny, seven-pound body in my big, clumsy arms—when Pearl went into surgery to stop the blood." He hung his head. "And all I could think about, all I could feel, was this great big love for you, something I'd never felt for anything or anybody before. It's like it took me over."

Wallis was still and quiet as those tossed husks. She looked at Daddy for a long time, then at me, then walked over to the rocker.

"I felt so bad for months after 'cause I hardly thought about Pearl until the surgery was halfway through. Of course, when she came out all right, I was relieved."

I had never heard Daddy make such a long speech.

Wallis placed her slender hand, coated with milk, on his shoulder, and he put his rough one over hers. They stayed like that for a few seconds, until Mama returned to the porch. Wallis put her hand on her tiny tummy.

"What's going on? We'll never get finished with you girls standing around."

"Daddy was just telling us about how cute Wallis was when she was born."

"That right? Yeah, she was a beauty all right. Both of you were."

Wallis and I started working the corn again. Mama told her version of the days of both our births, leaving out all private or distressing details, including Daddy's revelation.

Then, we girls began talking about what we wanted for our own future children—piano lessons for Wallis', open-classroom schools for mine, homes away from the towns that were filling up these mountains and valleys far and near, names like "Wesley" and "Joshua," "Melissa" and "Jennifer" that left no doubt as to gender.

"I'm going in and cook up some fried squash and green beans and slice up some tomatoes to go with this corn. Maybe bread some pork chops. You staying for dinner, Anne?"

"Yes, Mama, that would be nice." I didn't say that I was off meat. Matter of fact, I even decided to take some chops with me if there were leftovers.

Wallis looked at me and picked up the corner of her apron. "Better get that corn milk off your face before it sets. They won't know you in the valley."

We laughed, and she rubbed my forehead and my eyelids, then handed me my apron tail so I could finish the job.

A forceful wind swept down into the clearing where that old house rested. It flowed across the porch, ruffled our aprons, set Mama's hanging plants swaying, and brought the first heavy drops of a summer rain. ☕

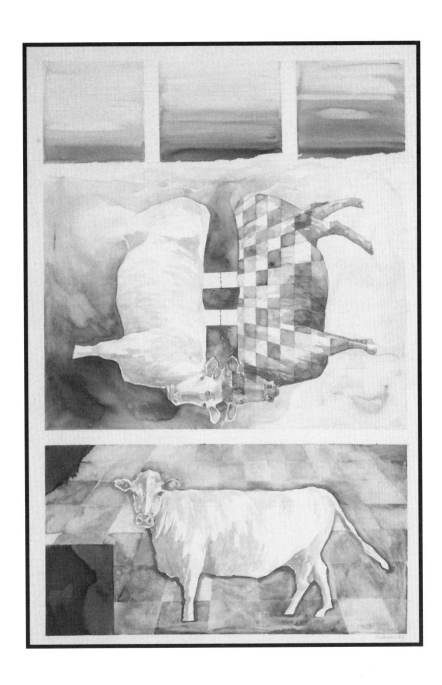

Margaret Scanlan / *Shot Cow*

September Sweets

by Simone Muench

You're a punctual man but today you're late.
Striding past Krispy Kreme you pause
mid-step and pivot. You're not
allowed sweets: *bad for your heart*
your doctor declares; *they'll kill you*
your family agrees. So they stuck you
on a diet. But today it's your heart
that clamors *gimme, gimme, gimme*
with the effectiveness of a pleading child.
You risk it: sliding into the shop
where the windows glisten
like indium and reflect the metallic
slate of lower Manhattan.

Cup of coffee—cream *and* sugar—and one
deliciously spongy Krispy Kreme donut.
Still warm. You can't wait to eat it.
You hike up your navy slacks, prop your leg
against a fire hydrant in the sun and savor
what you've been denied for months.

You're a punctual man but today you're late.
The evidence of your tardiness
stuck to your lips: powdered sugar, fine
as the tips of feathers and sweet as hallelujah.

Powdered sugar that switches to ash
as you approach your office,
coating you in a powdery shroud,
and is what you would have been
had you not paused, drawn
by the odor of fried dough dusted
with sweetness, glaze of grease, and coffee
steaming its burnt nut flavor. Krispy Kreme,
oh Krispy Kreme, hallowed be thy name.

Granny's Cabbage Patch Soup

by Sharon Auberle

Sunday, October 7th, the day Jack and Henry were born, the day we bombed Afghanistan, was a rainy, cold autumn day. I didn't know the twins were born, didn't know yet that they were in this world, I only knew I love this kind of day. Today was for looking out the rain-streaked window at the first snow on the mountain. To see a fox scamper across the road and disappear under changing oak leaves. To watch two young does and a fawn delicately tread a trail behind the house. I knew today was the first day after a long, hot summer that we could build a fire while reading the Sunday papers and cook soup—the first soup of autumn. Today was a day for comfort soup, seasoned with only salt and pepper. If the cook felt particularly daring, she might add just a pinch, mind you, of garlic salt or powder. A simple dish we grew up with, that brought back memories in each bite. Of our parents, how we miss them: Harry—a meat and potatoes man only, and Louise, cooking so precisely, serving in fine bowls in her dining room on Morningside Drive in Parkersburg, West-by-God-Virginia. The place where, to her, the sun *always* shone. Millie and C.J. in their little trailer beside blazing Ohio hardwoods, rather haphazardly throwing the ingredients together. Both kettles of soup filled with so much love, I'm thinking, as I brown 1½ lbs. of ground beef or turkey with onions, salt, pepper, and yes, lots of garlic powder. I throw this in a crockpot, along with 4 cups (or more, to taste) of chopped cabbage, 2 cups of chopped celery, a 28 oz. can of crushed tomatoes (undrained), 1 or 2 cans of dark red kidney beans, 4 cups of water and 1 can of chicken broth. Barley and more garlic are optional. And that's it. Pay no more attention to it for at least 7 or 8 hours on low, other than to relish the increasingly appetizing smell drifting through the house. Look out the window, dream, pray, make rainy Sunday afternoon love, watch football, phone an old friend, laugh, bake bread, paint a picture, write a poem, find out that you have just become the grandparents of two amazing boys: Jack Douglas and Henry James, weighing in at six pounds each, and twenty inches long. Give thanks as you eat the soup for all the love and blessings—past and present—in your life. Always.

Cindy on Television

by Leslie McGrath

Late one Sunday afternoon while in the kitchen
I turned the television on and saw a girl
I'd grown up with, buffed and bleached to what passes
for beauty in middle age. She was hostessing
a cooking show on a local cable station,
leaning over bubbling pots with cannibal zeal
and chatting up the chefs.

Cindy, a first-generation feminist,
who donated her bat mitzvah money to Planned Parenthood,
in whose car we'd skip school and drink beer for lunch
while sneering at our mothers' real estate jobs—
Cindy reading recipes on television.

I wiped my hands on my apron and turned the volume up,
but still I couldn't understand how the beast
we thought we'd tamed had turned up on the menu
as osso buco, how I could be here
rolling pastry for a bake sale, watching
Cindy scooping marrow with a spoon.

Julia Child's Kitchen

by Kay Newton

They've hauled it to the Smithsonian, walls and all:
the junk-drawer's flotsam—thumbtacks, tangled ball
of rubber bands, scotch tape, and hiding in a dark
and linty corner, a souvenir wine cork
saved from a special vintage she once shared
with a friend who'd come to cook with her—James Beard?
Ubiquitous fridge magnets pin up notes
and recipes, snapshots, cartoons, and jokes.
The lab where she once worked her alchemy
seems just as plain, as down-to-earth as she—
and just as dowdy; though a pinch of wit
and a soupçon of humor flavor it,
the ambience is homey, almost humdrum.
Like her, the place demystifies conundrums
intimidating to the rest of us.
She had the great gift of inspiring trust—
just watching her I knew: what she could do,
no matter how advanced, why, I could too.
Unworthy of this unearned intimacy,
I trespass on her sanctum's privacy.
The thought of my own crannies makes me shudder—
would I want someone snooping through my clutter?
Antique Hamburger Helper past its date,
Moroccan sardines no one ever ate,
Kraft Macaroni Dinner, cans of Spam
reveal the sorry sort of cook I am.
Perched at cross-hatched Formica as I dine,
I'm glad they took her kitchen and not mine.

Sarah McCarty / **Basket with Grapes and Currants**

Martha's Final Entrée

by David E. Joyner

Gone to rust are the pumps at Ferdie's Texaco, their glass globes long since filched by dealers from Atlanta. They have probably found a collector's market, along with the soda fountain from Tate's Pharmacy with its fixtures, mirrors and chrome-ringed pedestal stools. Twisted iron bars pierce a bed of gravel and concrete crumbs where the twirling pole outside Ed's Barber Shop once fascinated small boys. Even the stained glass windows and steeple of Gordville Freewill Baptist have been hauled away. The town has been ravaged, reduced to a whisper in the road from Craigtown to Tagboro. It cannot even be called a ghost town, as no apparition would tolerate the infestation of kudzu slowly creeping in from the south strangling the post-Victorian mansions on Willow Lane and the workers' clapboard row houses on Mill Street.

A bullet-riddled sign hangs loose, swinging by a single corner from a column which itself is no longer plumb. The wind beats a dirge of decadence against it, causing curious travelers to tilt their heads in passing. It reads:

> Welcome to Gordville.
> Population 1,327

There are still some, although their numbers are dwindling, who can pinpoint the exact day of Gordville's last breath and tell you about Martha Puggins, who was the instrument of its demise.

Martha monitored the social life of the town as skillfully as her husband, Jay Barton Puggins, controlled the Gordville Savings and Loan, the town's only financial institution.

J.B. had returned from a bankers' convention in New Orleans with his new bride back in the 'thirties. Martha, whose beauty and youth had won her the richest man in Delmore County, wasted no time in establishing herself as the Social Sovereign of Gordville.

Having securely ensconced herself in both marriage and community, Martha soon allowed herself to embrace a passion that had obsessed her since childhood, a passion that she had stifled in the interest of finding a husband who could support it. It was a passion for food; not just any food, but the best food, and not just the food itself, but its preparation, its presentation, and most of all, its consumption.

While others flaunted snapshots of their grandchildren, Martha accumulated pictures of gastronomic delicacies. Every Tuesday evening she stuffed herself into J.B.'s sixteen-cylinder Packard and drove to Craigtown, where she took lessons in watercolor from Miss Pettigail Simms, whose credentials included a stint at the Art Students League in New York. The subject of Martha's artistic efforts never varied. Bucolic landscapes or portraits of notables copied from photographs were not for her. Her genre was limited to the still life—not of flower arrangements or plaster casts, but of oyster chowders, curried stews, truffles, and racks of lamb dripping with mint sauces—subject matter not only from her own repertoire, but from her vast collection of richly illustrated coffee-table books and *Gourmet* magazines.

As Martha's beauty and youth gradually began to fade, her body expanded. Her small bud of a mouth became a gullet-bound culvert between once-taut cheeks gone flaccid. She traveled widely in quest of new delicacies, sipping, chewing, and swallowing her way across Europe, always returning several pounds heavier to brandish her culinary acquisitions. And as she grew heavier, J.B. grew more distant.

Shortly after attending a festival in Barcelona, Martha decided that what Gordville needed was an annual food event. It would be her magnum opus, the child she could never have. She would call it Foodfest. With J.B.'s resources and influence she immediately set to work. Full-color brochures were circulated throughout the state inviting any and all to bring their best regional dishes and recipes to Gordville. Participants would be eligible to compete in several categories.

While it could not be denied that, for Martha, Foodfest was self-serving—a theater for her own creations—she designed it so as not to discourage others. Categories were clearly defined, ranging from Martha's own culinary delights (Entrée category) to Hank Butterfield's seven-hundred-pound pumpkin and Red Parker's twelve-pound tomato, both of them pithy and inedible (Can You Top This? category). Both men were diminutive in stature, which left Martha to wonder if their drive to produce the largest of

their submitted species might have been to compensate for some hidden anatomical inadequacy.

No, she would leave for others the chow-chows, the barbecues, the watermelon pickles, even the desserts: pies, cakes, apple-pan-dowdies. She considered these unfit, lesser fare, although she would never admit it.

Foodfest became an immediate success and within two years attracted enough tourism to generate a substantial amount of Gordville's income. The festival took place on the grounds and terraces of the Puggins estate. Gardeners were hired and tents erected, and it is said that the collective aroma of the event wafted into the trees at the edge of the property where mill children hid in hopes of gleaning table scraps from the help. The highlight of the event, called "Tasters' Choice," was the judging of the competition itself.

Martha always competed in the Entrée category and, while all submissions were anonymous, there was never any doubt as to which selection was hers, if only because it contained ingredients which the judges had never before seen or tasted.

When the winner was announced, Martha invariably covered her mouth with her hand as if in shock. Her bracelets clattered and her eyes widened in feigned surprise.

As years passed, fewer Gordville dowagers participated in the Entrée category and Martha's competition was gradually limited to new arrivals and folks from out of town. In blithe naiveté they presented lasagna and chicken casseroles, while each year Martha's submission became more outrageous and complex.

The 25th anniversary of Foodfest was to be special. Winners would be awarded silver goblets engraved with the festival's crest: a knife, fork, and spoon foiled against the silhouette of a chef's hat. In preparation, Martha planned yet another trip, this time to the Iberian Peninsula in quest of something new—something to eclipse all past endeavors.

At a small café in the Basque country Martha discovered a dish called Kurfilla— a savory pie that combined various spices, nuts and filo with the finely diced flesh of pigeons. It was so delectable that she begged the chef for its recipe, finally offering him 50,000 pesos. "It comes," he told her, "from an ancient recipe first brought from Morocco to Portugal, and then into Spain. It is rumored to have been a favorite of Moorish noblemen. The recipe found its way into my grandmother's hands. She told me it would be even better," he added, "if I could add a certain ingredient which she had been unable to locate—a nut called talchaba."

The daughter of the chef, a dark-haired girl of twelve and a student at a nearby convent, spent a good part of the evening translating the recipe from Catalan into French, for which Martha gave her a ring which she had admired, and a pair of nylons.

"Kurfilla," Martha repeated to herself several times. "Kurfilla. It will be perfect for the 25th Foodfest."

Back in Gordville Martha decided she would not be satisfied until she could track down the elusive talchaba. She scoured specialty sources in New York and Chicago and, unable to find it, turned to markets in Europe. She was finally referred to a vendor in Marrakech who, after much confusion, shipped the talchaba to her by air at an astronomical expense.

For three days Martha supervised the assembly of the Kurfilla. In addition to Lily, her regular maid, she enlisted and swore to secrecy two of her closest friends—the girls, she called them, which was as much of an attempt at intimacy as she was willing to muster in order to recruit them. The talchaba would be added 24 hours before the presentation and care taken not to move the Kurfilla, which had been nested in a bed of chopped ice and covered with damp cheesecloth.

On Friday morning, Martha's hands trembled as she opened the small box. Inside was a wax-covered packet containing the talchaba. The instructions, which she had memorized earlier, were clear. Martha herself had translated them from French to English.

It took the four women, immaculately aproned in white, almost six hours to perform the delicate culinary procedure. At five Martha paid Lily and sent the girls home. She locked the French doors that opened onto the terrace and drew the curtains across them. She placed a small Wedgwood cup and a silver demitasse spoon next to the Kurfilla resting in the middle of an enamel-topped table. Unable to tuck her legs under the table, she sat sidesaddle in a Windsor chair and stared at the Kurfilla for several minutes. Though it contained no yeast it had almost doubled in size as predicted—spores in the air, she guessed. She heard a faint crackling sound as if it were a living, breathing thing. Again her hands trembled as she carefully lifted a corner of the cheesecloth. A pungent, spicy aroma emerged from beneath the shroud.

Martha's eyes feasted on the buttery, golden-sienna crust. She dipped the tip of her spoon into the Kurfilla and transferred it to her cup. With closed eyes she guided it past her quivering lips (amazing, she had often observed, that even with one's eyes closed the spoon always finds its target).

"I have surpassed myself!" Martha said to the Kurfilla. She tingled with ecstasy. Her tongue, palate, and nostrils were teased until her entire body was inundated with a pleasure beyond any she had ever known (and she had, in her indulgences, known many). No nectar of the gods or morsel of ambrosia could have touched it. She desperately wanted more. Tears trickled down her cheeks and into the corners of her mouth as she stifled the impulse to continue. She replaced the cheesecloth, caressing it as one might a pet, feeling its warmth against her fingers and the palm of her hand. She left the kitchen, locking the door behind her. The room was not to be disturbed until morning.

On the terrace, Lily had prepared a light supper for Martha and J.B.— a salmon soufflé with aspic. But Martha, basking in the exquisite aftertaste of the Kurfilla, would have none of it.

"I have a headache," she told J.B.

"I don't wonder," he replied. "You've been running yourself ragged."

Sleep did not come easily to Martha. Years before, a combination of ever-expanding bulk and snoring had driven J.B from their king-sized Beautyrest to a separate bed, and finally to a room at the opposite end of the hall.

That night Martha was visited by a series of images. In one, the Kurfilla floated up into the trees like a runaway balloon. In another she saw herself lifting the lid of a tureen only to find it empty. She awakened with a start, her nightgown soaked and clinging to her body. Finally she was swallowed into oblivion. There she remained until she heard Henry, the gardener, snapping the legs of the rented banquet tables as he assembled them on one of the terraces. She was an hour behind schedule but the headaches and sweating were gone.

Lily was already in the dining room polishing the silver. The sun was streaming through the glass doors on the south wall of the kitchen. An early-morning breeze filtered through the tulip poplars outside causing shadows to dance across the quarry tiles and up the legs of the table where they fluttered across the Kurfilla as if to tickle it into wakefulness.

Martha peeked beneath the cheesecloth.

"Perfect!"

Before transferring the Kurfilla to a large silver tureen, Martha carefully removed a portion for the girls and herself to be shared after the festival

—a reward for their tireless efforts and dedication. She covered it with a towel and placed it in the vegetable bin at the bottom of the refrigerator.

Martha felt blessed this perfect morning. September had withheld the blistering heat and sudden thunderstorms of previous festivals.

Three tables were placed end-to-end and draped with linen to form a single head-table for the judges. It was set with Haviland china and crystal wine glasses. Lily had been recruited to keep an eye on it. The remaining tables were covered with paper and laden with colorful napkins, plastic plates, cups, and utensils. Brass and copper braziers hovered precariously over cans of Sterno or candles and the tables wobbled and threatened to collapse under myriad casseroles.

Wearing a simple dove-gray shift, Martha breezed through a dizzy field of calico muu-muus, where she was by contrast, in spite of her bulk, conspicuously fresh and stunning.

Selections from Tchaikovsky were piped into speakers perched in trees like giant birdhouses, their wires threaded through branches like blackened umbilical chords to a mother tuner somewhere within the depths of the house.

A screening committee comprised of Gordville citizens had spent all morning and the better part of the afternoon narrowing down the entries. There were, besides Martha's Kurfilla (its presence a foregone conclusion), only three finalists.

The judges were seated and, although they were known to all, nameplates had been placed in front of each of them:

Bishop Kirkland (Delmore Episcopal Parish)
Wilma Carver (Superintendent of Schools)
Judge Thornton Perkins (Third District Court)
Bill Filmore (President, Gordville Mills)
Dr. Harvey Crenshaw (Chief Resident, Delmore County Hospital)

As Master of Ceremonies, J.B. joined them at the table. It had been announced that a conflict of interest would prevent him from participating in the judging. This happened every year.

Each submission was spooned onto small porcelain saucers and served by Lily to the judges, who were given pads and pencils. After tasting the entry, each put down a number between one and ten. Though it would be vehemently denied, it could hardly be construed as anything but deliberate

that Lily had saved the Kurfilla for last. The winner was announced and Martha accepted her silver goblet with predictable surprise and grace.

As had always been the custom after the ceremony, what remained of the winning entry was to be distributed by the winner to those at the judges' table. Lily had provided bowls for that purpose.

"Bon Appétit!" said Martha as she filled the bowls.

It was remarkable that this year the dignitaries were to display such animal behavior—digging into the Kurfilla like drunkards or street urchins until each had devoured several helpings. "Please Sir," Bishop Kirkland seemed to be saying, "Oliver Twist wants more!" while Dr. Crenshaw practically wrestled Wilma Carver to the ground for what little might be scraped from the sides of the tureen.

By ten o'clock the terrace was empty. The servants were taking down tables and cleaning up the littered lawn. The grass was trampled and ruined as it was every year, but it would be turning brown anyway as winter approached, and in the spring the gardeners would spray it with whatever substance they used to breathe life back into it until the next festival.

Shortly after midnight Judge Perkins was overcome by cramps and vomiting. He buried his fist in his belly and limped in agony to the phone to ring Dr. Crenshaw.

One by one the judges called in, all of them within a single hour and Crenshaw, now doubled-up in pain himself, called the Poison Control Center in Nashville. By the time a toxicologist and his assistant arrived by helicopter with a team of specialists and equipment, Perkins had already plunged into his swimming pool, preferring death to the torturous agony that had invaded every inch of his body.

The toxicologist was in constant communication with the Nashville Center by phone, but long before the laboratory results could be analyzed, all six—including J.B.— were gone. The economic, social, religious, political and financial bastions of Gordville were wiped out within a matter of hours.

News spread fast as townspeople, awakened by the sound of helicopter and ambulances, stepped into the streets, still in their pajamas and robes. Rumors spread that a new form of bubonic plague was kicking into full swing.

The final report from the Nashville Lab traced the source of the toxicity to a microorganism—a parasite hosted in a rare North African nut thought to have been extinct.

There were the grievers, Martha among them, who remained while the rest fled.

At four a.m. Martha, unable to sleep, waddled into the kitchen. She looked for a moment at the naked enamel tabletop, then went to the refrigerator and removed what was left of the Kurfilla. She scooped it into a chipped Fiestaware bowl with a wooden spoon.

It was still dark outside as she stared into the black panes of the French doors and studied her reflection. Her bloodshot eyes stared back from a bloated face that could not possibly be hers. "Bon appétit!" she said to the impostor as she shoveled the Kurfilla into her mouth.

It was every bit as good as she remembered. 🍮

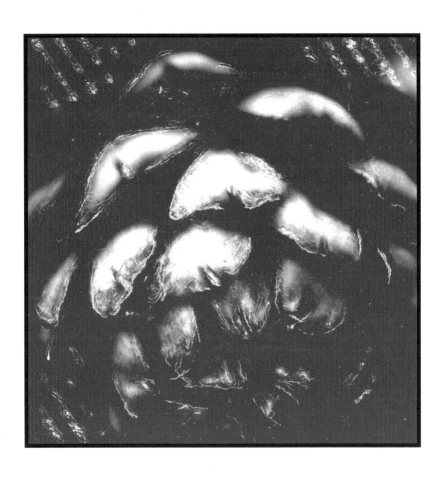

Lindsay Kromer / *Artichoke*

Tossing the Salad

by Sarah Maté

I read in *Better Homes and Gardens*
that couples need to communicate better about sex.

Right. I tear the iceberg
lettuce into bite-size
pieces and say adding oil
"I was just hoping . . ."
"Cute. I'm supposed to be Hemo the Magnificent
and juggle at the same time."
I slice the pepperoni.
Chop. Chop.
"Couldn't we just talk about clogged pipes?"

We are. Chop.
"We didn't have a problem
until you read it."
I toss in too much salt—
May your arteries harden. Suddenly,
I remember the night we were making love
and you said, "Look, don't you know
a woman's supposed to be
mysterious?"

Dinner goes down the disposal.

You can starve. I wedge shut the bedroom door,
practice my lines,
and cry my eyes into a clown face.
Just then, I hear you coming in the front door.
Whistling yet.
"Pizza, honey?"
How can you be THAT sure?

Lemons

by Blair Campbell

My father, an otherwise normal man, snacked on entire sticks of butter as a child. I learned this not from him, but from my disapproving Aunt Sandra in the context of a story about her courtship with my uncle. Sandra recalled dutifully shaking hands with three of her suitor's four brothers and recoiling in horror at the proffered hand of the butter-smeared youngest child.

When I confronted Dad with the truth, he deflected, quickly changing the subject with a story about his grandfather, who used to feed salted nuts to chipmunks straight from his mouth. During family vacations in the Poconos, Grandpa Goetze would sit on the back porch and let the rodents scurry up his arm, giving him what amounted to a little nut-stealing kiss.

Thankfully neither the butter-snacking nor the nut-sharing got passed down through generations, but as a child I did inherit another of my father's quirks of the palate—eating lemons whole. Following Dad's lead, I would halve the fruit, suck out the juice, then peel it like an orange and swallow the remaining flesh. Battling through the tartness made me feel bold, and I ignored all warnings about losing the enamel on my teeth.

My clearest lemon-eating memory is of a crisp late afternoon one Labor Day, when I was eleven or twelve. My family spent summers in a small seaside town, and we had the strange fortune to live across the street from a croquet court—a nod to the neighbors' Anglophilia. Over the long holiday weekend, the mixed-doubles tennis tournament was the hottest ticket in a town where your social standing depended on the strength of your forehand. Mixed-doubles croquet, on the other hand, was not such a draw, but for me it had the advantage of proximity. So on that Monday afternoon I grabbed half a lemon out of the refrigerator and headed across the street to watch the finals.

There was one other spectator—a boy we'll call Elliot B., my best friend's older brother. Elliot B. was not the cutest boy in town, but he had that 14-year-old-boy version of *je ne sais quoi*—a certain tanned, lanky ease—and he was by far the best tennis player in his age group. He had never spoken to me, so I sat down on the white-painted bench a respectful distance away.

A few minutes later, an incredulous, puberty-deepened voice asked, "Are you *eating* that lemon??"

"Yeah," I replied defensively before I'd processed the fact that the speaker was Elliot B.

"You eat the whole thing. Like an orange," he said, as though getting the details straight to later share with his friends.

"Yeah!" I said, with what I hoped was a tone of pride.

"That's *so* weird."

Suddenly Elliot B. scooted down the bench to sit next to me, as though my freakish behavior had earned, if not quite his respect, then at least his curiosity. We sat like that for over an hour, *talking.* I can't remember a single thing we discussed, but I know that that Labor Day, a day that has always made me catch my breath a little, was particularly beautiful and sad. The sky was a deeper shade than the bird's-egg blue of July and August, turning the green of the leaves and grass even greener. You could feel a hint of autumn chill and smell the smoke of the town's few year-round residents starting their first fires of the season. Kids with solemn faces took slow, final bike rides down the block, and station wagons loaded with trunks, bicycles, rafts, and coolers pulled out of driveways for the trip back to the city.

Add to this the feeling of awakening to a crush I never knew I had. Our talk continued until dusk, until shadows had fallen over the field and the croquet players had all gone home. Finally, with a "bye, see you next year," Elliot got on his Schwinn and rode away. I walked home, and when my mother saw me and asked where I'd been, I had to fight a smile.

The following summer, Elliot B. ignored me for three solid months. Unfazed, I believed there was a secret agreement between us and, on Labor Day, two hours before sunset, I walked across the street with half a lemon. No one else sat on the bench, so I bided my time, feigning interest in croquet.

When dusk fell and the players had packed up their mallets and gone, I was still alone, stood up for my first, albeit imaginary, date. I walked home and opened the refrigerator, hanging limply on its door. When my mother asked me where I'd been, I said "nowhere," then put the lemon back and searched for something sweeter. 🍵

Lord of the *Rugelach*

by Marilyn Kallet

Bubbe was a beautiful little old lady with a secret: she knew the ancient art of restoring human happiness through baking. She practiced good magic, the alchemy of turning humble ingredients into light and golden creations. But Bubbe was growing older, and she feared her art would die out, leaving the earth flat as a pancake. Her husband, the great wizard Gasoff, worked in his laboratory deep underground. The secret arts he practiced restored ancient machinery to humming order. He was a brother in the fraternity of tinkerers and engineers, and he was not at all interested in the culinary arts (except in the art of eating).

Bubbe and Gasoff had a beautiful son named Lou. When he was newly born, he smelled like cinnamon and raisins, like a little loaf of coffeecake. His parents should have suspected that he was "chosen" to rise. As a youth, Lou seemed to be interested in his father's workshop rather than in his mother's spells. But as he grew older, he turned more and more to his mother's secret arts. He became an apprentice baker.

"My son," his mother said, when he was old enough to understand, "the world is round like a *challah,* and we bake in order to maintain roundess, both in humans and in the cosmos. If the cake rises, the heavens stay high above, and the humans rest happily at the table. Earth was created at the kitchen table, and we renew its origins daily."

Lou was her son and her student. He could bake a *rugelach* to end all *rugelachs.* Whenever there was a celebration among the Jewish community, families called upon Lou to bake. Yet there were obstacles. Some felt that Lou should remain true to his mother's recipe, and that he must never, never add raisins. One night, in his sleep, a voice came to Lou: "Louis! Throw the fiery rum-soaked raisins into the mountain of rising dough!" Lou was deeply perplexed. But he followed the voice, rose and soaked some raisins, and then (as only adults can do), he lit them very carefully over the kitchen sink, and watched until the flames died down. He threw these into the bowl of dough, rolled, twisted, and cut the dough into cookies. While some of the old witchy women criticized these cookies ("*Oy vey!* I'm getting *ein bischen schnockered*—a little dizzy—just from one bite!"), they ate them all up at the next *Oneg Shabbat*.

Lou made his mother proud, and he made all of the *noshers* happy. Though wars continued on earth, some people were always sweet and gentle from their eating of Lou's *rugelach*. Those people took afternoon naps, and hardly ever quarreled. 🍵

A Month in Provence with Teenage Blues

by Margaret Pennycook

I massaged your aching heart
with ice cream.
Pink, green, chocolate or vanilla
packed in *cornettos*.
You draped your new long frame
over white leather sofas,
the shutters closed
to keep out the Mediterranean sun.
You watched French quiz shows,
German action movies
dubbed in a language
you didn't understand.
You suffered Pont-du-Gard.
Endured the Roman Theater at Orange.
Ignored the tapping sea
waving at your door.

Will you always remember
when you eat pistachio ice cream
when seagulls mewl
when you smell lavender
when you see black kittens
when you hear waves rolling
when you see azure water
when the Mistral blows
when you eat pizza
just as you were when the email came
how she crushed you?

I am surprised to see in photos
you smiled more than once
that month in Provence.

Make Love, Not Sausage

Judy DiGregorio

New relationships must be as carefully handled as spumoni ice cream on a hot summer day. Otherwise, they can easily melt away.

When my fiancé brought me home for the first time to meet his family many years ago, I resolved to put my best, if large, foot forward. My even temperament and sparkling personality would amaze them. They would immediately understand why their son had chosen me as his future bride. Dan's father inclined his head of thick black hair as he shook my hand. He had huge muscular arms from his years in the coal mines. Dan's mother wore her gray hair pulled back in a bun. Her smoldering green eyes stared intensely at me.

"*Piacere* (my pleasure)," she said, hugging me to her.

Dan's parents were a bit nervous, just like me, but I knew they wanted to make me feel welcome. They decided to do it by honoring me in a traditional Italian manner—by preparing and serving a meal with home-made sausage.

I'm a pastry lover, not a meat lover. I would have preferred home-made cannoli or *biscotti,* but I didn't want to offend Dan's family by telling them that.

To show what a special guest I was, they invited me to help make the sausage. Soon I stood in the blue and white kitchen with a muslin apron wrapped around me. I admired the copper pots and pans hanging on one wall as I inhaled the smell of fresh garlic and percolating coffee.

To my horror, Dan's mother directed me to stand at the sink and help wash fresh lamb intestines. I had no idea these were used to make sausage. The slippery, slimy gelatinous mass of intestines repulsed me. The kitchen looked like a scene from a horror movie with intestines flung everywhere— the table, the countertops, and the floor. They looked like primeval monsters struggling to metamorphose into a higher life form. I expected them to start crawling towards me at any minute. One of them had a dark spot resembling an eye. I felt it watching me.

We stood at the sink as we ran water through each intestine until it was perfectly clean and the water ran clear. Then we plopped the intestines into huge pots of boiling water. The stench was sickening. It smelled like a combination of road kill and camel dung. After the intestines were sterilized by boiling, we stretched them out like tentacles on the table and counter tops to cool them.

Next we ground up the lamb meat. We added black pepper, red pepper, chopped garlic, and salt. We poked the meat mixture down into the cooled intestines through a metal funnel. First we tied the bottom of the intestine with a piece of string. Then we inserted the funnel into the top, using our fingers or a metal spoon to force the meat to the bottom of the intestine. When the intestine was full, we tied off the top with another piece of string. It was a tedious and messy process. I hated doing it, but I kept a ghastly smile plastered on my sweaty face.

Finally, we fried the sausages in hot oil on a gas stove until every piece of sausage was crisp. My future in-laws were pleased at my efforts. They patted my back and repeatedly pinched my cheek murmuring *bella, bella.*

I looked properly grateful for the opportunity to learn to make homemade sausage. Finally, we finished frying all of them. I relaxed.

Suddenly, I remembered that I was expected to eat the sausages, too. Waves of nausea swept over me at the thought. At least I had several hours before the evening meal.

The smell of simmering tomato sauce soon replaced the greasy odor of the fried sausages as Dan's mother continued preparations for dinner.

That evening we sat down for supper and consumed platefuls of spaghetti cooked *al dente,* with just the right amount of chewiness. Fragrant sauce spiced with red wine, celery, garlic, and oregano covered the pasta. Hand-grated Parmesan and Romano cheeses topped each serving. Homemade red wine from zinfandel grapes filled our glasses. I began to forget the sausages.

Then Dan's mother left the table and returned with a huge platter of sausages. Dan's father passed a stack of crusty Italian bread.

"*Mangia, mangia* (eat, eat)," they encouraged me, offering me the bread and sausage.

In desperation, I stabbed a small sausage and wrapped it in a slice of bread. I took a teeny bite off the top as though I were eating toxic waste.

"You like?" asked Dan's mother.

"Um hum," I mumbled, gagging.

I continued to nibble on the bread while slowly squeezing the sausage out of the bottom of the sandwich. In my lap lay a large white paper napkin that became the repository for the sausage. I munched on until I had completely devoured the piece of bread, thinking that at last my ordeal was over. It wasn't.

"Judy, eat some more. Take another one," begged Dan's father.

Despite my protests and increasingly violent hand gestures, another sausage landed on my plate. We went through this same routine again and again until I felt as stuffed as the sausages. My napkin was now swollen with a pile of meaty monsters. I had no idea how to gracefully discard them.

Luckily, my future mother-in-law excused herself to answer the phone. Dan's father left the table to get more wine. I leapt from my chair holding the ends of my napkin tightly together. Dan shook his finger at me.

"I know what you've been up to," he whispered.

"If you tell on me, I'll force every one of these sausages down your throat," I muttered as I fled, pretending to have a coughing fit. I hid the sausages under my bed.

Later that night, I sneaked to the back yard and fed the sausages to the family dog, a black cocker spaniel. He looked at me with adoring eyes. At least I had impressed him, if no one else.

When our visit with Dan's family ended, I felt satisfied. Our relationship was off to a good start. I liked them. They liked me. They had honored me by making the meal of homemade sausage. I had honored them by eating it. I just hoped next time they would make *tiramisu*.

The Godfather II, the Italian Scenes

by Matt Cook

Little Italy is populated with fruit stands.
Fruit stands and undertakers, grapefruit, tangerines,
and religious processions, giant saints and virgins
teetering on the shoulders of masked revelers and brass
bands. Meanwhile, Vito played by DeNiro takes care of things
on the roof, makes an offer no one can refuse, becomes
a man who can return favors. He wraps his gun in towels
to silence a bullet.

I wonder if my father's father, Vincenzo, knew a man like
that, not in New York, but Newark. But Dad says
no. We didn't have any Godfather. We didn't owe
any favors. Vincenzo became Vincent, his brothers Giovanni,
Gieuseppe and Antonio became John, Joe and Tony. Cucco became
Cook—one who prepares food.

Still, I can't help but invent my own
Little Italy, like Coppola or Scorcese.
Sometimes I'm Sonny,
the angry one. Sometimes I'm Fredo, the weak one,
the tragic one. And sometimes I'm Michael, at first earnest
and naïve and later—after I blow away the enemy
in the restaurant—vengeful,
cold as stone.

We all have a favorite Corleone, like a favorite Beatle or,
in the old county, a patron saint.

The day after Christmas, Dad brings home
the cannolis. For twenty years he's been promising
the pastries, cheese and vanilla, soaked
in rum. They used to eat them all the time in Newark,
he says, the whole family gathering for dinner, the kids eating
off the bed because there was no room at the table, trying not to spill
meat sauce on the white sheets.

The first time he met my mother's parents, he brought
the cannolis. Dutch folk who prefer potatoes to
grapefruit, chunks of ham to paper-thin
proscuitto, they pushed it away after two bites.

I am Vincenzo's oldest son's oldest son,
in movie rules, the next Godfather. I hope I will be like Vito,
played by Brando, granting
favors with a gesture, punctuating with
the back of my hand on my chin.

Community Garden

by Patricia Wellingham-Jones

We plan our future, forget we were strangers,
dream over catalogs through winter rain.

Perfume our rooms with late roses, last season's
sweet peas, snapdragons, dried.

In July, we grew tomatoes to match the leaf lettuce,
tossed salads with each other,

grubbed on our knees, hoped the green slivers
popping through mud weren't weeds.

All summer after work we met with shovels,
bottles of water. Sweat helped our gardens grow.

Strangers no longer we tackled the city,
winkled more land, cleaned, hauled and dug.

Invited neighbors from the high-rise
to dig their fingers in rich soil.

Now we wait, impatient, for planting time.
Mother Earth waits 14 storeys below.

Apple Butter Psalm

by Jane Hicks

Rich brown primordial
ooze bubbles, boils, sweet
cedar smoke on October breeze.
Stirring autumn in copper
I lift my eyes unto the hills
from whence cometh my help.
Eight generations
of them that made me
crown the ridge,
feed ancient roots that
drop ripe gifts of sustenance.
The blue canopy deepens. Stir
rich cinnamon to spice the batch.
Mouths wide like
hungry birds, jars crouch
waiting to swallow autumn.

Lindsay Kromer / *Tomatoes*

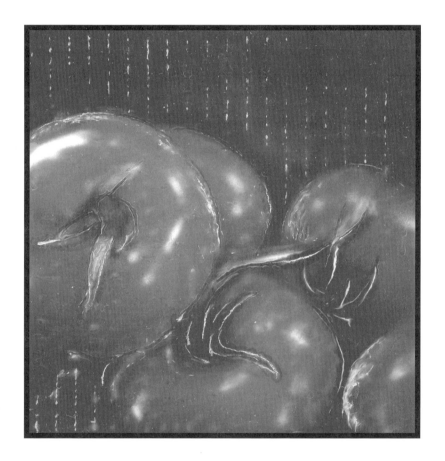

Life, Love, Fire, Fat, and Food
Are Mostly Four-Letter Words
Joseph Michael DeGross

Martin Stoker sat at the bar in the Fire in the Hole tavern. It was a dump; dollar bills stuck up all over the walls, the smell of stale beer, and everything in the place worn and threadbare. It was known as a gin mill. Martin's ass folded over both sides of the barstool like an amoeba trying to engulf food. He was six feet and three inches, one end to the other, but if you ran a measuring tape along his front surface, it added two and a half more feet to allow for his huge belly and chest. His neck was lost in chin-folds, and he had plenty of dark-brown curly hair on his head, back, chest, legs and arms. Naked, which was not a pretty sight, he looked like a great ape. His suit size was sixty-two and if you hooked two of his belts together, they could tie down a twenty-inch sewer pipe on a flatbed trailer.

Like most of us, he was flawed—had problems, this very fat man. Food, it seemed, was one. Martin Stoker needed a constant supply of food: cold food, hot food, raw food, cooked food, ethnic food, plain food, fancy food, seafood, spicy food, good food, bad food, fast food, junk food, vegetables, candy, meat, bread, sugar, fish, fruit, fowl, food high in cholesterol, food high in vitamins—he absolutely, without any reservation or self-control, needed to eat, and he knew why. His parents. Believing they were doing a good thing, they taught him to hate, and although he did not know what or why he hated, it was this hate that led to dark and deep far-reaching hunger which could not be sated, although the constant consumption of food did help to quiet this seemingly gentle giant.

Except for Rose, the lovely bartender, he'd been alone in the place since it opened at ten a.m. He preferred it that way. But now, it was lunchtime, and other regulars were showing up for their first drink of the day. The tavern served a small selection of simple sandwiches made daily and delivered by Vic's, a diner down the street. They were kept in the refrigerator behind the bar. If you wanted your sandwich hot, it went into the microwave for a few minutes. They also had chips and cheese-flavored fish crackers, but they weren't free. Nothing was free. The Fire in the Hole did a booming business at lunch and dinner because people didn't feel comfortable going to a bar just to drink, but when food was offered, Rose had suggested to her boss, it made for a perfect excuse to get that drink. Rose was much smarter than she appeared.

Why all the fuss, is what Martin thought—drink, eat, do what you need to do. Life is short. He had already eaten one of each kind of sandwich available that morning and was working on his sixth bowl of fish crackers and his seventh Seagram's and water. He never drank alcohol without eating. It made him dizzy and it could bring up other yearnings—yearnings to cook or damage things. He discovered that fact years ago.

"Hey, Fats, whadaya doin' here so early, campin' out?"

It was Albert. Albert was thin and small, five feet six inches from top to bottom. He worked and drank hard and looked older than his forty-three years. Albert owned the coin-operated laundry across the street and the building it was housed in—a rooming house from the second floor to the fifth floor. No cooking allowed. Tenants were mostly drunks—usually longshoreman or crewmen on freighters. Baltimore had plenty of both. Albert lived on the sixth floor, which was the top floor. He kept the rooms fairly clean—fumigated twice a year, washed the sheets and towels in the Laundromat weekly, swept the halls daily and cleaned the one bathroom on each floor on Tuesdays and Thursdays with a strong solution of Pine-Sol. You always knew if it was Tuesday or Thursday by the smell. Albert came to the tavern each day for lunch. Plus, on nights when the Orioles were in town, he went to the tavern so he could watch the game with some company, although he didn't like the crowds at the stadium. Albert wore a sweat-stained brown fedora. It came off only when he slept or showered, both rarities, and the smell it carried reminded Martin of elephants or camels at the zoo. Every day, Albert drank four beers with lunch. And when he came to watch a ball game, he drank two boilermakers each inning, one at the top, one at the bottom, more if there was excitement.

There was something about Stoker that scared Albert. He couldn't put his finger on it, but because Albert was so short, it made him feel courageous when he harassed Martin. "Fer chrisakes, Fats, dat barstool is gonna slip up yer ass," he said, and then laughed a raspy smoker's laugh.

Martin was not good at making friends. He was sullen and quiet. His parents caused him to fear people. They told him he was the Devil's child because he was much smarter than his parents, who ran a small chicken farm in Hagerstown when Martin was a boy. He read and learned things in school that they thought no one should ever learn because Blanch and Hardy Stoker were religious fanatics. They told Martin he'd burn in hell for his intellectual arrogance and after he graduated law school they went all out and finally got to him. His mother said she was going on a hunger strike to protest his academic accomplishments. He begged her to eat, but she wouldn't. He gave up his job at a prestigious Washington law firm, where he'd made a reputation in an unwanted court-assigned case by successfully defending several leftists accused by the FBI in a complex arson scandal. He moved back home, trying to convince his mother to eat; but she said he couldn't take back all of his education, and within a few months she died from starvation, he thought. Afterward, his father accused him of murdering his mother. Hardy would say it first thing in the morning when Martin helped him feed the chickens, and he'd say it last thing at night when he stoked up the wood stove to keep the old farmhouse warm as they slept. On one of those nights, Martin couldn't sleep and he found his mother's death certificate and discovered in the space marked *cause of death* the words "ovarian" and "cancer." So Martin moved out again and took the first available job he could find. It was at the Federal Bureau of Weights and Measures. That's when things started to go bad for him, when the weight began to accumulate on his bones and the desire to scorch things on large open fires took hold of him. He was also drinking heavily at the time.

Martin Stoker thought Albert was a cruel, shallow, and ignorant little man. Albert always called him "Fats," and reminded Martin of his father. Martin had been coming to this gin mill for a year because the one he used to go to when he needed to drink—the one he visited for almost twenty-two years—burned down. It happened during a time when Martin was trying to lose weight. Dieting was very difficult because it magnified the hatred, as did the fact that Martin believed he'd never have a relationship with a woman because first it was his parents, and then it was the fat. The owner of that other bar, the one that burned, had a drinking problem. When he got drunk, he'd call Martin a fat fag. He died in the fire. They had to identify him from dental records.

Martin edited statutes at Weights and Measures. The hours and the pay were good, but it wasn't challenging because Martin Stoker had graduated *summa cum laude* from Virginia Tech in 1953 and *magna cum laude* from Georgetown Law School in '56. He wasn't fat back then. He was tall and handsome and athletic. Martin first moved out of the farmhouse in 1949 when he got a football scholarship to college. He thought it might rescue him from his parents—from the fasting and the beatings to cleanse his soul. Martin was bigger than his father by the time he was fifteen, but he thought he needed or deserved the beatings until he read Dickens and Melville in the high school library. After that, Martin became a great football player because the fasting and the beatings had made him tough, and besides, he discovered that he loved to knock people down. In his senior year at Virginia Tech, he was an All-American linebacker. Martin's back was still covered with scars from the whip his father had used on him.

"You're a mean man, Albert. What do you know about being fat? You better be careful because you don't have any idea what you're messing with," Martin said.

"I'm shakin' in my boots, Fats."

"Look, Albert, just let him drink in peace, will you," Rose said, and she walked over to Martin. She stopped chewing and snapping her gum for a moment and leaned across the bar so she could whisper to him. "Ya wanna sit at a table, Mr. Stoker?"

"Thanks anyway, Rose. I'll be leaving in a few minutes—as soon as I finish this drink." Martin liked saloons with female bartenders. It was like a date, without having to ask.

Rose liked Martin Stoker. He came in once a week, usually on a Friday, drank quietly, was polite, always left a generous tip on the bar, and ran up a bill of thirty or forty bucks. Albert, on the other hand, was a beer drinker. He nursed his two or three beers and left a quarter or maybe, on a rare day, two quarters. She turned and frowned at Albert. "Why don't you behave yourself, little fella?" Then she winked all sexy at him just to keep him confused.

Albert liked Rose. She was thirty-something and she had a fine body. She wore blue jeans, spike heals, and tight-fitting low-cut jerseys when she worked. The jeans showed off her perfect ass, and the jerseys her perfect cleavage, and even her nipples when the air-conditioning got too far ahead of the temperature. (Martin had a good look when she leaned over to whisper to him.) Albert had fantasies about Rose, bedtime fantasies that played a major role in the only sex life Albert knew. So it hurt his feelings when Rose called him a little man because he believed this was the reason he never could get into a woman's pants, including Rose's. "Sure. Dat's right. You stand up fer Fats, why dontcha. But tell 'im he's gonna die young if he don't lose weight, Rosy, or areya scared he won't leaveya da usual big tip?" Albert said.

"Albert, you're no gentleman," Martin said. "You attack everyone. It's called a Napoleon complex."

"Fuck you and Napoleon," Albert said.

Martin rose from the barstool. "Look, you ignorant savage, don't speak like that in front of a lady," he said.

"Rosy here? She ain't no lady, Fats. Showsya how much you know."

"Apologize, Albert," Martin said, and he made a fist with his right hand that was almost the size of Albert's head.

"Like I says, *fuck you,* Fats."

For his fifty years and his 442 pounds, Martin moved quickly. He got Albert in a headlock—both his feet dangling above the floor—in seconds. The brim of Albert's fedora was folded down over his ears by Martin's gigantic arm. He looked like Popeye in a baby bonnet. Albert tried to kick Martin.

"Kick me and I'll snap your neck like a toothpick," Martin said. "Now apologize."

Rose came out from behind the bar. She had a baseball bat in her left hand. "Boys," she said, and she placed her right hand on her hip, "Enough!" Then she looked Martin straight in the eye and said, "Put him down before you kill him."

Martin slowly lowered Albert to the floor and released him.

"Ya fat prick, I oughtta sue yer fat ass," Albert yelled as he removed the fedora and reshaped it.

"Albert! Shut up," Rose said.

Albert looked at her and then kicked over a barstool and stormed out.

"I'm sorry," Martin said to Rose.

Rose walked back behind the bar and leaned the bat against the side of the refrigerator. "You surprised me," she said.

"I hate men who are disrespectful to ladies."

"Well, thanks for the taste of chivalry, Mr. Stoker, but I hear language all the time in this joint. It's part of the job." Then she smiled a broad toothy smile, like in toothpaste ads, and said, "But I do appreciate the thought."

"You know, I wasn't always a big fat slob," he said.

She walked around to the front of the bar and picked up the stool Albert had kicked over. Martin couldn't help a quick sideways glance at her perfect heart-shaped ass. Rose's long straight blond hair fell forward as she bent to lift the stool and Martin began imagining things he didn't want to imagine. Then she walked behind the bar, picked up a cloth and wiped some glasses. Martin knew she didn't want to hear his story; no one did, so he pulled a hundred dollar bill from his pocket and placed it on the bar. She totaled his bill: one BLT, one sausage and pepper sandwich, one ham and cheese on white, one fried egg sandwich, four bowls of fish crackers and seven Seagram's and water. "That's twenty-nine and a quarter," she said.

"I had six bowls of crackers, not four," Martin said.

"That's okay. They're on me." She smiled and handed him his change. He left a ten on the bar. She was already serving another customer and apologizing about the fight as he walked out the door.

Albert didn't like being pushed around. He didn't like being picked up like a sack of potatoes. When he was younger—always being a little guy—he learned to use a knife to protect himself in the tough neighborhood where he grew up. He still had this old switchblade and when he left the tavern, he went to his apartment to get it. He was waiting for Martin outside the gin mill door. "How . . . daya like . . . dis, ya big fat . . . shit," he said, still breathing hard from the run up and down six flights. Then, he stuck Martin in the abdomen with that knife.

Martin felt the burning sting of the blade. He grabbed Albert's wrist and broke it. The knife fell to the ground and Albert cried out in pain. Rose heard Albert shouting and ran out of the bar to see Martin holding his abdomen—the bloodstain growing on his yellow shirt. She saw the bloody knife resting on the sidewalk and Albert on his knees, holding a limp right wrist with his left hand.

The blade of that knife was four inches long and Martin's fat was almost four inches thick so only the tip cut into his abdominal cavity, but it nicked an artery and Martin almost bled to death. Rose thought fast, used some clean bar-cloths and her belt hooked to Martin's to tie around his belly and apply pressure. The doctors said she saved Martin's life. Martin went to Johns Hopkins University Hospital where the surgeon on call that afternoon was also doing some new experimental surgery for morbid obesity.

"As long as I'm in there," he said, "why don't you let me staple your stomach so it can't hold so much food. You'll lose lots of weight and feel much better."

Albert went to jail for assault with a deadly weapon. Rose told Martin that Albert was going to lose his building and Laundromat because he had no one to run it while he was in jail. She told him this while he was recovering from the surgery because Rose visited Martin at the hospital every day.

"I'll run it for him," he said. "I did provoke him." Martin had two years of unused sick days coming to him. Government jobs are good that way. So he took a leave of absence and moved into Albert's sixth-floor apartment. Every day for the next eighteen months he negotiated those stairs many times. As promised, the surgery worked and his fat shrank. He lost almost two hundred pounds. He still needed to eat, but he couldn't get more than a few mouthfuls down at a time because his stomach was all stapled up and only held a small amount of food, so, Martin got full very quickly. He ate ten or twelve times a day and sometimes he chewed and spit it out, but the total quantity swallowed amounted to less than one full meal.

The whole situation, in a way, turned into a kind of godsend. Rose loved the way Martin looked at two-forty and he had loads of money, it seemed to her, which he did because he'd never married, had no extravagances except the food, and of course his father had died in a fire that consumed the farmhouse, so, Martin got the insurance and the proceeds from the sale of sixty prime acres in Hagerstown, near the interstate. But Martin was a little uneasy. Although eating all the food he could eat and still losing weight, he was beginning to feel unsettled. He was actually losing his appetite. He'd even been going to a gym to work out, to dissipate the uneasiness—the need to cook or damage things.

"Really! You're losing your appetite?" Rose said, as Martin sat at the bar telling her how he felt. She was feeling his biceps. "Wow. You're really getting fit. How old did you say you were?"

"Fifty-one—almost fifty-two, and yes, I'm losing my interest in food, but I have this desire to cook things, especially flesh—meat. I never feel this way when I'm hungry and eating. This need to cook only hits me at certain times," he said.

"Go to a culinary arts school. Become a chef!" Rose said, and she was leaning way over the bar and Martin was getting aroused. Rose definitely had this idea that Martin was loaded with money and she kind of liked him. So, actually, looking at the various possibilities for her future, she was getting lots of ideas. "Why not come over to my place tonight and show me how you cook. I've got a great grill and you can do something fancy on a nice big fire. Just give me the money and tell me what to buy, and I'll get it on the way home. I'm done here at four."

Albert was paroled for good behavior after eighteen months of his three-year term (his lawyer plea-bargained). He returned home, Martin moved out, and the entire building burned down, Laundromat and all. It was an old building, and Albert, apparently, had been paying off the city inspectors, so the wiring was not up to code. That was the cause of the five-alarm blaze, according to the fire inspector, who said that Albert's body looked like a slice of charred bacon.

Next, the doctor called Martin and said the staples had to come out. "More than two years is dangerous," he said.

This statement made Martin, who seemed to be mourning Albert, uncomfortable. "Define dangerous," Martin said, and he laughed. He was sure that if the staples went, his fat would be back or other stuff might come up.

"Don't worry about it, Sweetie," Rose told him. "You've got me now."

The staples came out and he really tried not to eat. He worked out diligently at the gym and also below, behind, beside and above Rose—they were inseparable. Martin liked Rose to stay at home, so she did. They had a few drinks at home because Rose made it nice to drink at home. Martin went to culinary arts school where he developed extraordinary techniques for cooking meats over open flames. In 1980 they were married and they opened a restaurant. Martin called it Cooking with Fire as a kind reminder of his love for Rose and of his flaws. It was very successful and for some reason, no one ever wondered about those other fires. Every night Rose kissed the scars on Martin's back and life just went on—that was that. 🍵

Pears

by Judy Loest

S
R
A
E
P

||

Every summer
after the white blooms
of the pear tree have blown
away, revealing hundreds of
tiny green embryos, the dread
of all that bruised, rotting fruit
on the sidewalk and street next
October, the weeks-long tedium
of keeping it picked up prompts the
neighbors to renew discussions about
cutting it down. They bring in landscape
architects to confirm the annual prognosis:
the city is no place for a pear tree. But deep
in the dark burrows of ancient memory, they
know that if they destroy life in the name of
vanity, an invisible fiber or vein connecting
them to the infinite will be severed, a dark
indelible stain will appear on the walk
precisely the circumference of its
cool shade and all the mourning
doves will disappear.

Foiled

by Doris Ivie

On Valentine's Day my sister slips me a box of Godiva chocolates
as we settle in the movie theatre. It is mid-afternoon,
I have forgotten to eat all day, and my seldom-deprived stomach
rumbles, threatening to roar.

I focus on the screen, strain to catch characters' names,
strive to decipher British accents,
commit jewelry and furniture to memory,
and try to avoid judging the gentry and serving people,
who are all busy assessing each other from behind
silken and starched-cotton facades.

I think about the chocolates in my purse only five times the first half-hour.

My guts writhe and scream as the *elégantes*
munch on canapés, quaff tea, and sip whiskey.
I commit a necklace to memory and search
for a name for the green of a lady's dress.
Sage? Pistachio? Overripe lime?

Insufficiently distracted, I extricate the sweets from my purse,
slip off their broad ribbon, and pry off the lid.

Foiled!

The box and its dark prizes are encased in seamless plastic
—and the theatre, of course, is quiet and dark.

If they'll just shoot some more pheasants,
I can retrieve my Victorinox and liberate my prize.
While I'm rummaging, someone sneaks indoors
and stabs a man at his desk. *My* knife, thank God,
remains lost in my purse. I admit defeat
and busy my mind trying to unravel the murder.

A serving girl solves the mystery, and my sister and I hug goodbye.
The film lasted *three hours* and I am beyond starving.
My knees are weak and I see the world through black spots.
I toss the golden box to my car's floor
and drive, in search of real food.

Soup of Winter

by Marty Silverthorne

Hedged in by poverty,
he sired seven; offspring
slipped from his wife
with a pain named pride.
The stillborn went to the grave
with a cross and a prayer.

When the farm dried up
and the cow's ribs came to surface,
he lost his hand-me-down land,
worked for paper promises.

Morning brought light
to kill the half-fed stock.
She lit kindling under the vat,
salted meat for the smokehouse;
the bones she saved
for the soup of winter.

Saturday Breakfast

by Connie Jordan Green

He hefts the eggs, one by one,
cushions their tender weight
onto the counter. Sunlight
glints silver on hair
curling above his ears,
thinning at the crown.
He is warm as a summer morning,
gentle with the eggs
as a mother caressing her child.
On the eye of the range
the skillet waits, black and sturdy;
heat rises from its surface
like wisps off the winding river
that splits our view from meadow
to mountain. Into the skillet
he drops a pat of butter.
Up sizzles a scent
like toast, like fall evenings
by the fire, popcorn opening
to the heat. Now the metal
mixing bowl, brown shells crack,
golden yolk and clear albumen
slip down the side,
one egg, then another
until the bowl swims with color.
Strokes of steel fork
and steel bowl
sing their rehearsed song.

A splash of water for lightness,
he slides the yellow froth
into the skillet where fork
dances a hotter tune.
On the table strawberry jam,
hot biscuits, and soon the eggs,
scrambled airy as yeasty dough,
fluffy as bed pillows,
warm like his heart, like
our comfortable bodies
settling into our old chairs,
eating the perfect eggs.

Sarah McCarty / **Figs**

Kugela

by Marilyn Kallet

Once there was a very lovely and *zaftig* young maiden who lived not far from Minsk. The boys of her village had noticed that her skin appeared soft and milky. But Luchshen Kugel—or Kugela, as everyone called her—held herself as aloof as a cat.

One day a handsome strapping fellow named NiceJewishBoy arrived in town. He was a wealthy young man with his own beautiful black horse, Impala. "Come with me to the town dance," he pleaded to Kugela. "We'll have a lovely time, and I'll bring you home well before the moon rises too high, before there's any danger of Cossacks!" Kugela was tempted—it had been so long since she had danced. She couldn't even remember how. Her arms were sore from doing the daily chores. She needed to swing them, to loosen her poor muscles.

"I'll go!" she said. "But only if you bring me sweet berries from the woods. Blueberries from the forest," she insisted.

"Are you nuts?" responded N.J.B. "It's winter. Snow has fallen and has covered even the forest. There are no berries, my sweet."

Nevertheless, Kugela was firm. So N.J.B. had to use his wits. He went to the town winemaker and said, "Please, my good man, is there any chance that you have saved a few berries from your winemaking? Perhaps you have dried and pressed a handful?" N.J.B. was in luck. In exchange for some fine fabric cut by his father's hands, he received a packet of dried blueberries.

He took them home and gave them to his mother, who enrobed them in sweet cream from her blue cow. And then he presented them to his sweetheart. "Ms. Kugela," he swooned, "now will you dance with me?"

Lucky Kugela tried to answer him, but her mouth was full and blue. NiceJewishBoy knew, he had always known, that her answer would be "Yes!" They danced under the moon, and even the Cossacks had sweet dreams that night, dreams of potato pancakes with blueberry maidens dancing on top, on their beautiful blue toes. ☕

Fig, I crave

by Simone Muench

Fig, I crave
your hirsute body: a furred
purse for a stash of seeds—
achenes. Your bordello-
red flesh, proverbial

leaf of Eve. In the backyard,
you droop, swollen with juice
near hydrangeas' blue blooms.
Even when the season

folds, cobwebs of frost
sprawl across your leaves,
you remain steady in the smoky
sweetness of your preserves.

Fig, I have fallen
for your plump mahogany body,
concealing the seeds
of an orchard's worth of trees.

Emily Taylor / *Reaching*

Tasting the Memory

by Judy Pinkston McCarthy

A conversation last week about food and eating got me thinking about the best meal I ever had. It was such a long time ago, but I can almost still taste it. At least, I can still taste the memory.

I had grown up in Tennessee and, during the course of my youth, had left the state but four times, each time only briefly. Dennis and I were married on the first day of summer in 1965. I was nineteen; he was twenty-one. We went to Europe for three months, the first month in Ireland.

We had little money and stayed in the cheapest Bed & Breakfasts we could find. B&Bs were different in 1965: the sheets were changed once a week, no matter how many guests had occupied the room. And the food, at least in western Ireland, was dreadful. Greasy rashers were a treat.

On a beautiful evening in July, after weeks of wretched meals, we stopped at a little grocery in County Kerry. It had fresh-made bread, local cheeses, and tomatoes just picked from the garden. We bought a loaf of bread, some hard white cheese that crumbled in our hands as we broke it into pieces, and real tomatoes. Driving down the road in our rented VW bug, we spotted a newly plowed field. We stopped the car, got out, climbed across the stone fence, and spread our picnic on the edge of the field, inhaling that sweet smell only freshly turned ground has. We pulled the bread off the loaf in chunks, broke apart the cheese, and ate the tomatoes like apples. I wish I could say we had a jug of wine, but alas, it was only water. There was no book of verses either, but we did have a bough, an oak that was ancient when Wolf Tone arrived in Bantry Bay during the Year of the French. We stayed as the sun set below the field, propped against the oak, having eaten the most completely satisfying meal of our lives.

When it got dark we left, going on to the next B&B where the sheets would be changed in another two days, and we would eat yet another breakfast of eggs fried too hard in rancid grease, stale bread, and ever-present rashers.

The memory of those tomatoes comes back to me almost every summer as the tomatoes ripen in our garden. But the memory of that evening in County Kerry is as piquant as if I were, this very moment, in a County Kerry field, eating a magnificent meal of Irish bread, cheese, and tomatoes, washed down with spring water.

Oh, did I mention that we named our first child Kerry? 🍵

Too Much Plenty

by Heather Joyner

Tuscan hills ripple
Beyond sinuous stretches
Of aged wall, toeholds
Obscured
By cascading bougainvillea,

And everything is absurdly ripe:
Pears overwhelm baskets,
Breasts quiet infants
As candles weep rivers
Of wax in vast cathedrals.

Partaking of the ancient bread
From the more ancient stove,
I long for a place
Where nothing
Has ever happened.

The Cook's Memory

by Ashley VanDoorn

I want a recipe stripped of unnecessary ingredients,
body pared to its flavors—the metallic salt between
your breasts, the earlobe's sourness, the bitter
back of your knee and sugary fingertips. I love
even the silky blandness of your eyelids. O this
sweetness I can't get rid of—bowl of my hands held out
to catch the loss that spills from you, whip it to pleasure
then grate it onto your tongue. Skin's become a furnace.
The measure of beauty is the duration of mmm . . .
Minutes dice my hands into forgetting one good
grind of your hips could stretch that sound forever.
Memory's first bite is more delicious than any dish.
Tenderly I cupped your burning face. Tenderly
you shackled my sizzling heart to the flame.

Tongue

by Marilyn Kallet

Eight years old, I'm told
it's a delicacy
on Wonder Bread
with mustard

Munching someone else's
taste buds
the best damn argument
for vegetables
I ever chewed

This *thing* in my mouth
haunted by a huge animal
in the meadow

Haunted by poverty
by my grandmother
whose life was potatoes
by children with stick-like limbs

The era of tongue:
a house on Long Island
and a crowded deli department
in an upscale supermarket
waiting in line with ghosts
of the *stetl*—take a number!

Taste buds facing me
as if my own had been sliced
under a microscope

spread out like a lawn
Tongue-muscle
swallowing victory over Cossacks
and mad oratory
victory over watercress
little sandwiches
and crustless bread
over America and loathing the body
two tongues in every mouth

When the gods taste ours
they put aside disgust
our songs give them texture
our hunger blends with theirs
like mustard and mayonnaise.

Sarah McCarty / *Bowl of Artichokes and Cherries*

Grandma's Brave Cuisine

by Jeanne McDonald

Once upon a time, when I was four years old, my maternal grandmother came to visit us in Clarksburg, West Virginia, and ended up staying for twenty-four years.

Erica Jong once wrote that everybody, somewhere back in the family history, has a little Lithuanian grandmother. I had one of those, too, but this other grandmother, Augusta Pfister Schwegler, was thoroughly German, and her presence in the household forever altered the delicate balance of power in our nuclear family of five. Although she was demure in public, Grandma freely exhibited her Teutonic characteristics at home. She was intractable, frugal, and resolute. She had no time for pity or sentimentality; there was too much work to do. Her hands moved constantly, knitting, crocheting, or chopping food for dinner. I always remember her in sensible, lace-up black shoes and support stockings (for her varicose veins), a cotton print dress, and over that, a printed apron (always with a lace handkerchief in the pocket), and sometimes a ruffled dust cap. On Sundays she wore a black silk dress and a little black straw hat. She pulled her thin gray hair back into a tight bun, and she usually smelled of something she'd been cooking: onions, gravy, or carrots.

The one time I remember her exhibiting approval of me, or something close to it, was the day she sat crocheting in the living room while I practiced my piano lessons. After performing an energetic rendition of "Cruising Down the River," I heard a small sound from the living room: three claps. That meager applause was, in fact, the warmest validation I ever had from my grandmother. Clap. Clap. Clap. Not a word was spoken. Grandma went back to her needlework and I went back to my music.

When we moved to Virginia, my mother took a job teaching at the neighborhood elementary school, and Grandma became chief cook in the household. Thus, over the ensuing years, our family was introduced to unusual varieties of food that we would have preferred to leave to other, more adventurous eaters. It wasn't that Grandma was unpracticed in the culinary arts. Far from it. Born in Nuremberg, Germany, in 1875, she became the cook for her own family upon her mother's death, and later, for two successive stepmothers and all their children. But in 1892, when she was seventeen, she was offered what seemed like the perfect opportunity to escape all this servitude. Her aunt, Amelia Holtzinger, had emigrated from Germany to Pittsburgh, Pennsylvania, where she owned a saloon, and she offered Augusta passage to America and a job as a cook. In addition to selling alcohol, saloons in those days also served up three hearty meals a day for working men, and Mrs. Holtzinger had a thriving business. But on Augusta's arrival at Ellis Island in New York, she found that the golden opportunities her aunt had promised were considerably tarnished. First of all, Mrs. Holtzinger was not there to meet her, and when immigration authorities finally reached her, she instructed them to put Augusta on a train to Pittsburgh. After a twelve-hour journey across this strange new country, Augusta stepped off the train at Pennsylvania Station, where her fierce and formidable aunt immediately informed her that her wages would be $1.75 a week, with 75 cents to be deducted until her transatlantic passage had been paid for.

Her new regimen included rising at four a.m., scrubbing the floors of the saloon with lye, cleaning and polishing spittoons, cooking, and serving. It was a hard life, but Augusta was extremely resourceful. One weekend when Mrs. Holzinger went to New York to order brewery stock, Augusta was left in charge of running the saloon. Unfortunately, on the second morning, she discovered that she had forgotten to refrigerate the leftover meat the night before. Fearing her aunt's temper, she mixed the spoiled meat with all the leftovers in the icebox and made the mixture into a soup. And instead of charging the usual five cents a bowl, she priced it at fifteen cents, presenting the dish as a specialty. When Mrs. Holzinger returned and found the cash drawer full of money, Augusta shrugged and said, "Oh, I just put a lot of things together and called it Mock Turtle Soup." What happened to the unsuspecting customers, we shall never know.

Eventually Augusta found work as a cook in a more sanguine household, and on a return trip to Germany at age twenty-five, she became engaged to Heinrich Schwegler, a soldier in the Kaiser's army. The couple returned to Pittsburgh to start a life of their own.

In hindsight, I can recognize that Grandma exhibited bravery and ingenuity enough for someone twice her size, but as a child, I was ignorant

of her difficult personal history: I knew only that she was inordinately opinionated and exacting. If we left anything on our plates, Grandma would purse her lips and say, "Eat your supper. Some starving child in Germany would be thankful to have it." Sometimes I longed to push my dish toward Grandma's side of the table and invite her to take it to the post office, but we were always respectful of our elders. At other times, she would admonish me with, "Eat your meat. It will put hair on your chest." Or, when we refused to sample a strange new concoction, she would chide, "*Ach, Gott,* don't be so persnickety."

When she had lived in Pittsburgh, Grandma had a huge summer garden, and cucumbers were her favorite vegetables. Her daughter Louise, six years older than my mother, Carrie, was also addicted to them. But no matter how Grandma prepared her cucumbers, she and Louise would become "bilious," as she termed it, after eating them, which meant that they suffered lower intestinal problems. Finally, Grandma consulted the neighborhood doctor about her dilemma. "Dr. Orr," she said, "how can I fix cucumbers so Louise and I don't get bilious?"

Dr. Orr considered this question at length. "First," he advised, "peel off the skin, slice the cucumbers, put them in a bowl and cover them with salt. Then put another dish on top of that one, weight them with an iron, and let them sit for three days. On the fourth day, take off the iron and the top dish, cover the cucumbers with oil and vinegar, and then throw the whole thing out. That way you won't get bilious."

Despite her serious demeanor, Grandma loved a good joke, but Dr. Orr's story didn't stop her from experimenting with cucumbers. She finally came up with a delicious recipe that I still prepare to this day: Peel two cucumbers, add a large, fresh summer tomato and a small onion, all sliced paper-thin, and place in a bowl. Mix a dressing of equal amounts of oil and vinegar, and add a tablespoon of sugar. Stir dressing thoroughly until the sugar dissolves. Pour over vegetables, adding dill weed and salt and pepper to taste. I don't know whether that dish still made Grandma bilious, but she prepared it every summer and ate it with great enthusiasm.

In Virginia, my parents rented a house on the sunny shores of the Elizabeth River, a saltwater channel where my father and brother fished nearly every summer night. My sister and I grew tired of a constant menu of fried spot, but my grandmother always waited eagerly to review the night's catch. Once, when my father caught a baby shark off the fishing pier at Ocean View, Grandma was ecstatic. Although few Americans in those days considered shark a delicacy, my grandmother promptly fried it for supper. I remember thinking, "Thank God there are no snakes around here for Grandma to cook."

But there were eels. And often, one of us would snag one of those primordial-looking creatures on a hook intended for a more traditional fish. Most of the time my father unhooked them with as much dispatch as possible or, when that failed, he used pliers to pull the hook from their enormous jaws. But of course, if Grandma had anything to do with it, the eel would appear on the supper table. It wouldn't have seemed so repulsive if she had cut the eel into small pieces and fried or broiled it, but she preferred to pickle it and serve it up, with onions, in a quivering, gelatinous aspic. The dramatic show of gagging from my sister and me brought from my grandmother a weary dismissal of the strength of our characters: "*Ach, Gott,* you'ns are so silly."

Equally disturbing was the aspect of the pitiful carcasses of squirrels and rabbits my brother shot in the woods near our house. These animals Grandma gleefully boiled up in a huge aluminum pot filled with a broth highly seasoned with cloves and various other spices. The nightmarish memory of those tiny bodies sitting on a platter on our dining room table still makes me shudder.

When it came to food, Grandma had absolutely no sentimentality. The most horrendous story of her resolve happened in West Virginia when she first came to live with us, during those last years of the Depression. In those days, men still rode the rails looking for work, hoboes begged at doors asking for a meal, a sandwich, anything; people were desperate just to put food on the table for their children. One day a man carrying a tame chicken came to our back door. His children were hungry, he said, and even though they had this chicken, the family was too fond of it to eat it, so he wanted to sell it. When negotiations were settled—Mother can't remember the exact amount of the cash exchange, but it was probably less than a dollar— the man handed Grandma the chicken, which immediately laid its head on her shoulder and made a soft clucking sound in its throat. We children were too young to warn the chicken about making friends with Grandma, and as soon as the man was out of sight, she promptly wrung its neck and carried it into the kitchen, where she began to pluck its feathers in preparation for supper. Needless to say, my sister, brother, and I gazed tearfully at the succulent hen on the table and refused to eat a bite.

Grandma cooked other, less emotionally invested dishes that played havoc with our provincial minds and stomachs: tongue, liver, and occasionally chicken necks. On one shopping trip, Grandma discovered a real bargain: a bag of chicken necks on sale. She was so proud of her economical find that she told my mother, "If you'ns would let me handle your money, you'd come out a whole lot better." Imagine a scrawny pile of chicken necks served up as an entree, and you can understand our lack of enthusiasm for Grandma's penurious purchase. She chastised us for filling up on potatoes and corn and ignoring the "meat," but that night she became violently ill and, for a while at least, no chicken necks appeared on the supper table.

But some of my grandmother's concoctions were delicious. Her fruitcake, for example. To many people the mention of fruitcake is anathema, but Grandma's recipe was truly a treat. Every year, on the day after Thanksgiving, Mother and Grandma started cutting up dried fruit and nuts for the Christmas cake: English and black walnuts, red and green cherries, dates, raisins both dark and light, lemon and orange peel, and pineapple. When the fruit was ready, they began the process of mixing the applesauce cake base into which the fruit and nuts would be mixed. They always baked eight cakes in bread pans, some to send to relatives in Pittsburgh, and one large cake in a tube pan for the family. The recipe below makes one large tube cake:

Applesauce Fruitcake

4 cups applesauce, homemade if possible
2 heaping tsp. baking soda
1 cup solid shortening
4 cups all-purpose flour
1 tsp. allspice
1 tsp. cinnamon
1 tsp. cloves
1 tsp. nutmeg
1 large package candied fruit
¾ cup dark raisins
¾ cup light raisins
1 pkg. sugared dates
1 cup walnuts

Heat applesauce until hot. Add soda. When soda is dissolved, stir in sugar and shortening. With ¼ of the flour, add fruit and nuts in a separate container and coat the fruit with the flour. Sift remaining flour with spices and stir into sugar mixture. When mixed, add fruit and spoon into greased and floured tube pan. Bake 2 to 2½ hours at 275 degrees. If cake gets too brown during baking, cover with foil. After removing from oven, let cake sit 15 to 20 minutes before removing from pan. When cool, wrap in waxed paper, then cover with brown paper, and store in a cool place until ready to use. To freeze, cover tightly with foil.

Recently, while booking a hotel in Atlanta, I glanced through the restaurant section of the guidebook and noticed one that advertised "brave cuisine." If, as the Buddhists believe, we are reincarnated after death, I suspect that Grandma might be working there now as a chef. After all, the foods we considered disgusting as children are presently, under the guise of "the new cuisine," considered delicacies. And, yes, brave. Maybe not chicken necks, but shark, eel, rabbit, and squirrel. On my next trip to Atlanta, I plan to stop at that restaurant to say hello to Grandma and tell her how much ahead of her time she was.

Maybe I'll clap. One. Two. Three. For old times' sake.

(Thanks to my mother, Caroline Pratts, for information about Grandma's early life, which she has recorded in her book, Augusta.*)*

Recipes

by Linda Parsons Marion

Searching, searching for the ultimate brownie recipe
through my house of cards, wedding gift for this bride
in 1972, still child enough to believe a home well built
could not fall. Each card a day of trials, of errors,
circling stove to table to counter to stove. I should weed
out the ones I never got to: Polynesian pork, rhubarb
pudding, crab delight—but I keep stuffing them in,
snapshots ripped from newspapers and *Redbook,*
my overcrowded *Britannica,* avocado to zucchini,
candlelight to spongeware, girl to wife to mother.

So many meals to balance at once, and down they all
tumble in a delicious heap. What miscegenation—
wassail in the spinach casserole, lemon squares
in the dilled egg salad, tarragon in the seven-minute
frosting. What compotes of vinegar and honey:
cowboy stew on a hotplate in the attic apartment
my first three months of marriage, spoondoodles
for Scouts, homemade granola during my Mother Earth
phase, sifting of nineteen to forty-nine, one daughter to two,
grimy 3 x 5s dog-eared, buttered and salted, the lean
times and plenty worth their weight in Belgian chocolate.

Each tucked back in its tight row, I hear the scrape
of a biscuit cutter, *whumpf* of the gas flame coming
on in a Nashville kitchen, see the bloom of Martha White
flour above the Hoosier cabinet. These ingredients stir me
blood, flesh, and sinew: my grandmother's prune cake
in her own sure hand, before the iron bars of her mind

slammed shut; my ex-mother-in-law's cannoli, in strong
green ink, who taught me to wrap thread around thumb
and forefinger to slice polenta into yellow pillows
on a bowl of bean soup, but never entered my world.
I will save every scrap and scribble: this brown bread
cast upon our lives' restless waters, my offering plate
so sweet and sour, these loaves and fishes multiplying
one hundredfold to feed our deep and present hunger.

Sarah Kendall / **Roasted Zucchini**

Trafe

by Tamar Wilner

The alien textures enter uneasily.
Chewy mussels must be wrenched from their shells;
squid sticks on the way down.
At age two I almost choked on a hot dog.
The vendor swore it was all-beef,
but my throat resisted.
My father used the Heimlich
to dislodge the foreign object.
Now I was forcing down shrimp, clams,
each refusing to enter me.

In my mother's house I formed my flesh of fruit compote,
my lungs of matzo balls.
Her foods slide down the throat like milk.
Cheese blintzes fall into the mouth
soft as a nursing breast;
my veins beg for chicken soup.

Every shape commands cognizance:
rugelach pastries curl like *megillah* scrolls,
three-cornered *hamantashen* partition us from the enemy.
Jewish foods wrap, embrace, fold onto themselves
as fingers in a fist.
To confine, or protect;
most of all to declare
you are a product of this brisket,
slaughtered by a shochet.

Your body shall obey
circadian rhythms of flesh and dairy.
The Father watches our diets
and chops our food up small.

Their dough is thin, and I burst through
longing to taste she-crab soup, a plate of Memphis barbecue,
this Sicilian feast now fighting desperately for air.

I'd be willing to give up one part of myself,
to let my stomach roam.
But the forbidden shall consume me.
With an Italian heart, a Tennessee liver,
I'll have no place for Torah.
I know it from the *rugelach*
wrapped round my fingers
like a *tallith's* fringes
as I struggle with a mussel's shell.

My Mother's Pie Crust

by Barbara Crooker

Light as angels' breath, shatters into flakes
with each forkful, never soggy-bottomed
or scorched on top, the lattices evenly woven,
pinched crimps an inch apart.
My ex-husband said he'd eat grasshoppers
if my mother baked them in a pie.
Smooth tart lemon, froth of meringue.
Apples dusted with cinnamon, nutmeg.
Pumpkin that cracks in the middle
of its own weight. Mine are good,
but not like hers, though I keep trying,
rolling the dough this way and that, dusting
the cloth with flour. "You have to chill the Crisco,"
she says. "You need a light touch
to keep it tender; too much handling
makes a tough crust."

Gather the scraps, make a ball in your hands,
press into a circle. Spread thickly with butter,
sprinkle with cinnamon sugar, roll up, slice, bake.
The strange marriage of fat, flour, and salt
is annealed to ethereal bites. Heaven is attainable,
and the chimes of the timer bring us to the table.

The Feast Day of a Young Man

by Julie Auer

Before his death a few years ago, my grandfather Lajos Auer told me about the first time he ever got drunk, on his Confirmation Day, when he was thirteen, and on wine made by his own mother. In those days of Prohibition, Anna Auer had been a bootlegger. She was a short, squat, square-shouldered Hungarian peasant who spoke no English but spent half her life in the foothills of the Blue Ridge Mountains of Southwestern Virginia. Her husband—my great-grandfather, Ferenc Auer—had brought her there, chasing the European dream of America, on a desperate notion of finding his fortune. Their tiny house in a coal camp called Derby, near Big Stone Gap, stood alongside a dozen other gray-shingled shacks on a dirty lane smeared in soot.

For my grandfather, the story of his introduction to the excesses of manhood was an amusing reminiscence. For me it was as much a story about the times in which he lived as it was about a little boy's foray into debauchery at a feast made to honor a saint. It was about life lived between two worlds, one old and one new, one steeped in the rich earth of the Hungarian plains they had left behind, the other spread with coal dust.

The squalid coal mining towns of Virginia teemed with proud immigrant families from all over Eastern Europe: from Hungary, Poland, Slovakia, Croatia, and Romania. Most of these immigrants were Catholic or Orthodox, and life happened on saints' feast days. And life for any real Hungarian was all about music, food, and wine, especially when the feast day coincided with a holy season.

Lajos Auer's Confirmation fell on the Feast of St. Stephen the Martyr in 1924, so there had to be a big party for more than one reason. For one thing, it was Lajos's Confirmation day, and for another it was the day after Christmas, an important feast day on the Christian calendar, one commemorating the first martyrdom for the Faith, when a Greek named Stephen was stoned to death right after the Crucifixion. About a thousand years later, Hungary's patron saint, King Istvan—St. Stephen's namesake—would force all the Magyars to see the light of Christ. If you were smart, you saw it.

Everybody was coming to the feast. Where there were "Hunkies," there were people who played music. Old Man Horvath played the accordion, and his son Gyula played the fiddle. On the day of the feast, all the men worked together to decorate the small wooden building they had constructed a few years before as a community hall.

The hall held about a hundred people. It was their church, their school, their courthouse and their pub. The priest came twice a month and on holidays; the teacher came three mornings a week for the children; the circuit judge came once a month; and the men got together there a few nights a week. Tonight, the men tied festoons of holly, pine cones, and ivy across the ceiling, along all the beams and joists, and then ran colorful ribbons out from the center of the ceiling in every direction to the four walls.

Anna and a dozen other women worked like mules all day for the feast. They griped like mules, too. There wasn't any beef, but there was leftover pork from the Christmas suppers they had slaved over for their individual families the day before. And that pork had come from the smokehouse, because the women had slaughtered the hogs weeks in advance to get the business of preserving the meat out of the way before all the holiday toil. They had done all the slaughtering and the smoking because the men were in the mines all day long. Husbandry was left to the wives.

For St. Stephen's they killed two dozen chickens, cleaned them, and stuffed them with garlic and turmeric, because they couldn't find saffron and couldn't have afforded it anyway. They boiled tomatoes and peppers, onions, garlic, and paprika, and they complained about the quality of the paprika, but you couldn't find real rose paprika in this country and there wasn't anything to be done about it. Then they rubbed the chickens with salt and pepper and inferior paprika and put them in the kettles. They mixed heavy cream with butter and flour and hot sauce and added it to the stew.

They made a kind of pasta out of potatoes and flour and rolled them out into fat little bullet-sized noodles, dipped them in spicy breadcrumbs and fried them in butter. They made gallons of cabbage stew with tomatoes and garlic and caraway seeds. They made creamy noodles for the chicken, and cabbages stuffed with potatoes and the leftover pork.

They spared the occasion no expense of labor. In that tightly knit, impoverished village, hard work was as much a part of childhood as school or play. All during autumn, boys and girls alike had helped their mothers collect nuts that had fallen from the many walnut trees in the area. Afterward, men weary from working in the mines sat together on the porches of their homes on brisk November evenings, smoking their pipes and shelling the nuts.

Teenage boys, most of them having worked regularly in the mines since the age of ten, didn't mind a little kitchen work. They had the unenviable duty of crushing poppy seeds—tiny black beads, tough as metallic grains of sand—with mortars and pestles until the seeds were reduced to a black paste that could be spread with a knife. All this for the Christmas flat cakes, baked with layers of the poppy seed paste and crushed walnuts, apples, and nutmeg.

There was only one among them who had the guts to make the wine. It was illegal to make or sell wine, but that was only a problem if you respected Prohibition. If Prohibition hadn't stopped the hillbilly hooch stills all over the hollows of the Blue Ridge Mountains, it sure as hell wasn't going to stop a Hungarian woman like Anna Auer.

She made a curious blend of dandelion wine fermented with grapes that grew in summertime on vines along a sunny, well-drained hillside near the village. Growing grapes was expensive and labor-intensive, but collecting dandelions was easy and free. Anna had always made wine for her family, but when Prohibition became the law a few years before, she decided that she could make extra money for her family by selling it. So she began making dandelion wine by the gallons, using just a small portion of grapes to make her alcoholic confection more interesting, and bushels of dandelions to yield enough wine for a decent profit.

Lajos helped. The previous summer, the two of them pulled up every dandelion in the vineyard and in every grassy patch they could find. They pulled off the yellow blossoms and carried them by the bushel back to the house. There, Anna soaked the blossoms in hot water for a day, and crushed grapes she had peeled and seeded. Later she strained the mixture, added sugar and yeast to the liquid, and stilled it for a month before bottling it, aging it another few months afterward.

Everybody, immigrant and non-immigrant alike, knew what she was doing, and many of them became customers, including the mine bosses. It was good wine, and good extra income. And for goodwill, she provided bottles at no charge for the feast day of St. Stephen, and her son's Confirmation.

On the morning of St. Stephen's Day the Auer family made the short trip to Big Stone Gap for Lajos's Confirmation, where a bishop celebrated a Confirmation Mass for all the properly indoctrinated Catholic youth of the southwestern region. They got back to Derby in time for Anna to help with the cooking and for her husband Ferenc to load up bottles of her dandelion wine and cart them over to the hall.

At dusk the hall was ready. The torches were lighted, and coals glowed red and blue in the fire of the stove. They gave off warmth and an acrid smell that blended with the fresh cedar walls of the hall and the pinecones hanging amid garlands of ivy. It was a wintry aroma of blazing coal-coated caverns a mile deep in the earth and of the roots of pines and cedars crowning the snowy hillsides. The light of the coal fire and torches flickered off the purple, red, yellow and green ribbons spiraling out along the ceiling. The tables were decked out in brilliant white tablecloths sewn by the women, who had painstakingly embroidered and laced the trim with ribbons of the bright, rich colors these people loved.

Old Man Horvath, the accordion player, squeezed out gypsy melodies while his son Gyula sawed away at his slightly-out-of-tune violin. Everybody was dressed up in gaudy peasant outfits. One look at their heavy velvet, purple, green and yellow vests laden with colored beads and feathers and ornate embroidered patterns gave the impression that these were people with no concept of when enough was enough.

When Lajos arrived at the hall, everybody cheered for him. The men patted him on the back, the women pinched his cheeks, other boys rolled their eyes, and little girls smiled. The priest gave the blessing, saying that this was Lajos Auer's day just as much as it was St. Stephen's Day. The food was served, and the wine bottles uncorked. The music played, everybody danced and, thanks to Anna, a few people got good and drunk, including her thirteen-year-old, newly consecrated son.

Lajos felt so grown up with all the attention being lauded over him that he thought himself worthy of a glass of wine. His mother let him have a small glass, but admonished him to make it last. Even though he had been working two days a week in the mines for two years, he was too young to drink much.

Lajos enjoyed the taste of the wine so much that he found it impossible to make it last longer than a few minutes. The sweet, summery lightness of the wine contrasted starkly with the rich, heavy food. When the dancing and music reached fever pitch, and everybody's attention was diverted from the boy to the bacchanalia, Lajos grew bored and swiped a glass left unattended. He sneaked around the entire hall after that, picking up half-empty glasses and glasses with only one or two drops left in them. He killed them all, every last one left alone on a table or a stool, while unsuspecting adults danced and sang in the sweeping crescendo of festive folk music.

By midnight the women began to round up sleeping children and head for their houses, where they would wait until their husbands came staggering home. Anna looked for her son, whose posture was unlike that of one lulled into sound sleep. He was passed out cold, face down and spread-eagled on the floor. Anna tried to roust him, but Lajos only moaned and belched. Soon he was surrounded by people again, only there weren't as many smiles and whistles as there had been when he arrived earlier, in a state of grace.

His father pulled him up and slung the boy's thin, lanky body over his shoulder like a burlap sack. Ferenc was used to burdensome loads, but this one was embarrassing. An icy, upside-down world spun around Lajos as he rode his father's shoulder home along the hushed wintry lanes of Derby. He murmured incoherent pleas for help while his father warned him that a real man waited until he got home to get ill.

As he bumped up and down, his cheek slapping against his father's back, he thought about all that food. All the chicken *paprikas* and cabbage stew and pork and cabbage rolls and creamy noodles and fried potato noodles and poppy seed cake and how he had tried everything and it was all sloshing around inside his stomach with about a quart of home-stilled dandelion wine. He held it all in like a man, all the way home.

And when he got home, he staggered determinedly in back of the house, slipping on ice three times, hurtling around a chicken coop, past a well, through a thicket of pine trees to the outhouse, and puked like a martyr.

Breadman's Holiday

by Lynn Veach Sadler

So natural. The dark rye flour grown from the entire rye kernel—germ, endosperm, and bran. Do the very names not suggest human conception and birth? I teach my patients the links between *zygote* and what I choose to call *ryegote*. I sing to my patients "The Song of the Rye Bread," the life-giving, life-sustaining *Suomalaisruisleipä,* The Great Finnish Rye Bread. It is the song I learned in my mother's womb, where she *bran*ded me, I like to say. My patients are most surprised, I think, because I am male and do these things.

The sounds. Hearing is the first sense to develop in the fetus, you know. My mother's singing to woo The Sisu, Spirit of the Bread and Nature. The chopping. The smacking, in imitation of which my cheek muscles developed well before those of normal fetuses. You won't believe this, but the cracking of the loaves in the heat. The smell. Not just the starter—the soured dough—but the luscious dill. The feel. Her motion as she kept body's rhythm to her song—you don't knead rye bread, for it has little gluten and merely turns sticky if you do.

Mother died giving me life. My aunt, who never married, brought me to New York. She worshipped my mother. My aunt's facts were plainsong repeated until the yeast of her tears made it rise into what I still hear as a poem:

> My little sister, Anna The Virgin,
> was raped in the Virgin Forest
> that the bear hunters propitiate as
> "Gold-Glittering Gilded Hostess."
> By that act, the rapists turned
> The Lovely Woman Forest
> into a cold dark forest
> where Little Anna
> was left for dead.
> I found her, Little Anna,

laid her on pine branches,
dragged her home.
Our mother sewed her up.
Our father screamed and tore his hair
and rolled in the snow,
then took his gun
and went to find those
who had violated Little Anna the Virgin
those who had violated all Finland,
for Little Anna was Finland's Maid of the Bread.
Papa never returned.
After you came and Little Anna went,
our mother died of grief, went too.
When you were strong enough,
I sold all we had,
came here to New York.

I need some time to shape my aunt's lines into a loaf of rye, but that will come when I have planted the health, wealth, and wisdom of rye abroad in the world.

My aunt thought I invented "The Womb Story," as she called it. I did not. It is why I specialized in prenatal care, why I have published, to both acclaim and derision, so much on such topics as "In Utero Cognition," "Heightening of the Powers of the Senses from within the Womb," and "WombTime," the last my special coinage. But I could never convince my aunt. I searched for evidence, told her of medieval saints who had converted thousands when they preached from their mothers' wombs. Not that I was claiming such powers for myself, only for my mother and the Spirit of the Bread. My aunt sent me to a Madison Avenue psychiatrist when I was in my teens. Yet she had part of the secret in her narration. Ordinarily, Finnish children make their first contact with wood at their birthing in the sauna. Mine was, rather, at the moment of conception, when my virgin mother was raped in the Virgin Forest.

My aunt thrived in this new land. She began by peddling food from a cart as many in Finland still do. Her own sauna-cured leg of lamb between *rieska* (rusks) with sour dill pickles from her crocks on the side. Finally came "Anna's Sisu Shop," named for my mother and for the Spirit of the Rye Grain that brings health and strength to fight on, especially to babies and to the old. Does the rye not persist, against all odds, in the unfriendly land north of the 60th parallel? Have the Finns not endured and thrived through centuries of Swedish domination and through vassalage to the Russians? The Sisu brings well-being. To think of a woman, another like my mother, who is the embodiment of the Sisu . . . To have such a woman for my wife is a dream. A fixation, my aunt said.

My psychiatrist was kinder, more understanding. I believe he wished my dream woman for himself. He seemed to know already of Saint Elizabeth of Hungary, who fed the poor to the detriment of her own family. Once when she was slipping away with an apron full of bread, her husband demanded to know what she carried. She replied, "Flowers to decorate our church." At once, God changed her "flour" loaves to "flowers" in order that His saintly devotee should not be caught in a lie. "Flour" and "flower" have enjoyed many such interchanges, and even the poorest Finnish table intertwines flowers and rye-based food.

Yet, though my aunt never believed my talk of bread and womb, the most precious item among our luggage on the journey to America was the soured starter from a piece of fermented dough that dated back over a hundred years in our family in Finland. She tended it carefully, for she saw that the "moderns" here, as she called them, depended upon soaked rusks, stale bread, and buttermilk and that such could never have the vigor of our ancestral leavening.

The specialties of "Anna's Sisu Shop" were simple rye bread; *piima-limppu* (a sweetish buttermilk rye bread offered at Christmas); *karjalanpi-irakat* (Karelian pasties); *korput* (unleavened breads); *vorschmack* (the mixture of ground mutton, beef, salt herring, garlic, and onions favored by Field Marshal Carl Gustaf Mannerheim, Finland's national hero); the Karelian hot pot, *karjalanpaisti,* a stew of veal, pork, and mutton; and *piirakka* (our version of the Russian *pirog*) with egg-butter. My aunt's favorite was *kalakukko,* or "fish fowl," which can weigh up to eleven pounds and alternates layers of the fish *muikku* and strips of fat pork in a rye dough. During its hours of cooking, the fish bones melt away to their elementals. When she could acquire them, she served the two great delicacies, reindeer tongue and burbot caviar, but I encouraged her to be content with domesticated mushrooms. For, whereas in Finland, children are taught the art of picking the over fifty varieties, and Finns, so closely do they walk with nature, can eat even poisonous ones, the risk here was too great. On very special occasions, she provided a full *voileipäpöytä,* our adaptation of the Swedish *smörgåsbord.*

Always, one could buy fresh loaves of rye bread or the hard flat rounds strung on ropes around the restaurant. To my delight, people soon flocked to purchase from what I had jokingly called my aunt's "breadline." Her special drinks were the mild beer, *kalja,* and the liqueur, *mesimarja,* both of which she brewed herself, although she had difficulty coming by the honeyberries for the second. Such was also the case with the wonderful yellow cloudberries from which she distilled a golden liqueur tasting like caramel. And no self-respecting Finn would be without French Cognac or the specialized varieties of milk known as *viili* and *piimä.* The latter is "drinkable," and my aunt brought it with us from Finland as a dried cloth that had been dipped in my grandmother's own sour milk and was used by my aunt as a starter. On the other hand, one "eats" *viili,* which comes "short" or "long" in accordance with the size of the curds and the bacteria used as the culture. One of my aunt's best performances was cutting her elasticized "long *viili*" with scissors for her special customers.

When my aunt was murdered in her shop—beaten to death with loaves of rye she had shellacked to use as decoration—I closed it, once it was back in order, just as it had been when she opened it that last morning. It will remain as is until I have a wife to stand in my aunt's stead and daughters (or perhaps sons) after her. But, oh, after the attack on my adopted country on September 11, 2001, I did wish it open that I might give the comfort of our rye bread, its restorative, regenerative properties, to all in need. But I have not married ever, for I have not found the woman with the womb smell of my mother, Little Anna. When I take vacation time, it is a "breadman's" holiday. I turn from medicine proper to pursue the curative properties of rye bread and experiment, too, with a perfume to be called "Little Anna."

My family is from Finland's east country. Ovens were used there for the baking of soft, fresh, round rye bread. My mother was Queen of the Bread in our family (and afar!) and made it daily. My aunt assisted their mother in all else—housekeeping, growing, the lesser cooking—but my own mother was the one attuned to the rye bread. My aunt says that was often the way in Finnish families of old, and she was not jealous, though a true Queen of the Bread, particularly one as fair as my mother, was rare, and her position and powers were coveted.

No, despite my aunt's skepticism, I know that I knew my mother from my conception and from my time in her womb. Indeed, when I as embryo floated freely in the uterus of my mother, she sent forth her great Blue Light to lead me to where I should implant myself and to help knit the complex connections that formed the placenta. It emanates from the blue aura that is the Finnish atmosphere. When my mother had done her duties of the day by the bread, she would bathe at the wash stand in the small room that was hers alone because she was Queen of the Bread. As she gently touched, rubbed, and probed her emergent belly, a Burning Blue would flow from her fingertips straight to me. I now know it as the Od, the Odic Force that pervades all of nature but is manifested only in and to the most responsive and sensitive of humankind. If my aunt could not believe in it, how could a more modern and practical world? I tried to convince her on the basis that, whereas a fetus can sometimes cry at Week 26, I cried during the violent act of my very conception, abnormally knowing the precise moment when conception occurred.

I tried also to convince my aunt on the basis that the term *Od* itself was coined by a hard scientist, the forceful German, Baron von Reichenbach, though for such matters as magnetism and chemical reactions. She could not accept my version or vision even when I pointed out that *pito-ja-joulupuuro,* the great barley porridge of whole grain that she made in her restaurant for festive occasions, acquired its reddish color because its simmering of at least five hours caused the lactose in the milk to undergo a chemical change. Yet she who had always taken such care that "the bishop not come to visit"—the bottom did not blacken or burn—could not credit the wonder of the womb while lavishing love and beauty on that simple rye porridge, which she insisted upon serving always with nothing less than a rose-hip purée. She could not drive me from my faith, however, and I insisted that Baron von Reichenbach would have taken his ideas further could I have discussed with him the chemistry of the rye and how its natural operative spirit was sympathetic to my mother and she to it. When I told my aunt of the predestined link between the Baron and myself via the mnemonic for the twelve cranial nerves—"On Old Olympus' Towering Tops, A Finn And German Vindicated Ancient Hops"—she merely shook her head and walked away. I was glad I had not bothered to tell her that my version differed from the accustomed ". . . A Foolish Austrian Grew Vines and Hops." Nor would she listen when I tried to explain that the hop vine has cone-shaped female flowers dried and used not only to flavor beers, ales, and such but as medicine; that such dual views are world-wide, as in our Finnish blueberry soup used for stomach problems; and that she could look as well at America's own Native American population, where theology and medicine mingled as in drugs or herbs ingested or applied to invoke a supernatural agency to cure disease and insure success in some undertaking.

Perhaps I would have had better luck with my overly practical aunt had she not died before I began my e-mail correspondence with Dr. Carlos Correa, an Argentine pediatrician. He wrote of his experience in a letter to the editor of the *New England Journal of Medicine,* for no medical authorities would dare publish his story as article and data. Since he was a child (and he is now almost forty), he has visited the shrine of Difunta Correa, who is no relation to him, in the desert village of Vallecito. In a civil war of the 1840s, she followed her husband's battalion and died of starvation, heatstroke, and exhaustion. Passing mule drivers found her long-dead body with her infant boy alive and still suckling. When he was removed to safety, the mother crumbled into dust, which the mule drivers felt as a rain of peace. A saint of the people if not of the church, she symbolizes, like my own mother, the essence of motherhood. She gives to all who ask, be they travelers, girls desiring husbands, sportsmen, budding entrepreneurs, military officers in search of promotion and victory, or those in need of rejuvenated spirits and bodies. Last year, when Dr. Correa drove six hours from his home province to light candles at her shrine, his six-year-old daughter became querulous and complained of the journey. Immediately, the windshield wiper broke to show the displeasure of Difunta ("Deceased," as she is called by most of her visitors.) My latest communications reveal Dr. Correa's attempts to trace the economic disaster of his country to some more serious infraction against the esteem in which Difunta is held by most of her countrymen. He has suggested to me privately that, had Eva Perón added motherhood to her quiver, she would not have died at such a young age of cancer. She worked for women, labor, and the poor but gave herself to no child. Still, the *Descamisados* loved both of these women. At any rate, Dr. Correa and I will pursue the link between cancer and childless women. I have interested him in the possibility that a "blue baby" is something other than commonly perceived; and in my experiments with healthy additives, as pine bark to flour, I look to recapture that peculiar, zestful blend of "forest primeval" and urban living demonstrated in Tapiola, the Finnish "garden city."

There is something else, too, that links Dr. Correa and me, and this surely would have impressed my aunt. The statue of Difunta is dressed in bright red and her suckling boy baby in a flaming yellow blanket. I deem it comparable to the yellowish flowers of the dried dill plumes my aunt brought with us to America in the days before strict agricultural bans were in effect. It is also like our wonderful orangish-yellow arctic cloudberry, a wealth of Vitamin C in a land where the poor must depend on berries for their vitamins and on rye for not only fiber but lignans, antioxidants, the B vitamins, and minerals. The red calls out not just to the blood of my mother's rape and to the blood she shed as she died birthing me. We Finns are from a red land of earthly Mars. I have described the reddish *pito-ja-joulupuuro*. In our markets and kitchens sit giant bottles of the red blood of kine and swine that flavor and color pancakes and puddings as if they were brick. Our swamps and darkish landscape glint with the red of lingonberries, cranberries, raspberries, and strawberries, which we often beat into rosy foam the same way we whip our bodies with birch whisks to invigorate the circulation. Rust-red chrysanthemums are beloved if somber. Our strawberry jam adds a touch of liveliness and laughter. And not just the poor partake of Slaughter Soup, made not with meat alone but with entrails, as well as with dumplings flavored with blood (and a few roots-from-the-earth vegetables). Similarly, a-boil in lake water with dill and dill crowns, in which they steep often overnight, our crayfish go such a bright red that the water of their cooking stains the clothing.

My mother's link to the elemental force of all nature was heightened, too, by the fact that, because she was Queen of the Bread, she was fed, from the age of ten, Beastings Custard. This is beyond food. It is experience. It is said that otherwise sober men have become intoxicated when fed Beastings Custard made from the thick and enriched milk of a cow that has just calved. It happened that some was waiting for my mother at home on the day she was raped, and I tasted it then with her. The only life-giving force, beyond our rye, comparable to such milk is that of a mother nursing her child. The woman I marry will let me repast at one breast, our child at her other.

I like to think she came because I kept faith with my mother and her land of The Great Rye Bread. Instead of buzzing me in her accustomed fashion, my receptionist knocked and came in to tell me a "strange girl" was waiting to see me next. My heart leapt, for I felt in the instant my mother and her Odic Force take me. I stood in the doorway to my office as the girl walked toward me in the white apron and black boots of a Finnish peasant woman and in the blue haze of my mother and of Mother Finland. (If my receptionist noted the color, she has never mentioned it.) The girl's odor, as I fell back to let her pass through, was all that I had hoped but never perfected for the perfume I meant to call "Little Anna": a composite of baking rye bread, dill, chopped pine needles, resin, juniper berries, cranberries, aspen, birch, black earth, wet loam. I knew that she would taste, like true rye bread, tangy and a little sour, that her essence would be dense and chewy. She is like my aunt's *mämmi,* an Easter pudding of rye flour and rye malt, with molasses and slightly bitter orange peel. After being in turn boiled, whipped, and baked, it is finally offered with sweet cream, tasting still of the birchbark baskets in which it used to be baked and served.

I forgave my father-in-law for violating his professional ethics in my case. Had he not spoken to his wife of the strange lad imbued from the womb with a belief in the efficacy of the life force of rye bread and what it stood for, had his daughter not overheard what he said and sneaked to read my file, well, I would be single still. It is not for one who does not know his own father to blame another for shaping her life as she chose.

My wife is an architect in the tradition, if not the lineage, of Eero Saarinen, Alvar Aalto, Aarne Ervi, and especially women like Signe Hornborg and Wivi Lönn. She is preoccupied with the interplay of light with her structures, the light that is a precious natural resource in a northern clime like Finland. Like me, she is also captivated by the blue light/force she shares with my mother. She is a devotee of Reima Pietilä, who tried to make his buildings find the forms of Nature. She does not run my aunt's restaurant but is designing a domed structure for it that will marry the circular wooden shelter of the Finnish past with the modern interplay of form and function. And when our first child comes, I fully expect to exchange "beastings" for "breastings." But long before that, we will sing "The Song of the Rye Bread" to him or her in the womb, and when he/she teethes, it will be upon hard crusts of rye as I did pre- and post-natally. ☕

The Feast of the Fourth of July

by Angie Vicars

I blink rapidly as sweat stings one eye,
demand to know where my phone line is installed,
though I'm alone and ranting out loud.
A knock on the window of my new screen door interrupts me mid-curse.
The neighbor across the street holds a plate
covered with carefully tucked aluminum foil.
She asks what I'm doing.
When I confess to my attempt at wiring,
her face retracts into a puzzled look.
"On the Fourth?" she asks as she hands me the plate. "It's a holiday."
I uncover the most food I've ever seen on a plate, corn on the cob, baked beans,
potato salad, coleslaw, barbecued chicken and a barbecued rib.
The mixed scents of a Sourthern meal curl into the air.
I put down my pliers. It's a holiday.

Americana in Italy

by Pamela Schoenewaldt

Soon after we moved to a small town outside Naples, I came home one summer evening to find the sunset streaking bands of magenta across the violet Mediterranean just outside our kitchen window, backdrop to my husband Maurizio carefully arranging smoky-gray *tagliatelle* on our plates. I knew the pasta was homemade by the dusting of flour all over our kitchen counters and floor. We kissed, and then Maurizio went back to work, drizzling on a sauce of butter and sage, then meticulously decorating the plates with parsley. His face was decorated too, with a sly canary-eating smirk. I looked around, but saw no exposed ingredients, only flour. Rejecting sophistication, I settled for curiosity: "What kind of pasta is it?"

"*Tagliatelle.*"

For sure I knew that little pasta ribbons are *tagliatelle*. I was forgetting the street names in San Francisco, but I could identify dozens of pasta-forms. "I mean why is it gray?"

"*Is* it gray? *Interessante.* Well, *buon appetito.*" So I was supposed to guess. Something smoked, I thought at first, meat or fish? No, neither, and certainly not cheese. A dark taste, both familiar and strange, faintly spicy, not cinnamon. A fine grit of sweetness under bitter. Was it—? "Hum?" asked Maurizio mildly. "More sauce, bread, parsley?"

It could only be: "Unsweetened chocolate?"

"*Brava,* you guessed, *pasta al cioccolato.*" We toasted my cleverness with wine. Maurizio showed me the recipe, faithfully reproduced from *Il Grande Libro di Cucina Italiana,* a somber, encyclopedic cookbook whose thousand pages contained not only the just-demonstrated chocolate pasta, but also step-by-step guides to such terrible domestic circumstances as hosting a dinner party with no staff to help. A most useful book for us.

My father-in-law called that night and as always asked what we'd had for dinner. I told him bread, salad, and oh yes, *pasta al cioccolato.*

"What's that," he demanded, *"a schifezza americana?" Schifezza*—something disgusting.

Ha! "No, it's Italian." I named the weighty source, only to be informed I was lying or mistaken. "If you don't believe me, ask your son," I countered, passing the phone to Maurizio, my father-in-law's son who tells no lies, whose words are gospel. Energetic conversation ensued. I gathered its drift: Maurizio *used to have* good Italian tastes, but his American wife had ruined him. They had bought us a new bedspread; when were we coming to get it?

Schifezza americana. I heard about it constantly from in-laws, neighbors and friends, most of whom had never been to America, or at most spent two weeks in New York and Disney World, where they ate fast food and suffered greatly in the liver. "Is there any American cuisine besides McDonald's? How can you stand that *schifezza* every day?" Try to note that apart from teenagers, nobody eats fast food every day. Point out that America is bigger than Europe, with regions, cultures, and cuisines mixed like minestrone. Clambakes and chowders, New York pickles, pastrami and cheesecake, Maryland crabs and Jersey shore dinners, Pennsylvania Dutch salads and soups, two-handed Ohio peaches and Oregon blackberries as big as your thumb, Cajun fish and gumbo, blazing Tex-Mex, Southern home and soul food cooking, fresh Iowa corn run in from the field to boiling pots, farm breakfasts, pancakes, hush puppies, muffins and pies. Nobody wanted to hear about them.

Certainly nobody wanted to hear what "classical" Italian cuisine owes to American imports: tomatoes, potatoes, corn for the polenta so adored in Milan. Incredible but true: pizza and pasta languished pale before the first tomatoes appeared in Roman markets in the early 1800s—appeared then almost vanished when early chefs tasted the bitter leaves and declared the plant a pure American *schifezza*. Not a popular story, I only tried it once. If the truth makes you free, it surely doesn't make you friends, not if you're expatriate.

Turkey with fixings I tried to explain, my mother's stuffing with carrot, apple, onions and chestnuts, all mixed up, a tender, rich and indefinable goodness in your mouth, like home. "But fruit doesn't mix with poultry or meat," somebody would always remind me, *"Non si fa,"* it can't be done. There goes California nouveau, right off the map. "Besides, your desserts are much too sweet." Well, yes they're sweet, but every time my birthday came in Italy I remembered my grandmother's kitchen-bustling, sifting, creaming, grating, chopping and finally in its towering sweet darkness: German chocolate cake, oozing pecan and coconut frosting—how else do you know another year's gone round?

Not that I didn't appreciate *la cucina italiana,* one of the world's great cuisines, etc., etc. How could I not? The wood-oven pizzas of Naples, explosions of shellfish tangled in pasta, the glories of pesto and lasagna, Parmesan and all her marvelous sister cheeses, potatoes made celestial with rosemary and wine, gelato in summer like icy rich fruit in cones, rice balls like golden oranges, sublime minestrone that your mother-in-law swears is "just dried beans, some vegetables, water and salt," her lasagna and cannelloni with pasta as tender—there's no other way to put this—as a baby's skin. Our church-sponsored dinners, potlucks Italian-style; you thought you'd died and gone to heaven, served by signora-angels wielding long-handled spoons: try this, try this, I made it fresh this morning. No, there's no end of reasons to wish yourself *buon appetito* in Italy.

It's just that memory remains: there are other fine cuisines in the world besides this one. Not so, said my neighbors and the ladies of my church. Outside the cultural reach of Italy, the benighted suffer *schifezza* every day. Listen to travelers' tales over espresso—the constant delusions, stomach-insults and pure gastronomic folly of leaving Italy. A crescendo of culinary horrors. Mamma mia, what people eat, even in Europe! "You can't find decent lasagna in Sweden, forget it!" Luisa moaned. When I praised the salmon or pastries, a half-dozen women waved me silent. German pasta, how insipid and why make bread so dark *and* heavy? Don't they have white flour? Too much butter in French food, fish and meat in Spanish paella (very wrong), yogurt for dinner in Greece, don't even think about England. Mention of America brought giddy waves of "top this" even beyond the obvious crimes of convenience food, fast food, and the unspeakable McDonald's. Americans put cheese on fish, imagine! They eat their salads first and give you *raw vegetables* to dip in flavored cream—what's so hard about cooking carrots? Everything all piled on the same plate, what a mess. "They put this 'ranch sauce' on my salad," Luisa recalled with horror, "and I swear there was *sugar* in it." I cringed, knowing what came next: marshmallows on sweet potatoes when even sweet potatoes all by themselves are much too sweet to eat with meals.

Now the acme of horrors, macaroni and cheese in a box! The women all swiveled their heads towards me, speechless with disgust. What could I say to the truth? It happens, boxes are sold. Busy families—I floundered.

"Did *you* ever—?" Luisa asked. No, thank God, I never bought it myself. General sigh of relief. Yet now I confess that never in ten years in Italy did I ever tell a soul that yes, my own mother fed us even *that,* macaroni with cheese product squeezed from a tube, and more besides: Chef Boy-ar-dee, Tang and toaster pizza, Cheez-Whiz on hot dogs, TV dinners on a Saturday night. I ate them in my time, in my ignorance, with pleasure. And raw veggie dip besides.

Dinner over, espresso served, the women tackled cleaning while the men took on the folding chairs. I volunteered to shake the tablecloths outside, alone. Granted, my pain was small in the scheme of world pain, but it was mine and would not go away. I loved my husband and was loving my time in Italy, but like any sojourner in a strange land, if anybody's criticizing my country, it had better be me, not them. I swept the floor—carefully, so nobody would come after me to show how it's done.

I knew, I knew, there's no point losing sleep or friendships over who eats what how, and Maurizio was happy to try new foods, but nostalgia can melt to pettiness and snitty revenge. I wanted to plant myself before the church ladies and say: "Hey Signore, you want *schifezza?* Check out those sidewalk vats of rubbery octopus chunks floating in rancid oil. One near our first apartment was open 24/7—I heard guys on motorcycles roar up for a 3 a.m. octopus nosh. Or the cheese recently outlawed in Sardinia, that one with worms inside—quite the local delicacy. And speaking of worms, there's *cannolichi,* pencil-thin shellfish eaten not just raw but live; squeeze lemon on their little wormy heads and they writhe like tiny cobras before you pop them in your mouth. Pasta with *ricci di mare,* sea urchins, imagine a blackish slimy fish jelly with a heavy whiff of rot. Or wait! How about those stands in Naples, boiled pigs' heads festooned with lemons? Oh please, serve me some pig cheek, maybe a half-eyeball too and a bit of snout. Or that black-red mash of blood, liver and random innards called *sanguinaccio* (literally, "nasty bloody stuff"). What about lamb intestines still full of their milky infant shit, baked up in wine and rosemary, a treasure of my husband's region? Excuse me, I'll take macaroni with tube cheese any day." Of course I said none of this; I played the good guest, the nice, *simpatica* American wife and tried to stifle my kvetching.

But at home I pored through American cookbooks, searching for crossover foods. I mixed sweet potatoes half and half with white potatoes to make a winning puree—so long as nobody knew it was polluted with orange juice (one does *not* mix oranges and potatoes). Hummus (a.k.a. *crema di ceci*—chick pea cream) found its niche as well, made familiar with a dusting of chopped (Italian) parsley.

My second year in Italy, I produced a full Thanksgiving dinner which soon became tradition. Guests bore with cranberry sauce for the novelty of an exotic foreign ritual, the mega-turkey, the stuffing, the meat sauce whose name everybody learned, *gravee,* and rosemary bread I baked in various seasonal shapes—Pilgrim hats, an Indian who grew wildly wall-eyed in the rising, once a full-rigged Mayflower.

By the fourth year, mild hints started in September: "Are you doing that turkey and marmalade *festa* again?" meaning: "Will you invite me, can I bring friends?" I felt a vindication of sorts, a recompense for the loneliness of making stuffing with nobody there to ask, "Is this enough onion? How did *your* mother make it?" Nobody ever made turkey stuffing in Italy —not Dante's mamma nor Caesar's; for sure Romulus and Remus' wolf-mamma didn't know from stuffing.

Then there was my problem of seeming *rigida,* unyielding and inflexible. I was celebrating Thanksgiving on Saturday night, pushed up to Italian dinnertime, closer to midnight than noon. (And what would my Aunt Virginia have said to this incredible hour, she who had us assembled for grace sometime between 2:00 p.m. and 2:16 p.m., depending on the year's crop of babies and toddlers needing bibs and booster seats?) I'd serve the salad at the end the Italian way, give up candied yams and sweet corn relish, but if a guest wanted to bring *contorno,* a vegetable dish, the trouble began.

"I'll make my eggplant parmigiana," Claudia offered. Not that her version wasn't wonderful, spectacular in fact, but how about green beans just once? "You don't like my parmigiana?" And so I was *rigida* again. Yet—but I never could explain this—all year long I ate pasta boiled or baked, spoke another language, hung up laundry sock by sock because a drier, if you could ever find one, "ruins your clothes," made my sevens with little bars, drank espresso, molded the merest detail of life to a foreign culture, but one day in a year to have the home tastes and *just* those tastes, was that too much to ask? Still, there was Claudia before me, my friend whom I loved. Why load my foolish loneliness on her?

"Sure, bring the eggplant parmigiana."

"I could just grill the eggplant," Claudia offered anxiously, "or bake it with garlic or fry it without the sauce, or sautéed with tomato—"

"Parmigiana is fine," I interrupted, "really, Claudia, I'm serious." And it was fine. The turkey was tender, the *gravee* smooth and we polished off two pans of sweet potato puree laced with secret orange juice.

But my greatest crossover success was pecan pie, *torta di pecan*. I made cultural accommodations of course: halved the sugar, added lemon rind and rum and traced a heart in pecan halves on the top of every pie. Patrizia came back from a conference in Atlanta having tasted local pecan pies and found them all a scandal: "much too sweet, no lemon and no hearts on top."

"Come for dinner on Saturday," Francesco would invite us, meaning: "And bring the pecan pie." Once I assumed a dinner for four and brought a single pie. I remember Francesco's stricken face traveling from the pie in my hands to his milling crowd of guests—he'd have just a sliver at best.

My fifth year in Italy, I was missing my family and glumly approaching my birthday. Maurizio arranged a surprise party—the living room packed with friends when I came home from work. *Sorpresa!* Indeed, I was completely surprised. A mountain of pizza boxes appeared, wine, bread, salad and Claudia's eggplant parmigiana, her best so far. Alberto produced a *caprese,* a fine, slightly dry, dark chocolate cake dusted with sugar in an elegant design. Yes, yes, a wonderful cake, just not, well, not German chocolate. A trifle plain for a birthday, my grandmother would say. But why be *rigida* tonight?

Francesco, however, was never one to fear rigidity. As his eyes swept the now-chaotic kitchen, his thoughts were easy to read: if the hostess didn't know there'd be fifteen guests for dinner, what were the chances she'd have made enough (or any) pecan pie? Very slight. Yet one of Francesco's most appealing qualities was his tenacious optimism. He searched the counters, cabinets and refrigerator, inside and top. Finally even he had to ask: "*Allora, non c'e' torte di pecan, vero?*" Then it is true, there's no pecan pie? Conversation dimmed. Poor Alberto. I extolled his *caprese*. Yes of course, agreed Francesco patiently, *caprese* is good, but rather *tipico,* no? And he couldn't help noticing I had plenty of shelled pecans, eggs, and corn syrup—everything I needed.

With many hands to help, three pecan pies were quickly made, all with hearts on top. We ate pizza while they cooked. After dinner, Maurizio set out our little crystal shot glasses for his homemade *limoncello,* 100 proof lemon liqueur that goes straight to the head. The pies were done and cooled. We filled our plates—a slice of *caprese,* a slice of pecan. Then we ate and drank and all around the table, there was no *schifezza* at all. ☕

Contributing Writers and Artists

SHANE ALLISON is a graduate student at the New School University in New York City. His Pushcart-nominated poems have been published in over 70 journals, including, *Coal City Review, Chiron Review, Aura Arts Literary Review,* and others. He has work forthcoming in *Snake Nation Review.*

SHARON AUBERLE is a poet and artist living in the mountains of Flagstaff, Arizona. She combines poetry with her exploration of visual media. Her work draws on a wide range of subjects, including nature, Zen, spirituality and the Southwest. She is presently working on a children's book and a memoir.

JULIE AUER is a lawyer moonlighting as a writer of fiction and essays. She has published short stories, and currently has a mystery novel under contract at Alyson, due out in 2004. She once won a special merit from the National League of American Pen Women/San Francisco for her short story "Winnie's Wake," and first prize in the Knoxville Writers' Guild Essay Contest in 1999. "Feast Day of a Young Man" is a biographical essay based on reminiscences of her Hungarian-American family. She is also a pretty good cook.

MARYBETH BOYANTON was born on the Texas Gulf Coast and lived in Houston for many years prior to moving to Knoxville, Tennessee. She is an arts and humanities graduate of the University of Houston—Clear Lake. In addition to a variety of creative writing classes, she audited poetry classes in the Writer's Workshop at the University of Iowa during the late '60s. After a hiatus of many years, her recent work has been published in two editions of *New Millennium Writings* and included in a previous KWG anthology, *Breathing the Same Air.* In addition to her writing, she is a working studio artist and has operated as a freelance desktop-publishing specialist for over 12 years.

BILL BROWN directs the writing program at Hume-Fogg Academic Magnet School in Nashville. He, his wife Suzanne, and their cat live on a small farm north of Nashville in Roberston County. He was awarded the 1999 Fellowship in Poetry from the Tennessee Arts Commission. He has been a Scholar in Poetry at Bread Loaf and a Fellow at the Virginia Center for the Creative Arts. In 1995 he was awarded the Distinguished Teacher in the Arts from the National Foundation for

Advancement in the Arts. His latest collection of poems, *The Gods of Little Pleasures,* was published in 2001 by the Sow's Ear Press, Abingdon, Virginia. He has published work in journals such as *Appalachian Heritage, The Literary Review, The English Journal, The Atlanta Poetry Review, Passages North, The Asheville Poetry Review, Poem, Negative Capability* and *Slant.*

JEANNETTE BROWN has a master's degree in urban studies. Her work experience includes publicity for theatre, dance, and other arts groups, as well as writing copy for an ad agency. Her work has been published in the *Texas Observer, ArtSpace, Mother Earth, Breathing the Same Air, Suddenly IV, Bellevue Literary Review,* and other publications. She is the editor of *Literary Lunch.*

BLAIR CAMPBELL is a freelance writer and editor living in Santa Monica, California. A former editor at *Civilization* and *Fairfield County* magazines, her work has also appeared in *Mother Jones* and the *Washington Post.*

LISA COLLETT is a student at Davidson College in Davidson, North Carolina. A Nashville native, she attributes her love of poetry to Bill Brown, poet and teacher at Hume-Fogg Academic Magnet School.

MATT COOK is a recent graduate of Hope College in Holland, Michigan. He currently lives near Albany, NY, where he was born and raised.

CATHERINE CRAWLEY, a self-confessed foodie, has sampled black-pepper crab in Singapore, passion fruit in New Zealand, and grew up on her mum's Christmas pudd as a youngster in the United Kingdom. She has been a journalist, teacher and workplace consultant in California, Washington, D.C. and Nebraska. She is currently a doctoral student in the College of Communications at the University of Tennessee. She says she's never met a chocolate she didn't like.

BARBARA CROOKER's poems have been published in *The Christian Science Monitor, River City, Yankee, The Beloit Poetry Journal, Poetry International, The Denver Quarterly, America, Zone 3, Passages North, Negative Capability, Karamu, The Madison Review, Highlights for Children, Caprice, Appalachia, The Atlanta Review, The Chiron Poetry Review, Poet Lore, The MacGuffin, Nimrod, South Carolina Review,* as well as numerous anthologies. Her awards include First Place, ByLine Chapbook competition, 2001; First Prize, *New Millennium Writings* Y2K poetry contest, 2000; Grammy Awards Finalist, Spoken Word Category, 1997; First Prize, Karamu poetry contest, 1997; Pennsylvania Council on the Arts Fellowship in Literature; five-year Pushcart Prize nominee; and Fellow, Virginia Center for the Creative Arts. She lives in Fogelsville, Pennsylvania.

JOSEPH MICHAEL DeGROSS is an East Tennessee writer who obtained an M.F.A. degree from Goddard College after retiring from 30 years of medical practice. He is a professor of medical humanities at Mercer University School of Medicine and an adjunct professor of English at Chattanooga State where he teaches creative writing. He is also an associate fiction editor for *Carve Magazine.* His short stories have appeared in *MFA Pawprints* and *Carve.* His essays have appeared in *Southern Medicine* and were long running in *Valley Doctor* magazine. He lives and writes on Towee Mountain, in East Tennessee. When not writing he can be found fly-fishing for trout on the Hiwassee, or hunting grouse in the Cherokee National Forest.

EMILY DEWHIRST is a true nomad. Cycling through France at age 17, she caught the wonder of other cultures, communicating with many people in their native language. The entire world is her home, and her life experiences include unforgettable moments in Kazakhstan, China, Tibet, India, Nepal, the Middle East, North Africa and elsewhere. She has restored an historic building in the old Market Square of downtown Knoxville, where she resides and owns Nomad gallery, offering her own handweaving and beadwork along with the treasures she gathers from afar.

JUDY DIGREGORIO currently works as a training specialist for the Department of Energy in Oak Ridge, Tenn. She is also a freelance writer, workshop leader, and speaker. She has published nonfiction and light verse in print publications, such as *The Army/Navy/Air Force Times, CC Motorcycle NewsMagazine, New Millennium Writings, The Church Musician Today, Alabama School Journal, The Writing Parent, Inscriptions Magazine,* and *The Tennessee Writer.* She also publishes a monthly humor column for *Senior Living* magazine. She is a member of the Knoxville Writers' Guild, Tennessee Writers Alliance, and the National Writers' Union. She currently serves as vice-chairperson on the Tennessee Mountain Writers Board of Directors.

DONNA DOYLE says, "'First Fig' is a poem that startled me. Once written, I just read and reread it wondering if I had written it, because it was so unlike any poem I had ever written. I even gave the poem to a few people and asked them what they thought the poem meant! The origin of the poem—along with the question it asks—still haunts me. In a good way." She always gives the last bite of her banana to her dog, Sydney.

EMILY DZIUBAN was born and raised in Orlando, Florida. She holds a B.A. and an M.A. in English, the former from Winthrop University in South Carolina, and the latter from the University of Tennessee—Knoxville, where she currently teaches.

JIM EASTIN was a United Methodist minister for 19 years. He is now the program director for the Gospel Music Television Network, a freelance storyteller, singer, writer, and photographer. He wages peace against his enemies from Sevierville, Tenn.

NIKKI GIOVANNI was born in Knoxville, Tenn. Giovanni has recently published an illustrated "love poem" entitled *Knoxville, Tennessee,* for her grandmother, Louvenia Watson. Giovanni was graduated from Fisk University—Nashville, and is professor of English at Virginia Tech. Her most recent publications are

The Selected Poems of Nikki Giovanni (1996) and *The Love Poems of Nikki Giovanni* (1997), which was awarded the NAACP Image Award for 1998. Her most recent illustrated children's books are *The Genie in the Jar* with Chris Raschka and *The Sun Is So Quiet* with Ashley Bryan. The selected papers of Nikki Giovanni are held at the Mugar Memorial Library of Boston University.

Dr. Giovanni, the 1996 winner of the Langston Hughes Award, is a member of the National Advisory Board of the Underground Railroad Freedom Center. She recently edited two anthologies: *Grand/Mothers* (1996) and *Grand/Fathers* (1999). Her latest collection of poetry is *Blues: For All the Changes* (1999). Her most recent CD is *Nikki Giovanni in Philadelphia*. In the fall of 1999, the Board of Visitors of Virginia Tech appointed Giovanni University Distinguished Professor. In April 2002, she was awarded the first Rosa L. Parks Woman of Courage Award.

CONNIE JORDAN GREEN lives on a farm in Loudon County, where she grows, cooks, and consumes herbs and vegetables, fruits and berries. She writes stories and award-winning novels for young people, poetry, and a newspaper column. Her poetry has appeared in numerous journals and publications, including anthologies *Some Say Tomato; Voices from the Valley; All Around Us: Poems from the Valley; Breathing the Same Air; A Tennessee Landscape, People, and Places; HomeWorks,* and *To Love One Another.* Currently, she teaches a creative writing correspondence course for the University of Tennessee and volunteers as a writing instructor for various groups, including ORICL (Oak Ridge Institute for Continued Learning).

JANE HICKS is a native of East Tennessee and an award-winning poet and quilter. She recently won the Appalachian Poetry Contest sponsored by *Now & Then* magazine, published by the Center for Appalachian Studies and Services at East Tennessee State University. She has also won prizes from Tennessee Mountain Writers and Appalachian Writers Association. Her poetry has appeared in journals and literary magazines in the Southeast, notably *Wind, Now & Then, Sow's Ear,* and *Appalachian Journal.* Her "literary quilts" illustrate the works of playwright Jo Carson, Sharyn McCrumb, and Silas House, and she has toured with these respective authors. She is a teacher of intellectually gifted students in Sullivan County, Tennessee.

JENINE HOLMES is currently a copywriter in New York City for Spike DDB, an advertising agency headed by Spike Lee. For another creative outlet, Ms. Holmes writes poetry and is currently working on a book of fiction. Her hobbies include running, studying the cello, and reviving the lost art of letter writing.

DORIS IVIE, professor of psychology at Pellissippi State, writes poems occasionally, stuffs them in odd places, and seldom sends anything out for publication. She wrote the first draft of the "occasional poem" chosen for this anthology in the Knoxville Writers' Guild's monthly Writing Women group, which she has convened for three years in succession. She loves traveling to ancient European monastic sites and enjoys solitude at home with thousands of books and one

Sarah McCarty / **Butterfly with Cherries**

perfect tortoiseshell cat, Sophia. She edited the Guild's fourth anthology, *Breathing the Same Air* (Celtic Cat Publishing, 2001).

ALISON CONDIE JAENICKE earned her B.A. and M.A. in English from the University of Virginia. She taught English and coached basketball at a private high school in Bethesda, Maryland, for eight years, then moved in 1997 to Knoxville, where she stayed home to care for her two young children and to focus on writing. She currently lives in State College, Penn., and works part-time as a telecommuting editor for an admissions consulting company, Accepted.com. In 1998, her story "Shelter" won second prize in the KWG Leslie Garrett fiction contest, and in 1999, her essay "Finding Fireweed" won second place in the National League of American Pen Women's Soul-Making Literary Competition. Her stories and essays have been published in *Brain, Child: The Magazine for Thinking Mothers* and *Breathing the Same Air.*

ELIZABETH JOHNS was born in Marion, Virginia, and moved to Bristol, Tenn., when she was five. She graduated from Emory & Henry College in Emory, Virginia, in 1966 with a degree in sociology. While there, she studied drawing and painting under George Chavatel and, later, completed graduate work in painting and design at Teachers College at Columbia University. After living for nearly 20 years in Seattle, Wash., where her work was widely exhibited in Seattle and the Pacific Northwest, she returned to Bristol. Her work has been exhibited in numerous juried shows and solo shows in the area. She has illustrated children's books and CD covers. She lives with her husband in Bristol and has her studio in her home.

DAVID E. JOYNER, artist, illustrator and writer, is a retired TVA architectural designer who lives in Knoxville. His stories and poems have appeared in *New Millennium Writings.*

HEATHER JOYNER is beginning her sixth year as a biweekly columnist for Knoxville's *Metro Pulse.* She earned an M.F.A. in writing from Sarah Lawrence College in 1997. She also teaches art history and photography at Pellissippi State. Her interests include travel, and she is currently editing video footage she shot in China last year. She enjoys her cats, music, and napping, and would rather go somewhere than buy a new sofa.

MARILYN KALLET is the director of creative writing at the University of Tennessee and the author of eight books, including *Sleeping With One Eye Open: Women Writers and the Art of Survival,* co-edited with Judith Ortiz Cofer. Her poems have appeared recently in *New Letters, Now & Then, Sport Literate,* and *Prairie Schooner.* "Yom Kippur Remembrance" won the 2002 Robert Burns/Terry Semple Poetry Prize from the Knoxville Writers' Guild and the Scottish Society of Knoxville. She is the poetry editor at *Appalachian Life* and *New Millennium Writings.* In 2000, she was named Outstanding Woman in the Arts by the Knoxville YWCA.

SARAH KENDALL is a senior B.F.A. student at the University of Tennessee, Knoxville. Her main focus is in photo media, with a secondary emphasis in art history. Her work has been published in the *Phoenix Literary Art Magazine,* and shown in the Annual Student Art Competition, Dogwood Arts Photography Show, the Visual Arts Annual 2-Dimensional Show and, most recently, was selected to be in the Senior Honors Show at the Ewing Gallery. She has permanent work on display at Sunspot Restaurant in Knoxville. Her work explores food from a different perspective in photography and painting. The photos seen here were all taken in the kitchen at Blackberry Farm in Walland, Tenn.

DONNELL KING is associate professor of speech and journalism at Pellissippi State in Knoxville, Tennessee, where he also serves as program coordinator for speech. He is nearly finished with a doctorate in collaborative learning. He received the Excellence in Teaching award from Pellissippi State in 1999, and received an

Excellence Award for the year 2000 from the National Institute for Staff and Organizational Development. He is a member of the Knoxville Writers' Guild. A textbook he co-authored (*Responsibly Spoken*) will be published in the fall of 2002. Before becoming a college teacher, he spent 10 years as a minister, and continues to explore his interest in spirituality. He also spent 12 years in radio, newspaper, and magazine work and is a freelance writer.

LINDSAY KROMER taught art in the public schools in Pennsylvania, moved south and began raising her family. At the same time, she started her career as a studio artist and fine art photographer. In addition to her art education degree from Westminster College in Pennsylvania, she has a second degree in graphic design/illustration from the University of Tennessee. Through her skills, she has become involved in many regional organizations, juried exhibits, and has won numerous awards for her silk-screen printmaking, graphic design and photography. Most recently, she worked for U.T. in the Social Work Office of Research and Public Service as a graphic designer, and is currently the media production coordinator for the Frank H. McClung Museum, Knoxville.

JUDY LOEST was born in Snowflake, Virginia, and has lived in Knoxville for the past 25 years. Her poetry has appeared in the *Phoenix Literary Art Magazine, Now & Then, The Cortland Review* and in the anthologies *All Around Us* and *Breathing the Same Air.* Her awards include the Bain-Swiggett Poetry Prize, the Columbia Press Gold Circle Award, the Libba Moore Gray Poetry Prize, and the Vesle Fenstermaker Poetry Prize.

JEFF DANIEL MARION has published seven collections of poetry, the two most recent being *Letters Home* (Sow's Ear Press, 2001) and *Ebbing & Flowing Springs: New and Selected Poems and Prose, 1976-2001* (Celtic Cat Publishing, 2002). In 1978 he was the first recipient of the Literary Fellowship awarded by the Tennessee Arts Commission. From 1985-1992 and in 1994, he served as poet-in-residence for the Tennessee Governor's School for the Humanities, and in 1998 he served as Copenhaver Scholar-in-Residence at Roanoke College in Salem, Virginia. Now retired after teaching 35 years at Carson-Newman College, he lives in Knoxville with his wife, Linda.

LINDA PARSONS MARION is poetry editor of *Now & Then* magazine, published by the Center for Appalachian Studies and Services at East Tennessee State University. She has received literary fellowships from the Tennessee Arts Commission and the Knoxville Arts Council, the Tennessee Writers Alliance award in poetry, the Tennessee Poetry Prize, and the Associated Writing Programs' Intro Award, among others. She is co-editor of *All Around Us: Poems from the Valley* (Blue Ridge Publishing, 1996). Her first book of poems, *Home Fires,* was published by Sow's Ear Press (1997). Marion's poetry has appeared in *The Georgia Review, The Iowa Review, Poem, Asheville Poetry Review, Prairie Schooner, Apalachee Quarterly, Appalachian Heritage, Wind, Louisiana Literature, Negative*

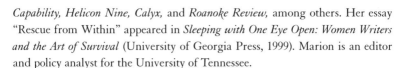

Capability, Helicon Nine, Calyx, and *Roanoke Review,* among others. Her essay "Rescue from Within" appeared in *Sleeping with One Eye Open: Women Writers and the Art of Survival* (University of Georgia Press, 1999). Marion is an editor and policy analyst for the University of Tennessee.

SARAH MATÉ is a poet and essayist, published over the last 20 years in a variety of journals, including *New Millennium Writings* and *Poet Lore.* She was named "Emerging Poet of the Year" by the Montpelier Cultural Arts Society several years ago and last year won an Award of Excellence in the Robert Burns Poetry Contest (Terry Semple Memorial). She came to Tennessee by way of Georgia and Maryland ten years ago after retiring from teaching. She is an avid student of food history; professionally, she owned a home-delivered grocery store for seniors, and was "weekend chef" for an upscale residential community for Alzheimer's patients, who loved her cooking while they ate it, but usually forgot it by the next meal.

JACK MAURO is the author of *Gay Street: Stories Of Knoxville, Tennessee;* the dark comedy novella *Spite Hall;* and, most recently, *Enola's Wedding,* a bilious account of love and courtship. He lives and works in Knoxville.

JUDY PINKSTON MCCARTHY was born and grew up in East Tennessee. She took a B.A. degree in pre-law at Michigan State University in 1966, a master's degree in weaving at the University of Tennessee in 1973, and a law degree from U.T. in 1982. She has lived in Michigan, Arizona, North Carolina, New Jersey and, briefly, in California. For the last 20 years she has practiced law in Knoxville. [Her husband says she is an outstanding cook.]

SARAH MCCARTY, a native Knoxvillian, has lived and worked as an artist in Santa Fe, New Mexico, since 1983. A B.F.A. graduate of the University of Tennessee, she continued her study of printmaking, etching, engraving, drawing, and painting in Scotland and Italy and in New York City at The Art Students League and The Printmaking Workshop. Her work has been in juried and invitational exhibitions in New York, Boston, Philadelphia, Albuquerque, and Santa Fe. She also designs gardens.

JEANNE MCDONALD has published short fiction in *Homeworks: A Book of Tennessee Writers; Worlds in Our Words: Contemporary American Women Writers; Special Report: Fiction; Kentucky Writing; Amelia; Phoebe; American Fiction;* and *Memphis Magazine.* Her work will be represented in *Women Writing in Appalachia,* forthcoming from the University Press of Kentucky, and her novel, *Water Dreams,* is forthcoming from the University Press of Mississippi. She has co-authored two books of nonfiction with her husband, Fred Brown: *Growing Up Southern: How the South Shapes Its Writers* (Emerald House, Blue Ridge Publishing, 1998); and *The Serpent Handlers: Three Families and Their Faith* (Blair Publishing, 2000). She is also editor of two collections for the Knoxville Writers' Guild: *Voices from the Valley* and *The Voice of Memory: A Collection of Memoirs.*

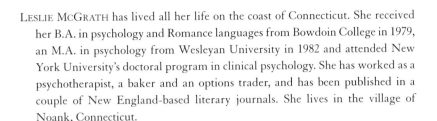

LESLIE MCGRATH has lived all her life on the coast of Connecticut. She received her B.A. in psychology and Romance languages from Bowdoin College in 1979, an M.A. in psychology from Wesleyan University in 1982 and attended New York University's doctoral program in clinical psychology. She has worked as a psychotherapist, a baker and an options trader, and has been published in a couple of New England-based literary journals. She lives in the village of Noank, Connecticut.

FLOSSIE MCNABB was born in Knoxville and has lived there ever since. She began writing poetry and essays while a graduate student in English at the University of Tennessee. She has been published in *Now & Then* magazine and in several Knoxville Writers' Guild publications, the most recent being *Breathing the Same Air*. In the spring of 2002 she won first place in the Libba Moore Gray Poetry Contest held annually by the Guild. She spends her time reading, gardening, taking care of her two dogs, and working as executive secretary of Old Gray Cemetery in downtown Knoxville. She is the assistant editor for *Literary Lunch*.

SIMONE MUENCH is an associate editor for ACM. She has poems published or appearing in *Paris Review, Phoebe, Pleiades, Indiana Review,* among others. She is a recipient of an Illinois Arts Council Fellowship, and has recently received the Charles Goodnow Award for Poetry. Her book *The Air Lost in Breathing* won the 1999 Marianne Moore Prize for Poetry and was published by Helicon Nine Editions in 2000. She is currently working on her Ph.D. at the University of Illinois in Chicago.

JACK NEELY graduated from the University of Tennessee with a degree in American history. In 1992 *Metro Pulse* debuted his column, "Secret History." Since then, the column has won several awards, including the East Tennessee Historical Society's "History in the Media" award and the East Tennessee Society of Professional Journalists' First Place award in the newspaper columns category. He joined the *Metro Pulse* staff as a full-time writer in 1995. He has also worked as a consultant and project writer for various historical and cultural projects, including the BBC's 1995 audio documentary about James Agee and Knoxville's live broadcast of *A Prairie Home Companion* (1999). His columns have been collected into two books: *Knoxville's Secret History* and *Secret History II*. He wrote the text for the photographic book, *The Marble City,* published by the University of Tennessee Press in 1999.

KAY NEWTON, world traveler, is in the midst of reorganizing her office and has no idea what she's written or published lately. However, she recently finished eating her way all over Northern Spain, Southern France, and Andorra; and she feels sure that her gastronomical gallivanting should sooner or later result in something more poetic than a belch.

CAROLINE P. NORRIS has been a teacher, editor, technical writer, career counselor, tax correspondent, poet and journalist. She has lived and worked in Japan and France and in many American cities and, for the past decade, in Maryville, Tenn., where she teaches English at Pellissippi State. Last year she published *A Small Price to Pay: Poems from East Tennessee and Beyond.*

TED OLSON is the author of *So Far: Poems* (1994) and *Blue Ridge Folklife* (1998, a volume in the University Press of Mississippi's "Folklife in the South Series"), and he is the editor of James Still's *From the Mountain, from the Valley: New and Collected Poems* (2001).

JO ANN PANTANIZOPOULOS has a sign hanging over her washing machine that reads: "I wasn't born in Tennessee, but I got here as fast as I could." After being raised in Roswell, New Mexico, eight years of living in Greece and Switzerland, and two new languages later, she eventually landed in Knoxville. She has published Greek lullaby translations in *Two Lines,* as well as several articles on young adult literature, poetry translation in the high school English class, and word play in various state English journals. Her personal essay "The Cornbread Legacy" was published in the Guild's *Breathing the Same Air.* In addition to her job as an administrator at the Division Street campus of Pellissippi State Technical Community College, she maintains the Websites for the Knoxville Writers' Guild, the Division Street campus, Celtic Cat Publishing, and others.

MARGARET PENNYCOOK moved to the United States from Britain twenty years ago. Since then, she has published numerous articles, from a weekly column on childbirth education to creative nonfiction travel features. She composes advice for writers, under the name "Ms. Penners," and published a poem in *Staple New Writing.* She has received many awards for writing fiction, nonfiction and poetry, but is most proud of the 2001 Sue Ellen Hudson Award for Excellence in Writing, from the Tennessee Mountain Writers Conference, and the 2001 Woodland Award for Poetry from Cookeville Creative Writers' Association. She lives in Oak Ridge, Tennessee.

JENNIFER POLHEMUS is a poet and writer living in Pennsylvania's Cumberland Valley with her partner, cat and dog. She holds a Liberal Arts degree from the College of Southern Maryland and is working on her first novel. Numerous poems and short stories of hers have been published in literary magazines. She has two collections of poems currently in print: *Borderlines* and *Women, Wounds and Kitchens.* The Vermont Studio Center has awarded her a grant for a one-month writer's residency.

JACK RENTFRO is a freelance writer and editor from Knoxville. Lately, he has been spending more time working on an anthology of Knoxville's pop music history than jobs that help pay the bills. After a publisher is found for that project, he plans to relax and take up farming. He thinks it will be easy. He is originally from Cleveland, Tenn., where one can no longer find the fabulous 25-cent Spot hamburger. Lest anyone be concerned, Jack and his wife Angie and their dogs' eating habits have improved a little over the years.

SUSAN RICH is the winner of the 2002 PEN West/Poetry award for *The Cartographer's Tongue/Poems of the World*. She has been a staff person for Amnesty International, an electoral supervisor in Bosnia, and a human rights trainer in Gaza. Her poems have appeared in *DoubleTake, Harvard Magazine, Massachusetts Review* and *Southern Poetry Review*. She lives in Seattle and teaches at Highline College and the Antioch University M.F.A. low-residency program in Los Angeles.

EVE RIFKAH is co-founder and artistic director of Poetry Oasis, Inc., and editor of *Diner,* a journal of poetry. She received her M.F.A. from Vermont College. Her poems have appeared in *The McGuffin, The California Quarterly, The Worcester Review, Porcupine* and others. She is currently writing a history of the grassroots poetry community of Worcester, Massachusetts.

CARLY SACHS is an M.F.A. candidate in poetry at the New School University, New York.

LYNN VEACH SADLER has a B.A. from Duke and an M.A. and a Ph.D. from the University of Illinois. Her academic publications include five books and some sixty-eight articles, and she has edited thirteen books/proceedings and three national journals. A chapbook, *Poet Geography,* is forthcoming in the Mt. Olive College Poetry Series. She won *The Pittsburgh Quarterly*'s 2001 Sara Henderson Hay Prize for Poetry. Her stories have been published widely and have won the North Carolina Writers' Network, *Talus and Scree,* and *Cream City Review* competitions. Her unpublished novel, *Tonight I Lie with William Cullen Bryant,* was runner-up for the 1997 Dana Award and a finalist in the 2000 Florida First Coast Writers' Festival; *Intending to Build a Tower* received Honorable Mention in the 2001 Florida First Coast Writers' Festival competition. She also writes plays and musicals.

JANE SASSER teaches English literature and creative writing. She lives in Oak Ridge with her husband and two sons. Her work has appeared in *The North Carolina Literary Review, The Sow's Ear Poetry Review, RE:AL, The Mid-America Poetry Review, The Atlanta Review,* and numerous other publications.

MARGARET SCANLAN was born in St. Louis, Missouri, in 1944, and has a B.A. degree from Webster University, where she studied with sculptor Rudolph Torrini. Her graduate degree is from the University of Tennessee, where she had her first solo gallery exhibition in 1981. For years she was affiliated with the Suzanne Brown Gallery in Scottsdale, Arizona, Abbott & Holder in London, England, and Kenny Galleries in Galway, Ireland. She has been represented by Bennett Galleries in Knoxville since 1988. She is a signature member of the American Watercolor Society, National Watercolor Society, and the Watercolor USA Honor Society.

DEBORAH SCAPEROTH's poetry has been published in *New Millennium Writings* and various literary magazines. She recently won the poetry award for the 2002 winter/spring issue of the *Yemassee Literary Journal.*

MATTHEW W. SCHMEER is an assistant professor of English at Francis Marion University in Florence, South Carolina, and edits the online journal, *Poetry Midwest.*

He holds an M.F.A. from the University of Missouri at St. Louis. He is the author of the chapbook *Twenty-One Cents* (Pudding House Publications, 2002), and his poems have recently appeared or are forthcoming in *River Oak Review, Re)verb, The Curbside Review, Good Foot, The Quercus Review, The Rio Grande Review, The Connecticut River Review, California Quarterly,* and other print and online journals.

PAMELA SCHOENEWALDT spent a decade living in a small town outside Naples, Italy, which provided the material for "Americana in Italy." She is current the Writer-in-Residence at the University of Tennessee library and teaches fiction and professional writing. Her short stories have been published in *Belletrist Review, Bianco e Nero* (Italy), *Cascando Review* (England, winning the Travel Writing Award), *Crescent Review* (winning the Chekhov Award for Short Fiction), *Iron Horse Literary Review, Mediphors, New Millennium Writings, Paris Transcontinental* (France), *Pinehurst Journal,* and *Women's Words.* Her one-act play in Italian, *Espresso con Mia Madre* (*Espresso with My Mother*) was produced at the Theater Cilea in Naples. Schoenewaldt is currently writing a novel set in 12th Century Sicily.

MARTY SILVERTHORNE lives in North Carolina.

STEVE SPARKS was born in North Alabama and has lived in Knoxville for six years. He has published poetry in *The North American Review, Now & Then,* and the Knoxville Writers' Guild anthology, *Breathing the Same Air.*

JENNIFER SPIEGEL has an M.A. in politics from New York University and is currently an M.F.A. candidate in fiction at Arizona State. Her piece, "Sartre Is Wrong and I Have The Scars To Prove It," is included in the 2002 anthology *In Our Own Words: A Generation Defining Itself, Volume 4.* Her most recent publications are an interview with author Douglas Coupland in *Hayden's Ferry Review* (No. 29), and an essay on U2 in *Image* (No. 31).

LAURA STILL's writing experience includes technical writing for dental patient education, screening poetry as assistant editor for *New Millennium Writings,* and screening novels for the Peter Taylor Prize, which is administered jointly by the Knoxville Writers' Guild and University of Tennessee Press. She is treasurer of the Knoxville Writers' Guild and administers the Young Writer's Prize. Her recent publications include *Aethlon: The Journal of Sports Literature, Breathing the Same Air,* and *New Millennium Writings.* She works part-time as a dental practice consultant and USTA certified tennis umpire, and is a member of the Knoxville Theatre Coalition.

LINDA SEALS TALBERT is the winner of the 1998 Leslie Garrett Award for Fiction, given by the KWG. Her published works include fiction and nonfiction, and she writes Christian poetry. She desires to, as Ms. O'Connor said, "[penetrate] the concrete world in order to find at its depths the image of its source, the image of ultimate reality." She lives in Knoxville with her husband, has three children and two "exceptional" grandchildren.

EMILY TAYLOR was born in New York City, and attended Hampshire College where she received her B.A. She then moved to Ithaca, New York, and studied painting until 1993, when she moved to Knoxville. She worked at the Knoxville Museum of Art and McClung Museum, and received a master's in art education and an M.F.A. in painting from the University of Tennessee.

INGA TREITLER moved to Knoxville some 13 years ago for a job as an environmental professional at Oak Ridge National Laboratory. "Authenticity Quest" is her first literary publication. Her previous publications are academic articles in the fields of cultural anthropology, linguistics, and environmental management.

AMY UNSWORTH graduated from Eastern Michigan University and currently resides in California with her husband and three sons. Her work can be found online at *Poet's Canvas, Poems Niederngasse, and Eclectica*. Her work also has appeared in the print editions of *The Best of Poems Niederngasse, Ibbetson Street,* and a forthcoming volume of *The Pikeville Review.*

ASHLEY VANDOORN received a B.A. in creative writing from the University of Tennessee in 2002. She is a recipient of the Woodruff Award and the Knickerbocker Poetry Prize. She has recently published poems in *North American Review, The Ledge, The Amherst Review,* and *Into the Teeth of the Wind.*

ANGIE VICARS is the kind of writer who has blurry words scrawled in her palm, a pen cap in her mouth and a cup of coffee too close to the keyboard. Her first novel, *Treat,* partially set in Knoxville, was published in May 2001. Her work appears from time to time in *Metro Pulse.* She also founded the Barnes & Noble Writers Roundtable and holds an M.F.A. in screenwriting from the University of Miami.

PATRICIA WELLINGHAM-JONES, a former psychology researcher and writer/editor, is a two-time Pushcart Prize nominee. She has work published in numerous anthologies, journals, and Internet magazines, including *The Tule Review, The Acorn, Poetry Depth Quarterly, Phoebe, Visions International, Manzanita Quarterly, Midwest Poetry Review, Nanny Fanny, mélange journal, Thunder Sandwich, FZQ.* She edited *River Voices: Poets of Butte, Shasta, Tehama and Trinity Counties, California* and *Labyrinth: Poems & Prose.* Her latest chapbook is *Don't Turn Away: Poems About Breast Cancer; A Gathering Glance,* one of Lummox Press's Little Red Book series, was published in 2002. She was named Featured Writer for March/April 2002 at www.OutStretch.net.

ALLEN WIER has published three novels and a collection of stories, and has edited a volume on style in contemporary fiction and an anthology of stories. He has received the Robert Penn Warren Award from the Fellowship of Southern Writers, and he is the recipient of a Guggenheim Fellowship, a grant from the National Endowment for the Arts, and a Dobie-Paisano Fellowship from the Texas Institute of Letters. In 2000, the Fellowship of Southern Writers elected him to its membership. He recently completed a long novel, *Tehano,* about the

Comanche Indian wars in Texas. He holds the English department's distinguished teaching chair at the University of Tennessee—Knoxville.

DON WILLIAMS is the founding editor of *New Millennium Writings,* an annual anthology of poems, stories and nonfiction. He is a columnist and former feature writer for *The Knoxville News-Sentinel,* where his awards included a Malcolm Law Award, the Sigma Delta Chi Golden Press Card and a National Endowment for the Humanities Journalism Fellowship at the University of Michigan. His short stories and articles have been anthologized. He is a founding member of the Knoxville Writers' Guild and directs the Leslie Garrett Fiction Prize. His just-finished novel, *Oracle of the Orchid Lounge,* is in search of a publisher.

LEO WILLIAMS is a technical editor living in Knoxville and working in Oak Ridge. Before going into technical communication, he spent 12 years as a newspaper reporter and copy editor. He moved to Tennessee from California in 1993.

TAMAR WILNER is the calendar editor at *Metro Pulse.* Some of the articles she most enjoyed writing were a cover story on area quarries, a depiction of *Star Wars* fanatics and an interview with Ralph Nader. She is a native of suburban Washington, D.C., and a graduate of Wesleyan University in Connecticut.

MARIANNE WORTHINGTON, a native of Knoxville, teaches communication studies at Cumberland College, Williamsburg, Kentucky. She is reviews editor for *Now & Then: The Appalachian Magazine,* published by the Center for Appalachian Studies and Services at East Tennessee State University. Her poems and essays have appeared in *Now & Then, Mossy Creek Reader, Appalachian Heritage, Arts Across Kentucky,* and *Appalachian Journal.*

JANET A. ZIMMERMAN writes about food and teaches cooking classes in the San Francisco Bay Area, where she previously worked in marketing communications. She is currently working on a nonfiction book, *Matters of Taste: Adventures for the Inquisitive Palate.*

Index of Contributors

Sarah Kendall / *Placement*

KNOXVILLE
WRITERS' GUILD